Data Analytics and AI

Data Analytics Applications

Series Editor

Jay Liebowitz

PUBLISHED (SELECTED)

Big Data and Analytics Applications in Government
Current Practices and Future Opportunities
by Gregory Richards
ISBN: 978-1-4987-6434-6

Big Data in the Arts and Humanities
Theory and Practice
by Giovanni Schiuma and Daniela Carlucci
ISBN 978-1-4987-6585-5

Data Analytics Applications in Education
by Jan Vanthienen and Kristoff De Witte
ISBN: 978-1-4987-6927-3

Data Analytics Applications in Latin America and Emerging Economies
by Eduardo Rodriguez
ISBN: 978-1-4987-6276-2

Data Analytics for Smart Cities
by Amir Alavi and William G. Buttlar
ISBN 978-1-138-30877-0

Data-Driven Law
Data Analytics and the New Legal Services
by Edward J. Walters
ISBN 978-1-4987-6665-4

Intuition, Trust, and Analytics
by Jay Liebowitz, Joanna Paliszkiewicz, and Jerzy Gołuchowski
ISBN: 978-1-138-71912-5

Research Analytics
Boosting University Productivity and Competitiveness through Scientometrics
by Francisco J. Cantú-Ortiz
ISBN: 978-1-4987-6126-0

Sport Business Analytics
Using Data to Increase Revenue and Improve Operational Efficiency
by C. Keith Harrison and Scott Bukstein
ISBN: 978-1-4987-8542-6

Data Analytics and AI
by Jay Liebowitz
ISBN: 978-0-3678-9561-7

Data Analytics and AI

Edited by
Jay Liebowitz
Distinguished Chair of Applied Business and Finance
Harrisburg University of Science and Technology

CRC Press
Taylor & Francis Group
Boca Raton London New York

CRC Press is an imprint of the
Taylor & Francis Group, an **informa** business
AN AUERBACH BOOK

First edition published 2021
by CRC Press
6000 Broken Sound Parkway NW, Suite 300, Boca Raton, FL 33487-2742

and by CRC Press
2 Park Square, Milton Park, Abingdon, Oxon, OX14 4RN

ISBN: 978-0-367-52200-1 (hbk)
ISBN: 978-0-367-89561-7 (pbk)
ISBN: 978-1-003-01985-5 (ebk)

Typeset in Garamond
by Deanta global Publishing Services, Chennai, India

Visit the [companion website/eResources]: [insert comp website/eResources URL]

To our seventeen-month old, first grandchild, Zev,
whose curiosity and energy amazes us all!

Contents

Foreword ix
Preface xvii
List of Contributors xix
Editor xxiii

1   Unraveling Data Science, Artificial Intelligence, and Autonomy 1
    JOHN PIORKOWSKI

2   Unlock the True Power of Data Analytics with Artificial
    Intelligence 21
    RITU JYOTI

3   Machine Intelligence and Managerial Decision-Making 31
    LEE SCHLENKER AND MOHAMED MINHAJ

4   Measurement Issues in the Uncanny Valley: The Interaction
    between Artificial Intelligence and Data Analytics 53
    DOUGLAS A. SAMUELSON

5   An Overview of Deep Learning in Industry 65
    QUAN LE, LUIS MIRALLES-PECHUÁN, SHRIDHAR KULKARNI,
    JING SU, AND OISÍN BOYDELL

6   Chinese AI Policy and the Path to Global Leadership:
    Competition, Protectionism, and Security 99
    MARK ROBBINS

7   Natural Language Processing in Data Analytics 117
    YUDONG LIU

8   AI in Smart Cities Development: A Perspective of Strategic
    Risk Management 133
    EDUARDO RODRIGUEZ AND JOHN S. EDWARDS

9 Predicting Patient Missed Appointments in the Academic
   Dental Clinic...151
   AUNDREA L. PRICE AND GOPIKRISHNAN CHANDRASEKHARAN

10 Machine Learning in Cognitive Neuroimaging..................................167
   SIAMAK ARAM, DENIS KORNEV, YE HAN, MINA EKRAMNIA,
   ROOZBEH SADEGHIAN, SAEED ESMAILI SARDARI,
   HADIS DASHTESTANI, SAGAR KORA VENU, AND AMIR GANDJBAKHCHE

11 People, Competencies, and Capabilities Are Core Elements
   in Digital Transformation: A Case Study of a Digital
   Transformation Project at ABB 183
   ISMO LAUKKANEN

12 AI-Informed Analytics Cycle: Reinforcing Concepts..........................211
   ROSINA O. WEBER AND MAUREEN P. KINKELA

Index 235

Foreword

Introduction

Analytics and artificial intelligence (AI), what is it good for? The bandwagon keeps answering: absolutely everything! Analytics and artificial intelligence have captured the attention of everyone from top executives to the person in the street. While these disciplines have a relatively long history, within the last ten or so years, they have exploded into corporate business and public consciousness. Organizations have rushed to embrace data-driven decision-making. Companies everywhere are turning out products boasting that "artificial intelligence is included." We are indeed living in exciting times. The question we need to ask is, do we really know how to get business value from these exciting tools?

The core of analytics hasn't changed much since Tukey wrote "The Future of Data Analysis" in 1962.* Statistics is still statistics. Linear and non-linear regression models, various flavors of classification models, hypothesis testing, and so on have been around for many years. What has changed is the vast amount of data that is available both inside and outside of organizations and the dramatic increase in computing power that can be called upon to process it. Moving well beyond the rigid structures of corporate data in relational databases, organizations are collecting, processing, and analyzing unstructured text, image, audio, and video data. Today's deeply technical analytical tools and techniques are truly wondrous. Are these wondrous techniques being translated to business solutions?

Data Science Life Cycle

Unfortunately, most organizations are confused about the difference between analysis, analytics, and data science. These terms are often used interchangeably. "Data science" groups within organizations are almost always staffed with statisticians

---

* Tukey (1962) The Future of Data Analysis. Ann. Math. Statist., Volume 33, Number 1, 1–67.

(what some companies call "quants"*) who analyze and model data. Analysis is a small part of the much larger data science life cycle† (DSLC) shown in Figure F.1. I've divided the DSLC into what is currently performed by data scientists and what is currently performed by database and information technology (IT) personnel.

"Quants" retrieve data from company data repositories and analyze it. They use statistics to build descriptive, prescriptive, predictive, diagnostic, and other kinds of models. This is analysis. Data science covers analysis plus everything else that has to do with the data. It is truly the *science of data*.

Data science starts at data generation. Today, data generation happens on a massive scale. We're at the point where data storage is so inexpensive (fractions of a cent per gigabyte per month on Amazon cloud storage‡) that organizations are storing anything and everything just in case it's needed someday. Video cameras are recording 24/7. Calls, emails, and documents are recorded and stored. With every smartphone having a camera, consumers are taking pictures and storing them at a furious rate. It's estimated that by 2025, 463 exabytes of data will be added to the

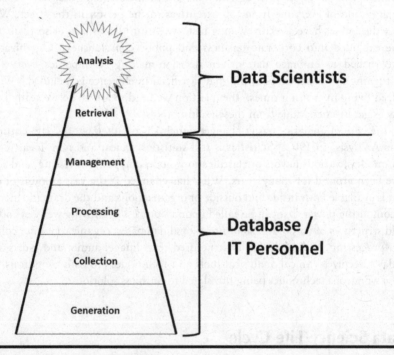

Figure F.1   Data science life cycle.

* IBM: The Quant Crunch: How the Demand for Data Science Skills is Disrupting the Job Market.
† *The Data Life Cycle*. MIT Press 2019. https://hdsr.mitpress.mit.edu/pub/577rq08d
‡ https://aws.amazon.com/s3/pricing/

global data storage swamp *daily*.* That's 463 million terabytes. Little thought is given to what happens next to all this data. How will the data be processed? What will it be used for? How can we model this data? AI will help us address these questions more every day.

We're just now trying to tackle the immense task of collecting the data that might hold something interesting for analysis. Entire industries are dedicated to collecting and organizing semi-structured data (for example, search engine industries, social media industries, and so on). For the most part, data collection relies on the data generator to tag and index just what is in that data. Hashtags must be used to figure out what a tweet means. Audio, video, and still pictures must have indexing keywords. However, vast quantities of data remain uncategorized. This is a big problem and will only get worse as companies realize the value of unstructured data. Deep learning might be a solution.

Deep learning is an advanced form of AI that is optimized for feature extraction in unstructured data and especially useful for classification tasks. For example, when trained on a variety of images, deep learning can classify what kind of leaves are present in a pile, can extract and identify various objects in a picture, and can perform facial recognition tasks, to name a few. In unstructured text, deep learning can identify messages and determine what kind of message it is, what the subject is, and relate that message to other similar messages.

Data must be processed. Missing, duplicate, and/or conflicting data needs to be resolved, known as "cleaning." Data scientists must be able to trust the data provenance. They need to know where the data came from. "Data wrangling" is the new data science buzzword. The tools and techniques and theories on how to do it right are rarely taught and therefore must be learned "on the job," something most data scientists are ill-prepared for. They are even less prepared to model data that has been gathered through AI (such as facial recognition) or analyzed by AI (for example, predictive search patterns).

Once we have clean data, data scientists must decide what is needed for analysis and, more importantly, what is missing. This is where data management comes in. How can we find the data that tells us what we need to know? Decades of work with structured data in relational databases has produced good results with optimized and provably correct data structures. However, unstructured data is proving difficult to manage. Not only is it difficult to wrangle, it's difficult to store, index, and optimize. The problem is made worse when unstructured data comes in at different velocities. AI can assist with this type of data by performing some of the wrangling by processing data through a "data lake."† The data lake, compared with the usual data silos, is a highly scalable, massively parallel data hub that smooths the torrent of data input. Unstructured data has incredible richness with far more detail than

---

* https://www.weforum.org/agenda/2019/04/how-much-data-is-generated-each-day-cf4bd df29f/

† https://www.cio.com/article/3406806/ai-unleashes-the-power-of-unstructured-data.html

structured data. Unfortunately, it's nearly impossible to collect, process, manage, or retrieve. This is where AI becomes critical for the advancement of data science into the future. Enter the domain of what I call *data science artificial intelligence* (DSAI).

AI has the remarkable capacity to scan the structured and unstructured data environments for relevant data, identify important elements, categorize and curate these elements, and store them for later retrieval. Deep learning is already attacking the problem of analyzing unstructured data. Fast image collection, categorization, and analysis has become commonplace. Other forms of AI such as voice recognition, processing, and analysis has entered the consumer marketplace with a myriad of household products (such as Alexa, Siri, etc.). Smart cars are collecting, processing, managing, and analyzing sensor data and making decisions in real time using AI.

DSAI in the future will take on many of the extremely difficult, currently manual tasks of data science. Today's true data scientists will move away from the data itself and will take on more responsibility for managing the DSAI. This will require data scientists who are trained in much more than statistics.

The Bigger Picture

In 2011, *The McKinsey Global Institute Report* stated that, "There will be a shortage of talent necessary for organizations to take advantage of big data. By 2018, the United States alone could face a shortage of 140,000 to 190,000 people with deep analytical skills."* In 2017, IBM predicted[†] that by "2020, job openings for data scientists and similar advanced analytical roles will reach 61,799" with a total shortage of 2,720,000 positions in all data-related fields such as database administrators and systems analysts. In 2018, the US Bureau of Labor Statistics[‡] expects that there will be an increase of about 50,000 technical data science jobs by 2028. The projections of the number of data science jobs keeps going down. Why?

During the early 2010s, companies realized that data science is where it's at. They went on a hiring spree for technical data scientists. Universities saw this shortage and created data science programs, strong on statistics. These programs were often simply existing statistics courses, repackaged and relabeled. By the late 2010s, companies had statistically strong data science departments but really had no idea what to do with them. Data scientists did what they were trained to do: mine data and create models. Hundreds of models. These models were passed on (often in indecipherable formats) to company management and executives who had no idea

---

* https://www.mckinsey.com/business-functions/mckinsey-digital/our-insights/big-data-the-next-frontier-for-innovation

† IBM: The Quant Crunch: How the Demand for Data Science Skills is Disrupting the Job Market. https://www-01.ibm.com/common/ssi/cgi-bin/ssialias?htmlfid=IML14576USEN&

‡ https://www.bls.gov/opub/btn/volume-7/big-data-adds-up.htm

what to do with them, so they were stored on a shelf in case they proved useful someday. Most of these models are still sitting on shelves gathering dust.

Today, there is a surplus of data scientists turning out models that are never used. Companies are reducing their hiring, and universities that were on the leading edge of data science education are closing their programs. All of this is caused by a basic misunderstanding: *Data Science is not Analytics.* Data science is data and analysis. Analytics is *the bridge between data science and business.*

Over the past year, I've interviewed data scientists and business managers in companies across the United States. Data scientists consistently say that managers can't ask the right questions and don't understand statistical models. Managers say that data scientists don't understand the business and can't give them what they need. Some companies are stepping up and creating a "translator" role to bridge the gap between data science and management. This is a step in the right direction, but only a baby step. Translators must understand both data science and the business. Period. Very soon they will also need to understand AI.

Today, in the early 2020s, this idea is spreading. The data science life cycle now includes a very important step: "Understand the business."* The problem is that this is not currently the data scientist's job. Data science departments are usually set apart from the rest of the organization. They have very little experience with the organization as a whole and even less with specific divisions or departments. Similarly, managers and executives are experts in their part of the organization but have very little experience with statistical models or the intricacies of data. Once again, business schools need to step up and provide training and re-training for both data scientists and managers.

Analytics must be recast not as a technical statistical field but rather as a discipline unto itself. Look at any current university's "Business Analytics" program and you'll see a lot of data science and very little business. This is not analytics as the term should be used. Whereas analysis is a small part of the whole of data science, data science itself is a relatively small part of analytics. The entire analytics life cycle is shown in Figure F.2.

The analytics life cycle (ALC) covers everything from start to finish all within a business context. The steps are straightforward and relatively intuitive. It's useful to go through a checklist of all the steps even if you *know* that nothing has changed. The littlest things may end up having tremendous impacts. The steps are:

1. Understand the business environment
2. Understand the business
3. Understand the business goals
4. Understand the business strategy
5. Recognize and understand the business problem(s)

---

* https://towardsdatascience.com/data-science-life-cycle-101-for-dummies-like-me-e66b47 ad8d8f

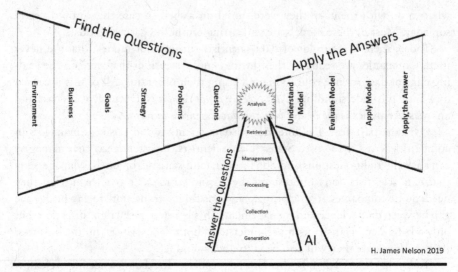

Figure F.2 Analytics life cycle.

6. Develop questions
7. Use the *data science life cycle*
8. Understand the analytic model through visualization
9. Evaluate the analytic model
10. Apply the model back to the questions
    (send unanswered questions by the model back through the process)
11. Apply the answered question(s) to the business problem

The ALC is far more than data science. It requires a deep understanding of the business, including what the business is, the business environment, its goals and its strategies, and what problems are being addressed. All this is required for generating questions that can be answered by data science and analysis. Only then will the two questions posed earlier be addressed: obtaining business value and business solutions from analytics.

What business manager or executive has the time or the skill for all this? If they could do it, they would be doing it. Managers and even top executives think they know what's going on in the organization and where the organization is headed. Many times, they are very, very wrong. What's needed is an AI application that can scan the organization's environment, internal processes, and structures to determine if the organization's strategy is indeed leading them in the right direction toward the desired goals. This is very similar in theory to DSAI. Enter management AI (MAI).

MAI can advise management and top executives about where the organization is actually headed. It can suggest changes to strategy or even suggest adjusting organizational goals. A continuously operating MAI can suggest organizational adjustments in real time. With a good idea of the proper strategy, MAI can scan for problems that are keeping the organization from executing strategy and develop questions that can be passed along to the DSAI for answering. MAI has the potential to mine things we currently view as ephemeral such as managerial intuition and hunches.*

DSAI has the potential to produce models that are accurate, relevant, and understandable in the business context. This can help managers and executives do what they do best.

Today, analytics is still in its infancy. It's a loose conglomeration of statistics, database/IT, and organizational management. Analytics brings all this together into a coherent whole. Supplemented with AI in the form of DSAI and MAI, we're moving into a very exciting future.

Harry (Jim) Nelson
Director, Pontikes Center for Advanced Analytics and Artificial Intelligence
Southern Illinois University

---

* Nelson, Clark, and Stewart. (2018) Hunch Mining. *Hawaii International Conference on System Sciences,* Waikoloa, HI.

Preface

As we continue to forge ahead in this data-driven and cognitive computing/artificial intelligence (AI) era, the question is what is next? With the demands for data-informed decisions, coupled with machine/deep learning techniques, we see the development and use of AI-powered analytics. At the same time, experiential learning (what I call "intuition-based decision-making") will also play an important complementary role in executive decision-making.

We are witnessing tremendous growth in data analytics, data science, and machine learning, but there is still ample room for creativity and future development. Currently, the analytics and AI communities have been a bit siloed. As we move forward, the two communities should share a more common bond as the integration between the two fields is essential for advancing the current state-of-the-art.

This book helps to shed light on the opportunities, challenges, issues, technologies, and applications where this integration can occur. Of course, this book presents only a sample of what is possible, but it at least helps to shape this integrative environment.

I am indebted to Jim Nelson for his Foreword and to those chapter contributors who provided their keen insights on their research and others. These contributors are highly respected individuals in the fields of analytics, data science, and AI. Their comments are insightful, and some provocative, and they will certainly get your neurons firing!

I am also extremely appreciative of John Wyzalek, Stephanie Place-Retzlaff, Randi Cohen, Rich O'Hanley, Kristine Mednansky, and all the Taylor & Francis team for their wonderful support and having the wisdom to create a *Data Analytics Applications* book series, adding this important volume to the other 21 books in the series to date. I am very grateful to Bryan Moloney and his colleagues at Deanta Global for their timeliness in producing this book.

I would be remiss if I didn't express my gratitude to all my students, colleagues, and professional contacts over the years who have helped me shape my own teaching and research agendas in my 37 years in academia.

Finally, I am very lucky to have such a fantastic, loving supportive family who wonders whether this might be my last book! I'll keep them guessing...

Jay Liebowitz
Washington, DC/Philadelphia

List of Contributors

Siamak Aram
Harrisburg University of Science and Technology
Harrisburg, Pennsylvania

Oisín Boydell
CeADAR
University College Dublin
Dublin, Ireland

Gopikrishnan Chandrasekharan
Marquette University School of Dentistry
Milwaukee, Wisconsin

Hadis Dashtestani
Eunice Kennedy Shriver National Institute of Child Health and Human Development, National Institutes of Health
Bethesda, Maryland

John S. Edwards
Aston Business School
Aston University
Birmingham, UK

Mina Ekramnia
Education Global Practice
World Bank
Washington, D.C.

Amir Gandjbakhche
Eunice Kennedy Shriver National Institute of Child Health and Human Development, National Institutes of Health
Bethesda, Maryland

Ye Han
Harrisburg University of Science and Technology
Harrisburg, Pennsylvania

Ritu Jyoti
Artificial Intelligence Strategies
IDC
Boston, Massachusetts

Maureen Kinkela
Drexel University
Philadelphia, Pennsylvania

Denis Kornev
Harrisburg University of Science and Technology
Harrisburg, Pennsylvania

Shridhar Kulkarni
CeADAR
University College Dublin
Dublin, Ireland

Ismo Laukkanen
ABB Northern Europe
Helsinki, Finland

Quan Le
CeADAR
University College Dublin
Dublin, Ireland

Yudong Liu
Western Washington University
Bellingham, Washington

Mohamed Minhaj
SDM Institute for Management
 Development
Mysore, India

Luis Miralles-Pechuán
CeADAR
University College Dublin
Dublin, Ireland

Harry (Jim) Nelson
Pontikes Center for Advanced
 Analytics and Artificial Intelligence
Southern Illinois University
Carbondale, Illinois

John Piorkowski
Asymmetric Operations Sector
Johns Hopkins University Applied
 Physics Laboratory
Laurel, Maryland

Aundrea Price
Graduate Health Data Analytics
 Program
Marquette University
Milwaukee, Wisconsin

Mark Robbins
Canadian International Council
Toronto, Canada

Eduardo Rodriquez
Department of Mathematics
Wenzhou-Kean University
Wenzhou, China

and

IQAnalytics
Ottawa, Canada

Roozbeh Sadeghian
Harrisburg University of Science and
 Technology
Harrisburg, Pennsylvania

Douglas A. Samuelson
InfoLogix, Inc.
Annandale, Virginia

Saeed Esmaili Sardari
Harrisburg University of Science and
 Technology
Harrisburg, Pennsylvania

Lee Schlenker
The Business Analytics Institute
St. Martin d'Uriage, France

Jing Su
CeADAR
University College Dublin
Dublin, Ireland

Sagar Kora Venu
Harrisburg University of Science and
    Technology
Harrisburg, Pennsylvania

Rosina Weber
Information Science
Drexel University
Philadelphia, Pennsylvania

Editor

Dr. Jay Liebowitz is the Distinguished Chair of Applied Business and Finance at Harrisburg University of Science and Technology. He previously was the Orkand Endowed Chair of Management and Technology in the Graduate School at the University of Maryland University College (UMUC). He served as a Professor in the Carey Business School at Johns Hopkins University. He was ranked one of the top 10 knowledge management researchers/practitioners out of 11,000 worldwide, and was ranked second in KM Strategy worldwide according to the January 2010 Journal of Knowledge Management. At Johns Hopkins University, he was the founding Program Director for the Graduate Certificate in Competitive Intelligence and the Capstone Director of the MS-Information and Telecommunications Systems for Business Program, where he engaged over 30 organizations in industry, government, and not-for-profits in capstone projects.

Chapter 1

Unraveling Data Science, Artificial Intelligence, and Autonomy

John Piorkowski

Contents

1.1 The Beginnings of Data Science 2
1.2 The Beginnings of Artificial Intelligence 3
1.3 The Beginnings of Autonomy 4
1.4 The Convergence of Data Availability and Computing 6
1.5 Machine Learning the Common Bond 6
    1.5.1 Supervised Learning 7
    1.5.2 Unsupervised Learning..10
    1.5.3 Reinforcement Learning 10
1.6 Data Science Today 11
1.7 Artificial Intelligence Today 13
1.8 Autonomy Today...16
1.9 Summary 17
References 18

Often in discussions on data science, artificial intelligence (AI), and autonomy, the terms become conflated. Recently, we have experienced hype cycles in data science, artificial intelligence, and autonomy. Although these fields share common technologies and algorithms, their history has evolved independently, and they employ different frameworks and address different real-world applications. This chapter explains the commonalities and differences in the fields of data science, artificial intelligence, and autonomy. First, we will provide a historical perspective for each of these fields, followed by an exploration of common technologies and current trends in each field.

1.1 The Beginnings of Data Science

Data collection and analysis have been around long before the advent of the computer. A notable example is the work of Matthew Fontaine Maury, who was known as the "Scientist of the Seas." Maury was a pioneer in the field of ocean navigation during the mid-1800s.* He joined the Navy at the age of 19, but a stagecoach accident forced him to give up traveling the seas and take an assignment with the Navy at the Depot of Charts and Instruments. The Depot of Charts and Instruments would later become the US Naval Observatory. By studying meteorology, collecting data from ship's logs, and creating charts, Maury revolutionized our understanding of oceanography and marine navigation. Figure 1.1 illustrates his 1851 Trade Wind Chart of the Atlantic Ocean, which assisted ship captains at the time with their cross-Atlantic journeys.

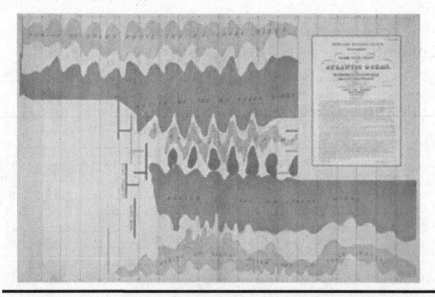

Figure 1.1 "Trade wind chart of the Atlantic Ocean," by Matthew Fontaine Maury, 1851. Geography and Map Division, Library of Congress.

* https://blogs.loc.gov/maps/2018/07/scientist-of-the-seas-the-legacy-of-matthew-fontaine-maury/

A second example involves security analysis created by Benjamin Graham and David Dodd at the Columbia Business School in the 1920s. Security analysis involves analysis of financial data to inform investment decisions. These professors coauthored the classic text "Security Analysis" (1934), which describes the technique. Long-time successful investors such as Warren Buffet have been stewards of this technique.

A modern history of data science enabled by computing is often credited to a paper by John Tukey in 1962 titled "The Future of Data Analysis." In this paper, he describes procedures for analyzing data, interpreting results, and planning for the gathering of data, as well as the statistics that apply to these procedures. Tukey's prophecy of data analysis motivated a shift from theoretical statistics and advocated for applied statistics to become data analytics. Tukey's paper has been reviewed more recently and still stands as a foundation for modern data science (Mallows, 2006).

In 1974, Pete Naur published the "Concise Survey of Computer Methods" and repeatedly used the term data science, defining it as the "the science of dealing with data, once they have been established, while the relation of the data to what they represent is delegated to other fields and sciences." Even with Naur's publication, many credit William Cleveland with coining the term "data science" with his publication in 2001. In his paper, he advocates for a substantial change to the field of statistics. To reinforce a significant change, he advocated for a new field called data science. He asserted that data science should include the following:

- Multidisciplinary investigations
- Models and methods for data
- Computational systems
- Pedagogy for education
- Evaluation of tools
- Theoretical foundations

Cleveland's paper is cited as the seminal data paper; however, the field did not gain popularity until the explosion of internet connectivity, the low cost of data storage, and the "Big Data" era. The Big Data term refers to large and complex data that cannot be addressed with traditional relational database tool sets.*

1.2 The Beginnings of Artificial Intelligence

Many authors trace the beginnings of AI to the work of Aristotle and Euclid, who promoted the idea of human intelligence being mechanized. The genesis of artificial

---

* https://en.m.wikibooks.org/wiki/Data_Science:_An_Introduction/A_History_of_Data_Science

intelligence using computers rose out of a workshop at Dartmouth in 1956. This spawned the first wave of artificial intelligence that extended into the mid-1970s. The first wave was characterized by symbolic reasoning (Gunning, 2017). Symbolic reasoning relies on rule-based engines and expert systems that require engineers creating knowledge for these systems. The field experienced the first AI winter in the mid-1970s due to several circumstances,* which included leading AI researchers identifying weaknesses in AI approaches and a summary report on the state of AI research published by the British government, the Lighthouse Report, in 1973. AI winters refer to increased skepticism within the field and reduced investment. Research funding diminished until the field of AI experienced another boom in the 1980s. The research of John Hopfield (1982) and David Rumelhart et al. (1986) described neural networks with back propagation, which renewed interest in AI research. These papers are credited with adding back propagation to neural networks. However, the original concept of back propagation was published by Paul Werbos a decade earlier (Werbos, 1974). A second trend fueling the boom was an effort to commercialize AI products.† A primary focus of new products was expert systems built upon rule-based engines. This was short-lived, as expert systems never achieved full acceptance due to the narrowness of the problems they could solve. So, the field experienced another winter in the early 1990s.

In the mid-1990s, the field of AI shifted from knowledge-driven machine learning (e.g., expert systems) to data-driven AI. Fueled by the exponential growth of data generated by computing devices and shared on the internet, researchers curated data for the development of machine learning algorithms. One significant effort was the development of the ImageNet data set (Deng et al., 2009) that commenced in 2009 and took 2.5 years to label 3.2 million images. The data set served as the foundation for the ImageNet computer vision competition that started in 2010. In 2012, Geoffrey Hinton and his team of researchers won the competition by a significant margin, and this result inspired the current AI boom (Krizhevsky et al., 2012). Their technique used neural networks that existed for decades. However, by applying neural networks with a large labeled data set and leveraging modern graphical processing units (GPUs), their work advanced the field.

Another recent milestone was the demonstration of an AI agent beating a human in a computer game titled AlphaGo. The AI solution combined neural networks with reinforcement learning, which outperformed traditional Monte Carlo search techniques (Silver et al., 2016).

1.3 The Beginnings of Autonomy

Today, the topic of autonomy is usually associated with robotics. To explore the genesis of robotics and autonomy, it is worth considering the history of automatons.

---

* https://towardsdatascience.com/history-of-the-first-ai-winter-6f8c2186f80b
† https://towardsdatascience.com/history-of-the-second-ai-winter-406f18789d45

Merriam-Webster's Dictionary defines automatons as "a mechanism that is relatively self-operating (especially: robot)" or "a machine or control mechanism designed to follow automatically a predetermined sequence of operations or respond to encoded instructions."

Examples of automatons can be found as far back as 250 BC with Ctesibius's water clock. During the 18th century, popular automatons included the Jaquet-Droz automata, which are the musician, the draughtsman, and the writer designs.

The term "automatons" was used for centuries. It was not until 1920 that the term "robot" appeared in the title of a play, *Rossum's Universal Robots*, written by Karel Čapek, a Czech writer.

In the 1960s, industrial robots emerged with the development of the Unimate robotic arm for factory automation. One of the early robots that involved computation was Shakey, which was developed in the late 1960s at the Artificial Research Institute at the Stanford Research Center. Shakey combined research in robotics with computer vision and natural language processing.

The current field of robotics and autonomy is enabled by sensors, actuators, and AI.* In 2009, the United States published the first national roadmap for robotics (Computing Community Consortium, 2009). The roadmap described broad critical capabilities to include robust 3D perception, planning and navigation, human-like dexterous manipulation, intuitive human-robot interaction, and safe robot behavior. For robotic systems to perform autonomously, the capabilities of perception and planning and navigation are critical. These are areas where AI has become an enabler. An update to the 2009 roadmap was published in 2016, and deep learning and reinforcement learning were highly emphasized (Computing Community Consortium, 2016).

---

* https://www.wired.com/story/wired-guide-to-robots/

1.4 The Convergence of Data Availability and Computing

In looking at the history of these fields, they all experienced modern data resurgence through the availability of data and speed of computing. Understanding the availability of data stems from the reduction of the cost of computer memory. In 2003, Morris and Truskowski provided a history of storage systems and concluded that digital storage technology is cheaper than paper and film. This trend led to an emerging field called "Big Data" that focused on processing structured and unstructured data, with most of the data being created by devices connected to the internet. The term "Big Data" was coined in 2005 by Roger Magoulas (Sreeja and Sangeetha, 2015). He was referring to a large set of data that, at the time, was almost impossible to manage and process using the traditional business intelligence tools available. Additionally, Hadoop, which could handle Big Data, was created in 2005. Hadoop was based on an open-sourced software framework called Nutch and was merged with Google's MapReduce. Because of this flexibility, Hadoop can process Big Data. Another shift that occurred in computing was the rise of GPUs. The world of computing benefited from Moore's Law, which states that computer processing speeds double every two years. From the 1970s through the 2000s, Moore's Law applied, but more recently, we experienced a slowing in performance improvements. GPUs emerged in the mid-1990s with 32-bit computer systems and the need for 3D graphics rendering. They provided high-speed polygon rendering and were optimized for mathematical processing instead of general-purpose computing. The performance of GPUs led to the current performance of machine learning algorithms. Machine learning is described in more depth in the next section.

1.5 Machine Learning the Common Bond

As previously mentioned, the AI community experienced a shift from a knowledge-based approach to a data-driven approach. Machine learning enabled this shift in the AI domain. In 1959, Arthur Samuel defined machine learning as a "field of study that gives computers the ability to learn without being explicitly programmed." At the highest level, machine learning algorithms can be categorized into the following:

- Supervised learning
- Unsupervised learning
- Reinforcement learning

Supervised learning involves learning patterns from labeled data. Examples of supervised learning include algorithms that would classify email as spam or identify cats in videos. Alternatively, unsupervised learning algorithms discover patterns in data without labeled data. Finally, reinforcement learning employs risk versus reward models to predict actions.

1.5.1 Supervised Learning

The process of supervised learning consists of two phases (Figure 1.2). The first is the training phase for the machine learning model. Training data must be curated and engineered, and this is generally the most resource-intensive part of creating the machine learning classifier. Once the training data are created, a supervised machine learning algorithm is applied to the data to create a machine learning model. The second phase is the classification phase, where new data are presented to the trained machine learning model and the new data are classified as one of the trained categories.

Popular supervised machine learning algorithms are Naive Bayes, support vector machines (SVMs), random forest, and deep neural networks. In addition, there are ensemble methods in supervised machine learning where different algorithms are combined in various ways to improve the classification results. The ensemble classification is illustrated in Figure 1.3. Combining the outputs of the individual classifiers can be achieved using different combination rules. Examples may include majority vote or probability-based solutions.

As previously mentioned, a boom in machine learning occurred with the results of the 2012 ImageNet competition (Krizhevsky et al., 2012). This work transformed the area of supervised machine learning by the application of deep neural networks (aka deep learning). Deep learning combines feature extraction with classification. In machine learning, a feature is measurable or observable data that can be used for analysis.

Figure 1.4 uses a simple example of feature engineering for classifying bicycles with machine learning.

Traditional supervised learning would require human feature engineering to create the machine learning classifier. In the case of designing a bicycle classifier, the designer would need to select features such as circles and triangles. For deep learning, the computer algorithm would discover the features by providing the

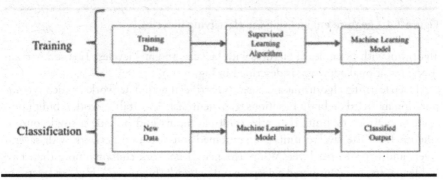

Figure 1.2   Two phases of supervised machine learning.

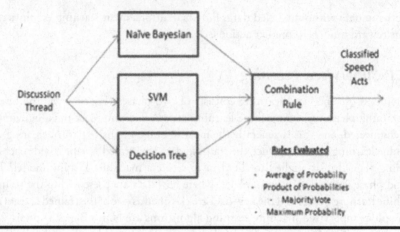

Figure 1.3 Ensemble methods for supervised machine learning.

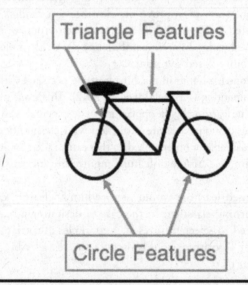

Figure 1.4 Feature engineering for classifying bicycles.

algorithm with examples of pictures with bicycles and no bicycles. This comparison to the traditional approach is described in Figure 1.5.

Deep learning algorithms are based on artificial neural networks, which is computation modeled on brain functions (e.g., neurons). A neural network is built upon a set of neurons or units that take multiple inputs and provide a single output (Figure 1.6). The layered units are combined into a neural network with several layers and neurons per layer. When the neural network contains more than two hidden layers, it is considered a deep neural network (Figure 1.7). Hidden layers are isolated from the input and output layers of the neural network. When designing

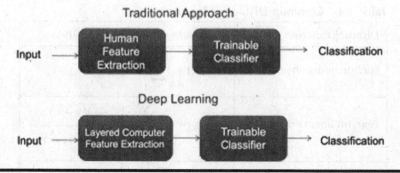

Figure 1.5 **Comparison of traditional supervised machine learning with deep learning.**

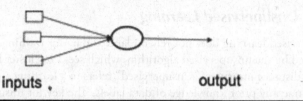

Figure 1.6 **Simple neuron model.**

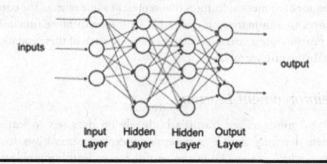

Figure 1.7 **Neural network.**

deep neural networks, the designer must decide on the number of layers, the number of neurons per layer, and the activation functions for the neurons. Common activation functions include the following:

- Step
- Linear
- Sigmoid (logistic)
- Tangent hyperbolic (TanH)
- Rectified linear unit (ReLU)
- Softsign

Table 1.1   Common Distance Measures

Distance function	Mathematical representation
Euclidean distance	$D(X,Y) = \sqrt{\sum_{i=1}^{n}(x_i - y_i)^2}$
Pearson linear correlation	$C(X,Y) = \dfrac{\sum_{i=1}^{n}(x_i - \bar{X})(y_i - \bar{Y})}{\sqrt{\sum_{i=1}^{n}(x_i - \bar{X})^2 \sum_{i=1}^{n}(y_i - \bar{Y})^2}}$
Cosine similarity	$C(X,Y) = \dfrac{X \cdot Y}{|X||Y|}$

1.5.2 Unsupervised Learning

Unsupervised learning does not rely on labeled data for training. Instead, data are processed by the unsupervised algorithm, which seeks to cluster like data based on various distance measures. "Unsupervised" refers to a learning algorithm that does not assume any prior knowledge of data labels. The key for unsupervised learning is to represent the data into a structure that allows for the application of distance measures. For example, the data will be structured into feature vectors. A feature vector is a vector of numerical features that represent some object. The common distance measures are summarized in Table 1.1. Common distance functions include Euclidean, Pearson linear correlation, and cosine. In each of these equations, X and Y represent the feature vectors.

1.5.3 Reinforcement Learning

Supervised and unsupervised learning both rely on data sets to learn patterns. Reinforcement learning uses a framework to explore alternatives to achieve a reward signal, which is the goal of the reinforcement learning problem. Another way to think about reinforcement learning is in situations when you can measure the goodness of a solution but do not have prior knowledge of the solution.

The architecture for reinforcement learning is illustrated in Figure 1.8.

The components of reinforcement learning include the following:

- Policy: mapping of perceived environmental states to actions to be taken when in those states
- Reward signal: goal for reinforcement problem
- Value function: the total amount of reward an agent can expect to accumulate over the future, starting from that state
- Model of the environment: provides for inferences to be made about how the environment will behave

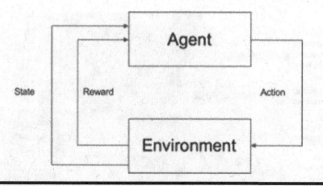

Figure 1.8 Reinforcement learning process.

The name reinforcement learning comes from the idea of reinforcing desired behavior. If the AI does something desirable, that behavior can be reinforced via a "reward signal." This reward is what the AI is trying to optimize. Specifically, it is trying to learn how to behave such that it gets as much reward as possible over time.

One of the limitations of reinforcement learning is when environment states become too large and computation becomes significant. Recently combining deep learning with reinforcement learning has advanced the field. By using a deep neural network to represent the state and observation space the learning performance is increased. The field of deep reinforcement learning (DRL) is rising in popularity and has been applied to robotics, natural language processing, and financial management (Yang et al., 2018).

1.6 Data Science Today

Leveraging the advances in data storage, computing, and machine learning, data science emerged as a popular field. Practical applications of data science are broad reaching, to include marketing, fraud detection, logistics, crime prediction, social engagement, sports team management, and health care.* For any data science application, you can consider the data science maturity model illustrated in Figure 1.9. The maturity model is adapted from the analytics value chain presented in Anderson (2015). The initial (and often the most resource intensive) step to mature a data-driven approach is the data engineering. Data engineering can also be described as data wrangling, curation, or extract, transform, load (ETL). As previously mentioned, the reduced cost of memory has led to creation of enormous amounts of data. However, the data are often contained in disparate systems and are not well-suited for modern data science algorithms. In the discussion of machine learning, the data must be engineered to allow feature representations.

---

* https://builtin.com/data-science/data-science-applications-examples

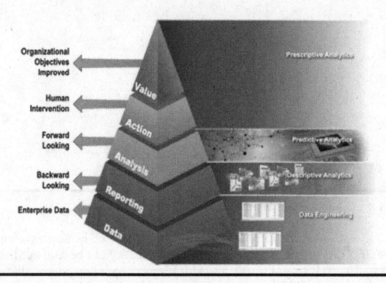

Organizational
Objectives
Improved

Human
Intervention

Forward
Looking

Backward
Looking

Enterprise Data

Value

Action

Analysis

Reporting

Data

Prescriptive Analytics

Predictive Analytics

Descriptive Analytics

Data Engineering

Figure 1.9   Data science maturity model.

Neil Lawrence offers a framework to assess data readiness for analytics (Lawrence, 2017). He uses three levels of data readiness (Figure 1.10). The lowest level (C-Level) describes the challenges with data engineering and wrangling. As Lawrence explains, many organizations claim they have data, but the data have not been made available for analytic use. He refers to this type of data as "hearsay" data. B-Level data require an understanding of the faithfulness and representation of the data. Finally, A-Level data are about data in context. With A-Level data, it is understood whether the data can answer organizational questions. Once data are made available in a data warehouse or data lake, reporting can be performed. Many organizations create reports using spreadsheets or text documents. This approach looks backward, reflecting what has happened in the past. The promise of data science is to move beyond backward-looking reporting to become forward looking. In the field of data science, analytics are typically described as descriptive, predictive, and prescriptive, although some include diagnostic after descriptive analytics. Descriptive analytics involves understanding the characteristics of the data. For numerical data, descriptive analytics includes statistical measures such as means, standard deviations, modes, and medians. Other analytics may include histograms. Descriptive analytics helps to discover anomalous and missing data examples. Descriptive analytics are backward looking too.

Moving from backward looking to forward looking can be achieved with predictive analytics. Predictive analytics uses data about the past to make predictions about the future. Supervised machine learning provides an analytical tool for predictive analytics. As previously described, supervised machine learning uses training data to create a machine learning model. The machine learning model can then be used to make predictions about new data sets.

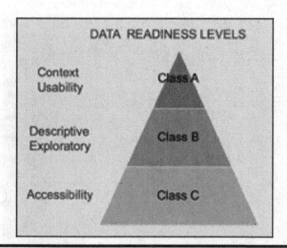

Figure 1.10   Data readiness levels defined by Neil Lawrence.

The third type of data science analytic is prescriptive analytics, which addresses the human intervention because it provides for decision options. Moving beyond predictive analytics, which describe a future state, prescriptive analytics offers courses of action to bring value to an organizational objective. Reinforcement learning is a machine learning approach that provides a foundation for prescriptive analytics.

1.7 Artificial Intelligence Today

We are in the midst of another AI spring driven by the results of the ImageNet competition (Alex Krizhevsky et al., 2012) and the AlphaGo results. These achievements motivated national-level initiatives with significant government funding.* AI has broad applications and, as previously mentioned, seeks to replace or augment human intelligence with computers.

To achieve practical results with AI techniques, AI needs to be considered as part of a systems concept, which can be specified as an AI-enabled system or intelligent system. A general framework for intelligent systems is described in Figure 1.11.

The framework captures the things intelligent systems need to do and the progressively sophisticated capabilities to enable them. Teaming is added because intelligent systems must ultimately be used by people, and because they have unique teaming challenges (both machine-to-machine and machine-to-person). Finally, it is critical that trust be addressed at every capability level. Trust deals with the need for assurance that an intelligent system will meet its performance objectives in the

---

* https://medium.com/politics-ai/an-overview-of-national-ai-strategies-2a70ec6edfd

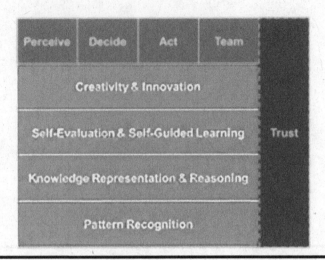

Figure 1.11   Intelligent systems framework.

face of uncertainty in real-world environments. The boxes represent the following families of techniques in the broad field of artificial intelligence. These techniques are described below:

> *Pattern Recognition. Using machine learning to recognize objects and patterns in data. Pattern recognition is most often applied to perception problems, such as classifying physical objects in imagery. Essentially, pattern recognition provides a level of triage for the human analyst to say, "there is something in the data." Both supervised and unsupervised learning play a significant role in pattern recognition. Pattern recognition does overlap with the field of data science.*
>
> *Knowledge Representation and Reasoning. Using computational techniques to put objects, patterns, and observables into context. Knowledge representation and reasoning requires upfront modeling, so the machine reasoning is constrained by the preprogrammed models. Traditionally, machine reasoning has been accomplished using techniques such as symbol processing (e.g., logic), semantic reasoning (e.g., ontologies), or probabilistic inference (e.g., Bayesian networks).*
>
> *Self-Evaluation and Self-Guided Learning. As compared with the previous categories, self-evaluation and learning allows the machine to adjust its programming and/or parameters based on its own observations. Although there are many classical techniques for progressive adaptation of the parameters of a fixed deployed algorithm, emerging techniques in machine learning (e.g., deep reinforcement learning) will enable a machine to evolve its actual algorithm over time in response to its environment and according to high-level objectives provided by a human. This is an area of*

active research and will be critical for national security as the real world is constantly changing, including the tactics of adversarial agents in the operating environment.

Creativity and Innovation. This layer is the highest aspiration in AI— emergent machine intelligence that autonomously realizes capabilities well beyond initial programming. In the lower layers, the AI algorithms are largely shaped by preprogrammed models and allowed to make adjustments from these models. Unlike machines, humans possess creativity and imagi- nation and can think outside the constraints of models. For this layer, the AI algorithms are demonstrating some degree of creativity. An interesting tangent here is the recent work of Pearl and Mackenzie (2018) on causality. He asserts causal discovery and the ability to reason about how "counterfac- tuals" represent key aspects of imagination in an intelligent agent.

With the boom of AI spawned by data-driven approaches using machine learn- ing achieving human-level performance in pattern recognition research, the field seeks to move beyond pattern recognition and leverage a combination of data- driven and symbolic reasoning techniques. In the future, the progression of the field can be mapped by deriving four technical areas. These areas can be described as follows:

Autonomous Perception
Systems that reason about their environment, focus on the critical aspects of the scene, understand the intent of humans and other machines, and learn through exploration.
Superhuman Decision-Making and Autonomous Action
Systems that identify, evaluate, select, and execute effective courses of action with superhuman speed and accuracy for real-world challenges.
Human-Machine Teaming at the Speed of Thought
Systems that understand human intent and work in collaboration with humans to perform tasks that are difficult or dangerous for humans to carry out with speed and accuracy.
Safe and Assured Operation
Systems that are robust to real-world perturbation and resilient to adversarial attacks with ethical reasoning and goals that are guaranteed to remain aligned with human intent.

It should be noted that the technical areas will require a combination of data- driven and symbolic AI techniques. Reasoning becomes more prevalent as machine abilities advance to perform pattern recognition. DARPA describes the next wave of AI as *systems constructing contextual explanatory models** which will require

---

* https://www.darpa.mil/attachments/AIFull.pdf

reasoning. In August 2019, the Computing Community Consortium (CCC) and Association for the Advancement of Artificial Intelligence (AAAI) published "A 20-Year Community Roadmap for Artificial Intelligence Research in the US" (CCC and AAAI, 2019). This roadmap identified three major research priorities that include integrated intelligence, meaningful interaction, and self-aware learning. For each of these priorities, the roadmap identified reasoning as an important research component.

Data-driven approaches to AI based on deep neural networks have been referred to as connectionism. Alternatively, a rule-based, logic, and reasoning approach to AI is referred to as symbolism. The AI field that explores the blending of both approaches is neural-symbolic computing (Garcez et al., 2019). Garnelo and Shanahan (2019) explain that the shortcomings of deep neural networks align with the strengths of symbolic AI. Their paper provides a survey of recent advances that seek to reconcile connectionism and symbolism in AI.

1.8 Autonomy Today

The field of autonomy today is dominated by modern robotics, driverless cars, and drones. Three main components of an autonomous system include sensors, reasoning, and actuators. Modern autonomous systems are enabled by AI. Figure 1.12 maps AI functions (i.e., perceive, decide, and act) to the components of an autonomous system.

In the field of robotics, there are numerous frameworks for developing robotic systems. Tsardoulias and Mitkas (2017) provide a comprehensive survey of robotic frameworks. Generally, these frameworks address the following:

■ Robot geometry library
■ Robot description language
■ Diagnostics

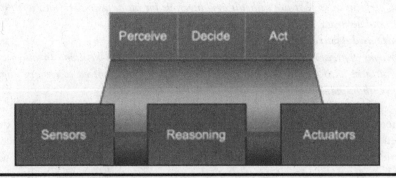

Figure 1.12   Mapping AI tasks to autonomy.

- Pose estimation algorithms
- Localization modules
- Mapping algorithms
- Navigation and path creation modules

A classification framework of key technologies for self-driving is described by Zhao et al. (2018). This framework includes car navigation, environment perception, path planning, and car control. The major components of drones include the flight mechanisms (e.g., fixed wing or rotary), the degree of autonomy, and the sensor payloads. The autonomy of a drone will rely on AI techniques.

1.9 Summary

This chapter describes the fields of data science, AI, and autonomy. Each of these fields is experiencing significant growth and interest as practical applications emerge. Machine learning is a critical enabler and provides tremendous capabilities with the availability of data and computing power. All three fields leverage the advances in machine learning with an emphasis on deep neural networks and reinforcement learning. Finally, there is a large amount of overlap in the fields of data science, AI, and autonomy. However, by considering the history of these fields and thematically what they seek to achieve, differences can be established, as summarized in Figure 1.13.

Figure 1.13   Comparison of data science, AI, and autonomy.

References

Anderson, C. (2015). *Creating a Data-Driven Organization* (1st ed.). Sebastopol, CA: O'Reilly Media, Inc.

Cleveland, W. (2001). Data science: An action plan for expanding the technical areas of the field of statistics. *International Statistical Review/Revue Internationale De Statistique, 69*(1), 21–26.

Computing Community Consortium (2016, October 31). *A Roadmap for US Robotics—From Internet to Robotics* (2016 ed.). Washington, DC: Computing Research Association.

Computing Community Consortium (2009, May 21). *A Roadmap for US Robotics—From Internet to Robotics*. Washington, DC: Computing Research Association.

Computing Community Consortium and Association for the Advancement of Artificial Intelligence (AAAI) (2019, August 19). *A 20-Year Community Roadmap for Artificial Intelligence Research in the US*.

Deng, J., Dong, W., Socher, R., Li, L., Li, K., & Fei-Fei, L. (2009). ImageNet: A large-scale hierarchical image database. *2009 IEEE Conference on Computer Vision and Pattern Recognition*, Miami, FL, 2009, pp. 248–255.

Garcez, A. S., Gori, M., Lamb, L. C., Serafini, L., Spranger, M., & Tran, S. N. (2019). Neural-symbolic computing: An effective methodology for principled integration of machine learning and reasoning. *IfColog Journal of Logics and their Applications (FLAP), 6*, 611–632.

Garnelo, M., & Shanahan, M. (2019). Reconciling deep learning with symbolic artificial intelligence: Representing objects and relations. *Current Opinion in Behavioral Sciences, 29*, 17–23.

Graham, B., & Dodd, D. (1934). *Security Analysis*. New York: McGraw-Hill.

Gunning, D. (2017, October 10). The promise of artificial intelligence—Again. *Presented at the MIT Washington Seminar Series: Artificial Intelligence and Machine Learning*.

Hopfield, J. J. (1982, April). Neural networks and physical systems with emergent collective computational abilities. *Proceedings of the National Academy of Sciences of the United States of America, 79*(8), 2554–2558.

Krizhevsky, A., Sutskever, I., & Hinton, G. E. (2012). ImageNet classification with deep convolutional neural networks. *Proceedings of the 25th International Conference on Neural Information Processing Systems (NIPS 2012)*.

Lawrence, N. D. (2017). *Data Readiness Levels.*, arXiv.

Mallows, C. (2006). Tukey's paper after 40 years. *Technometrics, 48*(3), 319–325.

Morris, R. J. T., & Truskowski, B. J. (2003). The evolution of storage systems. *IBM Systems Journal, 42*(2), 205–217.

Pearl, J., & Mackenzie, D. (2018). *The Book of Why: The New Science of Cause and Effect* (1st ed.). New York, NY: Basic Books, Inc.

Rumelhart, D. E., Hinton, G. E., & Williams, R. J. (1986, October 9). Learning representations by back-propagating errors. *Nature, 323*(6088), 533–536.

Silver, D., Huang, A., Maddison, C., Guez, A., Sifre, L., van den Driessche, G., Schrittwieser, J., Antonoglou, I., Panneershelvam, V., Lanctot, M., Dieleman, S., Grewe, D., Nham, J., Kalchbrenner, N., Sutskever, I., Lillicrap, T., Leach, M., Kavukcuoglu, K., Graepel, T., & Hassabis, D. (2016). Mastering the game of Go with deep neural networks and tree search. *Nature, 529*(7587), 484–489.

Sreeja, S., & Sangeetha, A. K. (2015). No science no humans, no new technologies no changes: 'Big Data a Great Revolution'. *International Journal of Computer Science and Information Technologies, 6*(4), 3269–3274.

Tsardoulias, E., & Mitkas, P. (2017). Robotic frameworks, architectures and middleware comparison. *arXiv*, Retrieved from https://arxiv.org/abs/1711.06842.

Werbos, P. (1974, November). *Beyond Regression: New Tools for Prediction and Analysis in the Behavioral Sciences* (Dissertation). Cambridge, MA: Harvard University.

Yang, Z., Xie, Y., & Wang, Z. (2018). A theoretical analysis of deep Q-learning. *arXiv*, Retrieve from https://arxiv.org/abs/1901.00137.

Zhao, J., Liang, B., & Chen, Q. (2018). The key technology toward the self-driving car. *International Journal of Intelligent Unmanned Systems, 6*(1), 2–20.

Chapter 2

Unlock the True Power of Data Analytics with Artificial Intelligence

Ritu Jyoti

Contents

2.1 Introduction 21
2.2 Situation Overview 22
    2.2.1 Data Age...23
    2.2.2 Data Analytics..23
    2.2.3 Marriage of Artificial Intelligence and Analytics 24
    2.2.4 AI-Powered Analytics Examples 27
2.3 The Way Forward..28
2.4 Conclusion 29
References 30

2.1 Introduction

Artificial intelligence (AI) is the study and research of software and hardware that attempts to emulate a human being. AI is poised to be more prolific and span every aspect of our daily lives. The International Data Corporation (IDC) forecasts that worldwide spending on AI will grow at a compound annual growth rate (CAGR) of 28.4% for 2018–2023 will reach over $97.9 billion. AI disrupters will drive better customer engagements and have accelerated rates of innovation, higher competitiveness, higher margins, and productive employees. The majority of the AI spend is driven by digital transformation (DX) initiatives. This is driven by the fact that all the data that comes from the DX initiatives will have limited value without exploiting the power of AI to extract valuable, accurate, and timely insights from them. AI will be the key technology that will propel organizations through DX. It is changing how customers buy, suppliers deliver, and competitors compete. Organizations of all size and industry are feeling the pressures to move rapidly and to digitally transform using AI. The power of AI lies in its ability to gain knowledge from data and market intelligence, not only to help the individual but also to scale a company's ability to improve performance and efficiency. By 2021, 75% of commercial enterprise apps will use AI. By 2022, 75% of IT operations will be supplanted by AI. By 2024, AI will become the new user interface by redefining user experiences where over 50% of user touches will be augmented by computer vision, speech, natural language, and augmented reality/virtual reality (AR/VR).

2.2 Situation Overview

AI-powered analytics is a relatively young, though already proven, technological advancement. Many companies have invested heavily in deep learning, a subset of machine learning (ML), which is itself a subset of AI. Deep learning and artificial neural networks enable image recognition, voice recognition, natural language processing (NLP), and other recent advancements. We have already come to take these for granted in our personal lives in the age of the internet and big data, but such features are hardly commonplace in analytics software. Modern analytics solutions have just started supporting NLP that enable end-users to use everyday language to ask questions of the data. But in just a few years, AI-powered analytics will help organizations create and deliver on all their most important strategies. With AI-powered analytics, businesses can concentrate on the initiatives that really matter instead of burying themselves in reports. Basic analytics packages report what has happened and helps to investigate why. But to stay relevant today, businesses must do more. They need to get on top of the mountains of data their customers generate as they engage through an ever-growing array of channels and devices. And then they must turn around and use that data to create compelling experiences on every channel that delight their customers and exceed even their highest expectations. Action is the goal. Analysis and insights are means to an end, not an end in themselves. AI and machine learning can identify the best action, and businesses can decide on situations where they want to automate business processes. AI and machine learning assist, augment, and amplify work. And when done right, these insights can empower everyone in the company, not just a few specialists.

2.2.1 Data Age

Successful DX relies on converting data into actionable insights, and this reliance on data is contributing to a new era of the data age. As per the IDC's Data Age 2025 study (Doc #US44413318) sponsored by Seagate, the IDC predicts that the global "datasphere" will grow from 33 zettabytes (that's one trillion gigabytes) in 2018 to 175 zettabytes in 2025. All this data will unlock unique user experiences and a new world of business opportunities. While we see an explosion in data creation, the sad reality is that a very small percentage of global datasphere is fed into AI, as they are not useful unless they are tagged, labeled, or annotated. We have an acute shortage of training data sets. In fact, AI is being used to create synthetic data to feed into AI training.

2.2.2 Data Analytics

As we know, data analytics is a broad field. There are four primary types of data analytics: descriptive, diagnostic, predictive, and prescriptive analytics. Each type of data analytics has a different goal and a different place in the data analysis process (see Figure 2.1).

- Descriptive analytics analyzes raw data from multiple data sources to give valuable insights into the past—what's happening or what happened in my business. However, these findings simply signal that something is wrong or right, without explaining why.
- Diagnostic analytics gives in-depth insights into a problem—why is it happening.
- Predictive analytics tells us what is likely to happen. It uses the findings of descriptive and diagnostic analytics to detect clusters and exceptions, and to predict future trends.
- Prescriptive analytics tells us what we need to do. It is to literally prescribe what action to take to eliminate a future problem or take full advantage of a promising trend. The prescriptive model utilizes an understanding of what has happened, why it has happened, and a variety of "what-might-happen" analysis to help the user determine the best course of action to take. A prescriptive analysis is typically not just with one individual response but is, in fact, a host of other actions.

The applications of data analytics are seemingly endless. One of the earliest adopters is the financial sector. Data analytics has a significant role in the banking and finance industries, used to predict market trends and assess risk. Credit scores are an example of data analytics that affects everyone. These scores use many data points to determine lending risk. Data analytics is also used to detect

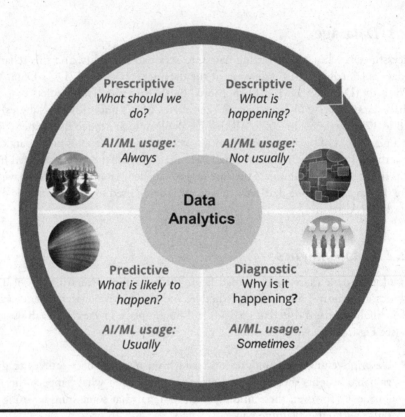

Figure 2.1   Types of data analytics.

and prevent fraud to improve efficiency and reduce risk for financial institutions. The use of data analytics goes beyond maximizing profits and return on investment (ROI), however. Predicting patient outcomes, efficiently allocating funding, and improving diagnostic techniques are just a few examples of how data analytics is revolutionizing healthcare. The Internet of Things (IoT) is a field that is exploding. These devices provide a great opportunity for data analytics. IoT devices often contain many sensors that collect meaningful data points for their operation. Devices like the Nest thermostat track movement and temperature to regulate heating and cooling. Smart devices like this can use data to learn from and predict your behavior. This will provide advance home automation that can adapt to the way we live.

2.2.3 *Marriage of Artificial Intelligence and Analytics*

For decades, AI was out of reach because the requisite compute scale and processing capabilities did not exist. Even when computational processing power advanced to adequate speed, costs kept AI development beyond the reach of many otherwise-interested parties. Now in the age of big data and nanosecond processing, machines can rapidly mimic aspects of human reasoning and decision-making across massive volumes of data. Through neural networks and deep learning, computers can even recognize speech and images.

When first introduced to AI-powered analytics, most people tend to jump right to the potential for predictive analytics. However, there are far more potential use cases for front-line knowledge workers surrounding the diagnostic capabilities of AI-powered analytics—"why did something happen?" Because data is constantly moving and growing, augmented analytics is crucial to more quickly diagnose root causes and understand trends. An analyst may need hours, days, or even weeks or months to develop and evaluate hypotheses and separate correlations from causality to explain sudden anomalies or nascent trends. With AI-powered analytics and machine learning techniques, they can sort through billions of rows in seconds to diagnose the indicators and root causes in their data, guiding and augmenting their work to deliver consistent, accurate, trustworthy results. By leveraging AI-powered diagnostic analytics, you get valuable insights on the current state of the world faster. This yields a competitive advantage to businesses trying to stay ahead in dynamic marketplaces.

Beyond opening new opportunities outside of descriptive and diagnostic analytics, AI and machine learning bring other significant benefits to an analytics practice. For example, they can take over tedious tasks that deflect their attention from strategy. Many of these tasks involve building and maintaining rules that guide the analysis of data. These tasks are critical, but by automating them businesses can focus on the message, the creative, and the content, as well as responding to what is happening. Businesses can move from rules-based to AI-powered analytics and reap significant benefits. With rules-based analytics, the investigation of why an event happened and possible actions are manual. With AI-powered analytics, evaluation of what factors contributed to the event and suggestion of a cause and action is automatic.

AI and machine learning analyze data, makes assumptions, and learns and provides predictions at a scale and depth of detail impossible for individual human analysts. AI and machine learning systems work with fuzziness. They predict. They will consider a path but can abandon it if new data negates a line of reasoning—then begin looking at a new direction. Machine learning systems get smarter as more data is given to them and are well-suited to identifying anomalies over time. For example, digital businesses with high-risk exposure are adopting AI-based online fraud analysis and detection platforms. First, supervised machine learning algorithms are used to finetune decades worth of transaction data to minimize false positives and provide extremely fast responses to inquiries. Second, unsupervised machine learning is used to find emerging anomalies that may signal entirely new, more sophisticated forms of online fraud.

Advanced analytics provides companies new means and abilities to better understand the past and to predict the future. Innovations in machine learning, advanced learning, and NLP make it even easier for business users to understand quicker than before about impacts to the future. AI can enable you to sort through mountains of data, even uncovering insights to questions that you didn't know to ask—revealing the proverbial needle in the haystack. It can increase data literacy, provide timely insights more quickly, and make analytics tools more user-friendly. These capabilities can help organizations grow revenue, improve customer service and loyalty, drive efficiencies, increase compliance, and reduce risk—all requirements for competing in the digital world. AI-powered analytics can help automate tasks in the analytics lifecycle, augment human intelligence, or support human-machine collaboration (see Figure 2.2).

Here are examples of how AI-powered analytics can transform businesses:

- *Intelligent search.* To make analytics and data available to everyone, systems must adapt to the way humans work, not the other way around. With intelligent search, digital workers can easily find the right content by searching via text or speech. AI-powered analytics can determine the best answer to their question, dynamically generating it or suggesting predefined content. Intelligent search is available on any device or format—laptop or mobile, spoken or text.
- *Smart data discovery.* In today's dynamic business environment, getting to the right—and unbiased—answer quickly is critical. With smart data discovery, the system automatically analyzes and generates explanations to

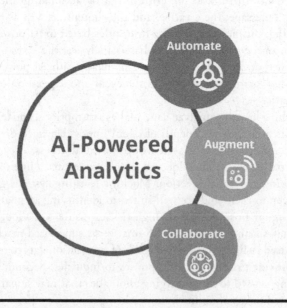

Figure 2.2 AI-powered analytics.

any attribute, generating facts about their data, including the drivers of the results, key segments that influence behavior, and anomalies where the data is not aligned with expected patterns. Smart data discovery expands the explaining capability of AI-powered analytics, beyond analyzing an attribute or measure, examples include explaining an entire data set, explaining specific data events, or automatically understanding the links to related data.

■ *Auto Suggest.* Business analysts and consumers often don't know where to start their insights initiatives. Auto Suggest embeds suggestions intelligently throughout the analytics life cycle, using ML behind the scenes, personalized to user needs, and fast-tracks the cycle to quicker actions. It's a valuable time-saver that helps users get to the data, visualizations, or content they are looking for. Auto-suggestions are just that—suggestions, not mandates, and users are still able to override the suggestions with the click of a mouse.

■ *Automated insight-generation.* Insight-generation is a key application of AI in analytics. Rather than relying on a user to ask the right questions, AI-powered analytics solutions can traverse massive data sets at the click of a button—or via a scheduler—and find interesting insights on their own. With user feedback, machine learning can help determine which insights are interesting and which are just noise to individual users and groups.

2.2.4 AI-Powered Analytics Examples

AI-powered analytics is already transforming a diverse group of industries, including healthcare, retail, financial services, and manufacturing. Though we are in the early days of AI-powered analytics, analytics infused with AI will generate greater benefits for the organizations that take advantage of this disruptive combination in their decision-making.

One of the most popular use cases for industrial IoT is predictive maintenance, a specific type of predictive analytics. Here, systems collect streams or regular batches of data from machines and look for patterns to predict when equipment or components might fail. In retail, merchandising teams have been some of the heaviest adopters of AI-powered analytics. For example, merchandisers at a popular convenience store chain had very little access to point-of-sale data and loyalty data in its data lake with its traditional BI solution. With its AI-powered analytics solution, it is not only privy to this data—it is asking natural language questions like, "Who is signing up for the loyalty program but not using it?" "How are points being redeemed in various regions?" and "How frequently are different segments using the loyalty program?" In finance, one of the world's largest investment management companies cut time-to-insight by 50% with AI-powered analytics.

2.3 The Way Forward

IDC predicts by 2022 46% plus of global GDP will be digitized, with growth in every industry driven by digitally enhanced offerings, operations, and relationships. While DX is becoming more prolific, and spanning all aspects of business, Intelligence is still occurring in silos. Within the next five years, new AI-oriented architecture will allow businesses to do things in a more integrated, holistic way and move away from being stuck in machine learning models and data science. The shift to business outcomes will occur because AI will be integral to all parts of the business. This is like the way the cloud was treated five years ago. There is no longer talk about hardware, networks, and data centers. It's about cloud-enabled outcomes. This sort of evolution is coming soon, and it will insert a new measure of business success.

As per the IDC Global AI Survey conducted in May 2019, primary business drivers for AI initiatives across industries are balanced between tactical and strategic objectives and range from improvement in operational efficiencies and customer satisfaction to increasing existing product revenues to improving profit margins to launching new digital revenue streams. Data is foundational to AI and over 80% of the organizations report using 10–30% of external data for training their AI models.

For digitally determined organizations, data that is created in DX initiatives has limited value if an organization can't extract valuable, accurate, and timely insights from it. And it's not enough to have just a small team able to get at that data and plumb it for insights. Data access must be democratized, with stakeholders from across the company able to access intelligent, self-service solutions and find the answers that matter most to them, as well as perform surprising and game-changing analyses. Augmented analytics is the future of data and analytics. Augmented analytics uses machine learning/artificial intelligence techniques to automate data preparation, insight discovery, and sharing. It also automates data science and ML model development, management, and deployment. Augmented analytics uses machine learning automation to supplement human intelligence across the entire analytics lifecycle.

Disruptive companies can integrate AI across the enterprise, uncover insights and patterns in customer behaviors, and generate accurate predictions to find the most appropriate interaction to optimize for revenue and profit. It can be used to predict who is most likely to become your next best customer and to focus your resources on the right people. Everyone has lots of data about their customers, but often miss context outside of their relationship with the customer. i.e., a bank only knows their customer from a banking perspective (not anything outside that lens)—filling in blind spots in their data is difficult. Advanced machine learning techniques can be applied to first-party data to better anticipate customer needs and behaviors and boost prediction accuracy by leveraging third-party intelligence from tens of billions of interactions across industries. Businesses can see between a 23% and 50% sizeable increase over their current conversion rates, which translates into millions of dollars in revenue growth.

We are at a market disruption point. With modern analytics platforms, insights and actions are moving to real time. AI-powered analytics will provide organizations with knowledge on how to develop, invest, monetize, and release products more than previously done before. Enterprise economies and the nature of competition have changed. While still important, economy of scale has been augmented with economies of scope and economies of learning. Now, leading companies are pursuing "economies of intelligence," the continual improvement, innovation, and variation based on leveraging data and AI technologies to identify and fulfill changing needs to enhance scale, scope, and customer engagement. This is changing the nature of intellectual property, whose value has shifted to where it's created rather than where it's realized and contributing to an asymmetrical accumulation of capital and innovation where an organization's capacity to learn has a distinct competitive advantage.

2.4 Conclusion

AI is not new. In fact, it is over 60 years old, since John McCarthy together with Alan Turing, Marvin Minsky, Allen Newell, and Herbert A. Simon coined the term "artificial intelligence" in 1955 and organized the famous Dartmouth conference in the summer of 1956. This conference started AI as a field. After decades of experiencing a slow burn, artificial intelligence innovation has caught fire to become the hottest item on the agendas of the world's top technology firms. Today's flurry of AI advances wouldn't have been possible without the confluence of three factors that combined to create the right equation for AI growth: the pervasiveness of data (from IoT, social media, and mobile devices), seemingly infinite scalability of cloud-based compute power combined with the emergence of powerful graphics processing units (GPUs) for complex computations, and the re-emergence of a decades-old AI computation model—deep learning. Understanding and sophistication of the algorithms have expanded as well. While many ML algorithms have been around for years, the ability to apply complex mathematical calculations to data, and process them quicker than ever before, is a recent development.

DX is reaching macroeconomic scale and spanning all aspects of business. Artificial intelligence is at the heart of digital disruption and business strategies for companies of all sizes. Today, AI is embraced by businesses in silos. By 2024, innovations in the digital economy and newer AI-powered enterprise architectures and solutions will lead to the employment of AI across the business holistically and much beyond basic ML models. AI will transform companies to a business outcomes approach. Increasing productivity and capacity, improving efficiency, and reducing the cost of operations are some of the first business outcomes to be expected from AI. Ongoing sophistication of AI technologies will drive the development of AI solutions that can be leveraged to increase the accuracy and effectiveness of business processes.

It's time for AI-powered analytics. To be successful, businesses must ensure that their analytics tool includes AI capabilities. AI-powered capabilities should be usable across the organization, not just by specialists. With AI-powered analytics, businesses can pull ahead of competition and win the hearts and minds of every customer.

The benefits of AI-powered analytics are many. Data analysts have more time to focus on deep data insights (that they might not have uncovered previously) rather than data preparation and report development. Decision-makers can explore much deeper and faster than they were ever able to with predefined dashboards. Perhaps the most important ingredient to adopting AI as part of your analytics strategy is trust. For AI-powered analytics to gain people's trust, there are three key considerations: accuracy, relevance, and transparency. These are paramount concerns if business leaders are to make decisions and act based on the results of AI-powered analyses.

Technology providers are working on innovative tools and technologies to address each of these concerns. With these bases covered, expect to see more and more companies adopting analytics strategies that take advantage of artificial intelligence as a significant component.

References

Artificial Intelligence Global Adoption Trends and Strategies (*IDC Doc #US45120919, June 2019*).

IDC FutureScape: Worldwide Artificial Intelligence 2020 Predictions (*IDC Doc #US455 76319, Oct 2019*).

https://www.seagate.com/files/www-content/our-story/trends/files/idc-seagate-dataage-whitepaper.pdf (*An IDC White Paper I Doc #US44413318 I November 2018*).

Chapter 3

Machine Intelligence and Managerial Decision-Making

Lee Schlenker and Mohamed Minhaj

Contents

3.1 Managerial Decision-Making 32
    3.1.1 What Is Decision-Making? 33
    3.1.2 The Decision-Making Conundrum 33
    3.1.3 The Decision-Making Process..34
    3.1.4 Types of Decisions and Decision-Making Styles 34
    3.1.5 Intuition and Reasoning in Decision-Making....................35
    3.1.6 Bounded Rationality..36
3.2 Human Intelligence 36
    3.2.1 Defining What Makes Us Human...36
    3.2.2 The Analytical Method...38
    3.2.3 "Data-Driven" Decision-Making 39
3.3 Are Machines Intelligent?..41
3.4 Artificial Intelligence..41
    3.4.1 What Is Machine Learning? 42
    3.4.2 How Do Machines Learn? 42
    3.4.3 Weak, General, and Super AI 43
        3.4.3.1 Narrow AI 44
        3.4.3.2 General AI 44
        3.4.3.3 Super AI 44

3.4.4   The Limitations of AI 44
3.5   Matching Human and Machine Intelligence 45
    3.5.1   Human Singularity...45
    3.5.2   Implicit Bias... 46
    3.5.3   Managerial Responsibility 47
    3.5.4   Semantic Drift...48
3.6   Conclusion 49
References 51

Can machine intelligence improve managerial decision-making? Artificial Intelligence is based on the idea that human decision-making can be analyzed, modeled, and improved. One potential use of machine intelligence is to replace part or all managerial decisions. A contrasting scenario would be to leverage machine intelligence to help managers better leverage analytics at all levels of an organization. If the second scenario appears more sensible, we need to understand in what situations, and in what conditions, human and machine intelligence can work together.

In this chapter, we will explore how machine intelligence can improve human decision-making. We base this discussion on a certain number of normative assumptions. Analytics requires different types of "intelligence" that extend far beyond rational thinking. The objective of information technology isn't to replace humanity, but to enrich human experience. Each new iteration of technology introduces new ethical challenges that management needs to address. In the end, the data and algorithms of machine intelligence don't add value to an organization, people do.

To develop our vision, we will begin our discussion in reviewing the foundations of managerial decision-making. We will then turn our attention to the singularity of human intelligence. With this foundation in mind, we will then analyze the nature and the conditions in which machine learning and artificial intelligence can improve management. We will conclude with several considerations that should be taken into account when leveraging machine intelligence in business.

3.1 Managerial Decision-Making

Every decision has a consequence.

—Damon Darrell

Decision-making is an essential component of management and plays a pivotal role in achieving the goals of any organization. Irrespective of the nature of management and the rungs of an organization, one critical success factor in any organization is the quality of its managerial decision-making.

Good decisions save time, money, and stress ("The Anatomy of a Great Decision," 2019). People take multiple decisions daily in response to both personal and organizational challenges. The outcome of these decisions is either good or bad for the decision-maker, the organization, and society. A "good" decision is a course of action that will capture the most value or get the most of what you are seeking given the uncertainties and complexities of the real world (Neal and Spetzler, 2015). While every decision-maker would like to take good decisions, is there a secret formula for that? With so many factors influencing the decision-making process, what should be an ideal approach to make better decisions in the limited time available? This section of the chapter endeavors to address some of these questions.

3.1.1 What Is Decision-Making?

Decision-making involves the selection of a course of action from among two or more possible alternatives in order to arrive at a solution for a given problem (Trewatha and Newport, 1976). In both personal and organizational decision-making, the objective is to choose the best available option within a given time constraint. it is generally observed that when it comes to personal decisions, most people go with their gut feeling, hunch, or intuition. However, when it comes to organizational decisions, many managers are very careful and slow: they discuss, deliberate, get into finer details, and only then arrive at a decision.

Why do people react differently when faced with organizational decisions? Obviously, they are worried about taking a poor decision, and its repercussions on them, the business environment, and society at large. Each manager's approach to decision-making is marked by their own personality: some are quick in their decisions while others are risk averse and are very hesitant in taking any concrete decision. Some are astute at arriving at a logical conclusion from the available figures and facts, while others struggle with data-based decision-making.

3.1.2 The Decision-Making Conundrum

Decision-making is part of everyone's life and all of us have to make decisions every moment. All of us are confronted with "What," "Why," and "How" for everything that we do in our personal and professional life. What makes the decision-making a difficult task is not only the numerous options that we have but also the limited time and pressure to act decisively. Particularly when it comes to organizational decisions, it becomes trickier as many more dimensions are added to the decision-making environment. Information systems, advanced search engines, and globalization multiple the number of potential alternatives. Government regulations, market instability, competition, and changing consumer demands produce further uncertainty, making it more difficult to predict the consequences of our decisions.

3.1.3 The Decision-Making Process

Managerial decision-making is a course of action over the short term or long term to solve a problem or leverage an opportunity. This entails the act of choosing one option from two or more alternatives and in the context of organizational culture and processes. Managerial decision-making generally involves multiple steps, starting with definition of the problem and then exploring the alternative course of action, followed by the evaluation of alternatives, and finally selecting one alternative. This approach, which is consciously or unconsciously followed by most decision-makers, is described as a three-step process by Herbert Simon and is popularly known as Simon's decision-making model (Simon and March, 1976) (Figure 3.1).

3.1.4 Types of Decisions and Decision-Making Styles

Decisions are taken at every level of management to achieve organizational goals. While some decisions are clear-cut responses to organizational processes, others are difficult choices to ill-defined problems. In a similar vein, the impact of the decision taken will either be beneficial or not for organizational stakeholders in either the short or the long term. In this light, managerial decisions can be broadly classified into three categories, namely, strategic, tactical, and operational (Figure 3.2).

Strategic decisions are major choices of action that influence all or a major part of an organization. It involves setting a direction and allocating resources to pursue a stated vision. They have long-term implications on the company, administration, or market.

Tactical decisions are broadly related to the implementation of strategic decisions and involves short range, current operations of various parts of the organization. These decisions are usually taken by the middle levels of management.

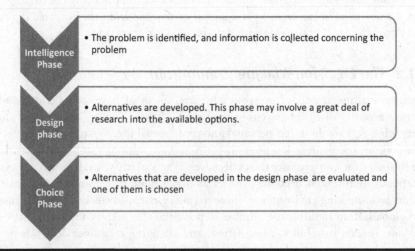

Figure 3.1 Simon's decision-making model.

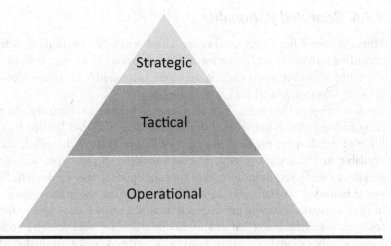

Figure 3.2 Types of decisions.

Operational decisions are related to the day-to-day operations of the organization and are taken at the lower rungs of management. Among the three categories, operational decisions are the simplest as they are based on facts regarding the events and do not require much organizational judgment.

3.1.5 Intuition and Reasoning in Decision-Making

Traditional psychological theory describes the decision-making process as an action based largely on intuition rather than logic or reasoning. In other words, managers often interpret the facts to align them with their gut feelings. Does this imply that intuitive decision-making is irrational or illogical? In his book, *The Power of Intuition*, Gary Klein suggests that 90% of critical decisions are made using our intuition (Klein, 2007). Intuitive decision-making is basically based on something that is known, perceived, understood, or believed by instinct, feelings, or nature without actual evidence, rather than by use of conscious thought, reason, or rational processes.

The intuition-based decision-making (Liebowitz, 2019; Liebowitz et al., 2019) is good or bad depending on the scope and ramifications of the decision. If the decision is relatively minor and the impact of the decision is limited, intuition-based decisions may be preferred. If, on the other hand, the impact of the decision is substantial and has far reaching repercussions, organizational stakeholders may expect that managerial decisions are based on more than just gut reactions.

Beyond flawed information and insufficient consideration of alternatives, another major problem with intuition-based decisions is the erroneous application of personal convictions. People that have a rich experience, expertise, and intuition in one area can become overconfident and apply their intuition in unfamiliar or unrelated areas, which may not match the reality of the decision context.

3.1.6 Bounded Rationality

Humans have different personality traits and deal with situations in different ways according to their natural instincts. Our emotions drive our behavior and can cloud our reasoning when making decisions. Is it possible for all decision-makers in all situations to assess all decisions rationally?

According to Herbert A. Simon's theory of bounded rationality, the rationality is by nature limited: managerial decision-making is always limited by the tractability of the decision problem, the cognitive limitations of the mind, and the time available to make the decision. Decision-makers, in this view, act as satisficers, seeking a satisfactory solution rather than an optimal one. Herbert A. Simon proposed bounded rationality as an alternative basis for the mathematical modeling of decision-making widely prescribed in political science, economics, and the hard sciences. It complements "rationality as optimization," which views decision-making as a fully rational process of finding an optimal choice given the information available (Gigerenzer and Selten, 2002). This limited rationality leads to systematic errors in the decisions that we make. Kahneman, in his extensive work on this domain, refers to these limitations as *cognitive biases* and has experimentally proved how cognitive biases like *framing* or *anchoring* can lead to poor decision-making (Kahneman, 2011).

3.2 Human Intelligence

Can the essence of humanity be captured in an algorithm? Before discussing how human and machine intelligence can potentially work together, it can be useful to ask what separates humanity from machines. If the visionaries of artificial intelligence promise to use technology to augment what makes us human, the proponents of Dataism argue that little differentiates us from the technologies we produce to mimic our behavior (Briggs, 2016). Are human thought and feelings nothing more than programmed biochemical responses to environmental stimuli? Let's consider four unique human traits before asking how machine intelligence can make us better: the notion of human agency, the capacity for abstraction and empathy, the multiple forms of human intelligence, and the capability to differentiate right from wrong.

3.2.1 Defining What Makes Us Human

One fundamental characteristic of humanity is the notion of human agency: the capability to make informed, uncoerced decisions and thus act independently of our environment. Agency is often classified as either a subliminal, involuntary behavior or a purposeful, goal-directed activity. The degree to which one can act independently of his/her environment is open to debate: the primacy of social structure versus individual will in determining one's scope of action has been regularly discussed in the social sciences. For example, to what degree are our actions conditioned by the technology we use, i.e., do we communicate differently through the telephone than we do on Twitter, Facebook, or Instagram? That said, most of us would agree that humanity has at least some degree of free choice: people are self-organizing, proactive, self-regulating, and engage in self-reflection, rather than reactive organisms shaped and shepherded by external events (Bandura, 2001).

A second characteristic of humanity is our capacity for abstraction (the conceptual process where concepts are derived from experience) and for empathy (the ability to understand and to relate to the world around us). Abstraction allows us to act in accordance with our ideals rather than events where empathy "is basically the ability to understand others' emotions." Empathy can be either cognitive (concerned with thought and understanding), emotional (concerned with feelings and sensations), or compassionate (focusing on Intellect and emotions). Abstraction, for example, allows us to consider HAL 5000, WALL-E, and RD-D2 all to be robots, and empathy allows us to identify with the challenges they faced in each respective film's storyline.

The third distinguishing feature of humanity is our use of multiple forms of intelligence—our ability to think both intuitively with the heart, and logically with the mind. Human intelligence undoubtedly extends far beyond these two forms of expression, various authors speak of five, seven, or even nine forms of human intelligence. Linguistic intelligence evokes the ability to think conceptually and to use language to explore complexity. Intra-personal intelligence is the capacity to understand oneself, one's thoughts and feelings, in applying knowledge in everyday life. Spiritual intelligence implies a sensitivity and capacity to explore metaphysical questions about human existence and condition. Does augmenting humanity infer enhancing one of these forms of intelligence, and if so, which one?

Finally, a fourth feature of humanity is ethics—shared values that help us differentiate right from wrong. Business ethics are commonly associated with several moral concepts including honesty, integrity, transparency, accountability, and privacy. Data ethics involves the study and adoption of data practices, algorithms, and applications that respect fundamental individual rights and societal values. Because technology influences these ethical standards—i.e., artificial intelligence reflects the visions, biases, and logic of human decision-making, we need to consider to what extent technology can be isolated from the larger economic and social challenges it has been designed to address. Emerging issues such as personal privacy, which metrics allow us to evaluate human progress, and what is the relationship between information and governance suggest that data condition how we see and evaluate the world around us. Can advances in machine intelligence alone help us understand what it means to be human?

3.2.2 *The Analytical Method*

Improving human intelligence isn't an end in itself. In the context of managerial decision-making, human intelligence plays a role in helping managers and their customers improve their ability to take pertinent decisions. Intelligence in the field of data analytics is less about technical knowledge or skills than about analyzing how to interpret data to seize opportunities and address personal and organizational challenges. Let's explore the foundations of the analytical method: evaluating the context, evaluating the available data, applying the appropriate methodology, and creating the conditions for individual or collective action.

The first step of the analytical method concerns exploring the context of the market or the organization to understand the nature of the problem at hand. This context, also referred to as a "decision environment" includes the available information, alternatives, values, and preferences at the time of the decision (Harris, 2012). Four types of decision environments are of interest here. Simple decision environments involve problems or opportunities that are rule- or process-based—both the causes and solutions are readily apparent to the decision-maker. Complex decision environments concern "wicked problems" like business strategy, ecology, and subjective well-being whose causes reflect multiple competing perspectives with no readily apparent solutions (Camillus, 2008). Deterministic environments like geolocating a consumer suggest that the decision-maker has fully incorporated all the parameters of the problem, and that the solution can be found using the data at hand. Finally, stochastic environments, like predicting future corporate performance, imply that the decision-making environment cannot be fully understood due to either a lack of, or too much, information.

The second step of the method involves evaluating the quality of the data at hand. Several questions must be addressed here. To what extent does the available data adequately reflect the problem or the opportunity? What type of data do you have to work worth (qualitative, quantitative, discrete, continuous, nominal, ordinal, etc.)? Is the data labeled and is this metadata clearly understood? What type of biases may be present in the collection of the data? How is the meaning of the data conditioned by the manner in which it is stored? Our mental models, let alone their application in machine intelligence, will never be better than the quality of data at our disposal.

A third step of analytics requires identifying the heuristic (mental model) or the algorithm that is best suited to address the problem. In working with data, four basic models are used to determine or predict solutions. Classification models help us sort the data using class labels (metadata) to produce categorical or discrete outcomes ("yes" or "no," etc.). Clustering is a similar process of organizing objects into groups without labels in attempting to group members who share common characteristics. Regression models on the other hand elucidate linear, quadratic, polynomial, non-linear relationships in the data to produce continuous or numerical predictions (like stock price, temperatures, etc.). Dimensionality reduction infers reducing the number of random variables under consideration in order to provide more intelligible features of the problem.

The final step of the analytical method involves transforming the predictions into action that effectively addressed the problem or opportunity. Customers and managers often either don't decide or choose poorly based on their perceptions of the risk, uncertainly, or ambiguity of the decision at hand. On a "subjective" level, a manager determines risk when he or she understands the probabilities and outcomes of the choices before them. A manager confronts "uncertainty" when for one reason or another the probabilities and outcomes cannot be precisely determined. The factor of "ambiguity" weighs into the equation when the decision-maker questions the clarity of the problem itself. As a result, *the goal of management is rarely about finding the right answer, and largely about helping managers and customers take better decisions through reducing the sources of risk, uncertainty, and ambiguity.*

3.2.3 "Data-Driven" Decision-Making

People don't act on data, but on their perceptions of what the data represents. The human brain isn't wired to store dates, formulas, or statistics but rather its synapses process colors, feelings, and sensations that are tied to human experience. When presented with new data, human beings compare what they "see" with these records of experience in recognizing the need or not to act. Understanding how customers, employees, and managers interpret the data they see is fundamental in understanding how human and machine intelligence can work together to inspire action. In managerial decision-making there is no direct link between data and action, but rather four steps of perception, prediction, evaluation, and action worthy of our attention. Using the AI Roadmap, we can map out the challenges and opportunities of matching human and machine intelligence based on specific business contexts (Figure 3.3).

Perception refers to the way in which data is regarded, assimilated, and interpreted. No two customers, employees, and managers interpret data in exactly the same manner, for their prior experience is used in accessing, selecting, qualifying, and organizing sensory information. Using the example of a business dashboard of last quarter's sales figures, the human brain uses this information to build a mental picture or story of what is going on in the organization or in the market. Perception is thus much more than just "information coming in," it is an interactive process in which prior experience is used to interpret the facts, and the facts are eventually used to reinterpret experience.

Prediction is a second step in the decision-making process. A prediction is a conclusion that a decision-maker makes about what they believe is going to happen. Predictions are based on the hypothesis that if we understand the roots of an opportunity or a challenge, history most likely will repeat itself. Unfortunately, predictions are made using imperfect information: we may not have access to all the

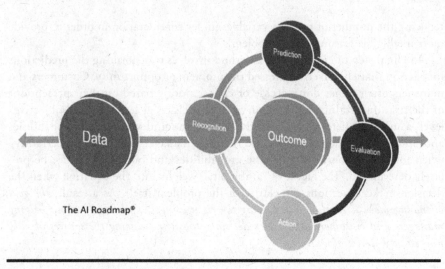

The AI Roadmap®

Figure 3.3 The decision-making process.

explanatory variables, and we often work in "stochastic" decision environments in which there may be several potential outcomes. The validity (or confidence index) of our prediction will depend not only on how we perceive the data, but also on the pertinence of the heuristics or algorithms we use to process the data at hand.

Evaluation is the third step in the decision-making process. An evaluation is an appraisal of something to determine the extent of the opportunity or challenge. There are three main types of evaluation: process (are we satisfied in how we have produced the results), impact (has the process under evaluation produced the desired impact), and outcome (has the impact of the process provoked the targeted outcome). An example here can be found in reviewing the data of a sales process—should we evaluate the sales tasks and activities, the impact of the sales campaign, or changes in consumer purchasing patterns? Will improving the sales process imply doing things more efficiently, more effectively, making better use of organizational resources, or responding more precisely to customer needs?

The final step of the process involves transforming data into action. Action involves one or several activities designed to solve a problem or seize an opportunity. Human perception, prediction, and evaluation is of little practical use if we can't "use" the data to spur action. Consumers, managers, and stockholders can be convinced of the challenge, and yet "decide" not to do anything about it out of fear of risk, uncertainty, or ambiguity. Challenges or opportunities may not involve just the decision-maker him/herself, but they depend on bringing teams, communities, or public opinion on board. These concerns are at the heart of using data science and data analytics to improve management, for a manager's job isn't behind a computer, but out in front of his or her customers and colleagues.

3.3 Are Machines Intelligent?

Intelligence is the ability to adapt to change.

—**Stephen Hawking**

Human intelligence is about responding to environmental opportunities or challenges using a combination of several cognitive processes like thinking, knowing, remembering, judging, and problem-solving. When we speak of machine intelligence, we refer to computer algorithms that are either programmed or learn to mimic human behavior.

The intelligence in humans is innate as humans by birth are gifted with degrees of intelligence which grows with the knowledge absorbed from books and institutions, acquired skills, and the slings and arrows of life experiences. Do man-made machines acquire intelligence mechanically or is it something that must be embedded artificially? If machines are capable of learning on their own, from whom or what do they learn? This section of the chapter endeavors to address these questions.

3.4 Artificial Intelligence

Machine learning (ML) is no longer a subject of fiction depicted in movies and science novels. It has become a reality and has provided remarkable business applications. Besides *Siri*, *Alexa*, or *Cortana* becoming household names, we notice that most industries have embarked on the road to artificial intelligence (AI). Personal assistants used in healthcare, the recommendation engines used in retail portals, and Internet of Things (IoT) data to detect quality issues in manufacturing are all examples of how businesses are leveraging machine intelligence.

The notion of machine intelligence is as almost old as the computer itself. In 1950, in his seminal paper "Computing Machinery and Intelligence," computing pioneer Alan Turing laid out several criteria, known since as the "Turing test," to assess whether a machine could be qualified as intelligent (Turing, 1950). The term *Artificial Intelligence* was first used by John McCarthy in 1956 to describe the research focused on problem-solving and symbolic methods. Subsequently, the domain of AI has grown in both breadth and depth and has contributed significantly to the world of business. Some notable outcomes of AI research and development include Deep Blue and Watson. Deep Blue was the first chess engine to beat reigning world chess champion, Garry Kasparov, on May 11, 1997. Watson is a question answering system from IBM which defeated champions of the challenging television quiz show *Jeopardy!* Another notable AI system is AlphaGo, which can play a board game considered to be more complex than chess and in fact defeated the world's top ranked Go player.

Many industries like healthcare, logistics, retail, and financial services are using AI to enhance the speed, precision, and efficiency of human interactions in business processes. The key point to observe is that all these industries who have embarked on AI are dealing with large amounts of data which is spawned from their digital initiatives. The bottom-line is AI has become a mechanism to create value from data by aiding organizations in either tapping new opportunities or solving their business problems.

3.4.1 What Is Machine Learning?

Machine learning is a subset of AI that provides computing systems with the ability to learn without being explicitly programmed. ML focuses on the development of computer programs that can change when exposed to new data. Technologies such as RFID, GPS, Social Networks, IoT, and so on enable rich details of micro-level data pertaining to employees, suppliers, customers, and their behavior. The tremendous data emanating from these IT applications, stored in multiple forms like documents, images, audios, videos, and so on, are predominantly unstructured in nature. While organizations conventionally have been taking business decisions primarily based on transactional, structured data stored in relational databases, in recent years, they have realized that the non-traditional, loosely structured data generated from weblogs, social media, emails, and sensors are a trove of useful business insights. It is this phenomenon that fueled the growth of analytics.

In the present landscape of business, general data analytics capabilities no longer provide a competitive advantage. This has forced organizations to look deeper into their data to increase competitiveness and hence ML is becoming part of a broader analytics strategy. ML (as well as deep learning) is a method of data analysis that automates analytical model building and works on the idea that systems can learn from data, identify patterns, and make decisions with minimal human intervention.

3.4.2 How Do Machines Learn?

Do machines really learn or is machine learning just another marketing pitch to sell software services? If machines are indeed capable of learning, can we speak of machine intelligence?

Any form of automation entails a fixed algorithm that takes an input and returns an output as a response to a given problem. For example, given a list of numbers that needs to be sorted in ascending order, how does a computer address this problem? Obviously using some type of process or a set of rules commonly referred to as an algorithm. The algorithm takes the list of numbers as input and by employing some rules and manipulation returns the sorted list as output. The challenge in this approach would be to develop the algorithm and test and refine it to get the required output in the most efficient manner. However, once such an algorithm is ready, it can be used for sorting any set of numbers and can be executed any number of times without any variation in accuracy.

On the other hand, there are some business problems which cannot be automated using traditional computer programs. Historically, algorithms were programmed to follow a fixed set of instructions in a specific context. If there is change in the inputs or conditions, the algorithm cannot modify the instructions or rules on its own and requires human intervention to correct the program. For example, what if we would like to develop a system to detect fraudulent transactions on an e-commerce portal. In a traditional approach, a rule-based system would be developed to test each transaction against all the rules defined in the algorithm. The system would not be capable of detecting any implicit correlations nor incorporate new rules deducted from the online transaction's environment. The ML approach on the other hand can detect subtle and hidden events in consumer behavior which may be a signal of possible fraud. This is possible because the ML algorithms are designed to process large data sets to detect hidden correlations between user behavior and the likelihood of fraudulent actions. After identifying a transaction as fraudulent, this is fed back to the system for factoring these features into the future processing of fraudulent transactions. This is what is referred to as machine learning: the correlations or relationships are recorded as new data points to improve the working of the machine/system.

Based on the different approaches used to discover the patters from data, machine learning can be broadly classified as **Supervised** and **Unsupervised**. Machine learning requires past figures, facts, and experiences given in the form of data for it to predict or act on the new set of data. The idea behind supervised learning is to make the system or machine learn a task by giving it a set of questions along with an answer. The training process is continued until the model achieves a desired level of accuracy on the training data. The supervised learning methods include regression, decision tree, KNN, and so on.

In unsupervised learning, unlike supervised learning, we do not give the answer to the questions, and the model is expected to find the inherent patterns or answers from the given data. Clustering and association are popular examples of unsupervised learning methods. Without any labeled prior knowledge, the unsupervised algorithms explore and discover interesting hidden structures in the data.

The choice between a supervised and unsupervised machine learning algorithm typically depends on factors related to the structure and volume of data available and the specific purpose. In most cases, data scientists use supervised learning and unsupervised learning approaches together to address a use case.

3.4.3 Weak, General, and Super AI

AI systems used today in different industries for different purposes exhibit different degrees of intelligence. Considering the type and scope of the intelligence that these AI machines have they are broadly classified into three types—Weak or Narrow, General, and Super AI.

3.4.3.1 Narrow AI

The term "Narrow Intelligence" stems from the fact that this kind of intelligent system is explicitly created for a specific task. They are limited and are focused on doing only one or one set of tasks well. Owing to its ability to perform specific tasks automatically, narrow AI is meant to stimulate, rather than replace human intelligence. AI-assisted chess engines, smart digital assistants, recommendation engines, and spam filtering systems are some examples of narrow AI. In a variety of markets, businesses can employ narrow AI today to automate and integrate business processes more efficiently than ever.

3.4.3.2 General AI

Artificial General Intelligence (AGI) is broad and adaptable and is meant to replicate human-level intelligence. So, it can understand, think, and act the same way a human might in any given situation. This includes tasks such as vision and language processing, cognitive tasks such as processing, contextual understanding, and a more generalized approach to thinking as a whole.

With extensive efforts from the global research community, AGI has reached to a relatively higher degree of maturity. But unlike narrow AI, there are few major functional use cases today. The key constraint for implementing AGI is Transfer Learning, a term used to denote applying knowledge learned in one domain (attending a business school) to another (managing a business unit). While Transfer Learning is naturally imbued in humans, such attributes in a machine have yet to see the light of day.

3.4.3.3 Super AI

Super Artificial Intelligence is a term used to denote an AI that exceeds human intelligence and capabilities. Nick Bostrom defines Super AI as any intellect that greatly exceeds the cognitive performance of humans in virtually all domains of interest (2014). Super AI is more conjecture today than of practice, though the adversaries of AI often refer to a form of super AI that will one day enslave humanity.

3.4.4 The Limitations of AI

Today, organizations are investing heavily in AI in the hope of automating and optimizing a long list of time-consuming and costly manual tasks. Does this success in chess, smart cars, and drones mean that AI can replicate human intelligence? AI's superior and ever-improving capabilities in different fields has evoked a hope from the global tech community as well as the general public. Specifically, the use cases like AI detecting cancers better than human doctors can lead us to believe that AI can massively benefit humanity by raising our standard of living.

For the organizations that are procuring and implementing AI, in addition to limitations like availability of data, cost, and lengthy implementation cycles, several ethical issues have arisen. As we will see in the next section, privacy, security, responsibility, and dealing with the unintended consequences of machine intelligence are all concerns worthy of a manager's attention.

3.5 Matching Human and Machine Intelligence

Machine intelligence alone can't improve management because humans are not cold calculating machines. Having explored the notions of human and machine intelligence, we can now turn our attention to whether organizations can replace managerial decision-making with forms of artificial intelligence. We will argue that this is a risky proposition for the organizational benefits of machine learning hinge on recognizing the unique contributions of human decision-making. Let's consider four points here: human singularity, implicit bias, managerial responsibility, and semantic drift.

3.5.1 Human Singularity

We have argued that one of the characteristics that separates man from machine is the notion of human agency, the very human capability of thinking and activity independently. Although this affirmation has been debated over the years, our ability to act of our own accord is fundamental to our economic, social, and political systems. Nonetheless, because such decision-making is both energy and time consuming, we have naturally developed mental shortcuts, in the form of rules of thumb, mental models, and heuristics to save both time and effort. Machine intelligence is little more than an extension of this practice, a translation of our mental models into algorithms that can be processes with little human intervention.

Slowly but surely, these algorithms are becoming increasingly pervasive in our daily lives. Google's PageRank algorithm conditions how we search and rank information on the internet, our GPS guides our sense of orientation and direction, and Facebook and LinkedIn provide structure in how we see our social and professional relationships. In an ever-increasing frequency, algorithms are used to evaluate our aptitude for employment, for credit, and medical care. Will this push to support human decision-making lead us to one day believe that algorithms will one day rule the world? Dan Brown, the author of the novel *Origin* investigates this trend in exploring the duality of *Where we come from? / Where we are going* (Brown, 2018)? His protagonist, Edmond Kirsch, preaches the end of human singularity, where we will be replaced by a different form of intelligence based on some blend of human and artificial intelligence.

How plausible is this vision? As we have seen previously, human decision-making relies on two distinct forms of cognition: intuition and bounded rational thinking. When is intuition critical to decision-making and in which situations should intuition be replaced by data-driven machine learning? Noah Yuval Harari suggested provocatively that machine algorithms would soon be able to compose music as well or better than their human counterparts (Cave, 2018). His argument hinges on the possibility of programming musical scores that adapt to the specific personality and mindset of each individual listener. Is our appreciation of music simply a programmed response to acoustic stimuli or do song writers attempt to transmit messages that transcend programmable responses?

3.5.2 Implicit Bias

As the recent example of Microsoft's chatbot Tay demonstrates, one of the major concerns of artificial intelligence is the institutionalization of implicit bias that can seriously comprise the purported advantages of machine intelligence (Vincent, 2016). When we evoke implicit bias, we are referring to unconscionable attitudes or stereotypes that influence our understanding, actions, and decisions in both repetitive and exceptional events situations. Although this bias can be potentially either favorable or unfavorable, these implicit evaluations or beliefs can severely limit our ability to be objective. In reference to machine intelligence, there are four potential sources of implicit bias: in the data, in the algorithms, in our own logic, and in our definitions of ethical behavior. Let's explore each in turn.

We have argued that machine learning involves specifying a data set that is used to train (test) the algorithm that will subsequently be used in real-world conditions. Although as a rule the more data you collect to train the model, the better the results, several sources of implicit bias can significantly compromise the pertinence of your work. Sample bias occurs when the data used to train the model does not accurately represent the problem space in which the model will operate. Prejudicial bias occurs when training data content is influenced by stereotypes or prejudice coming from the population. Finally, measurement bias can result from faulty measurement of the outcomes. The algorithms at the heart of machine learning will never be better than the data used to test them.

A second source of implicit bias is found in the way in which algorithms are constructed to explain or to predict real-world phenomena. For the data scientist, bias, along with variance, describe an algorithm property that influences prediction performance. Since bias and variance are interdependent, data scientists typically seek a balance between the two. Models with high variance tend to flex to fit the training data very well but may not generalize well to data outside the training data set. Finding the appropriate balance between these two properties for a given model in each environment is a critical data science skill set.

A third source of bias can be found in the means in which human beings induce and deduce logical arguments. A cognitive bias is a systematic pattern of deviation from the norm or rationality in judgment. Some cognitive biases are presumably adaptive. Cognitive biases may influence perceptions of similarity, judgment, memory, and action. Although cognitive biases may lead to more effective actions in each context, they often lead to misleading representations of personal and business challenges. Furthermore, allowing cognitive biases enable faster decisions which can be desirable when timeliness is more valuable than accuracy, as illustrated in heuristics. Other cognitive biases are a "by-product" of human processing limitations, resulting from a lack of appropriate mental mechanisms (bounded rationality) or simply from a limited capacity for information processing. Gigerenzer argues that human rationality isn't riddled with irrational cognitive biases, but rather that human intelligence is an adaptive tool that defies the rules of formal logic or mathematics (Gigerenzer, 1991).

A final source of bias comes from our views of ethics. Ethics can be understood as a set of moral principles that guide our individual behavior. Ethics reflect our perceptions of what is right and wrong, our beliefs about justice, as well as our convections of what is acceptable in terms of human behavior. According to the theory of cultural relativism, there is no singular truth on which to base ethical behavior, our interpretations of the limits of what is acceptable are conditions of existing social norms, cultural practices, and religious influences. Ethical considerations are often in conflict with our perceptions of self-interest: and as a result, people often cross the line without being aware that they are doing anything wrong (Bazerman, 2011).

3.5.3 Managerial Responsibility

A manager's job is to take decisions. On one hand, machine intelligence should greatly assist management in providing timelier, more pertinent, and more insightful data to understand the past, analyze the present, and predict future performance. The introduction of machine intelligence in core business processes challenges the traditional definitions of managerial command and control. On the other, managers at all levels will have to adapt to the world of smart machines. What exactly are these challenges and how can management adapt to the needs of human and machine intelligence?

Machine intelligence will soon be able to execute many administrative tasks automatically, more quickly, more efficiently, and at lower cost than their human counterparts. It is estimated that managers at all levels of an organization spend more than half of their time working on administrative coordination and control processes (Kolbjørnsrud, 2016). According to the consulting group Accenture, middle management will need to focus on "judgment-oriented" skills beyond the scope of AI to enhance their value to the organization: creative thinking and experimentation, data analysis and interpretation, brand management, and strategy development (Accenture, 2019).

Managers needs to have some familiarization of data analytics to ensure they are asking the right questions to address the potential ethical issues when applying machine intelligence to business. The potential dangers of machine learning regarding digital citizens are specifically addressed in emerging government regulations including Europe's General Data Protection Regulation (GDPR) and the State of California's Consumer Privacy Act (CCPA). These government regulations seek to legislate the conditions in which organizations can hold and use customer data and to ensure a citizen's digital bill of rights, which includes rights of access to digital records, rectification, portability, and the right to be forgotten.

The use of machine intelligence to automate decision-making, especially in human resource management and risk analysis, is of particular concern here. Managers need to provide leadership within their organizations in defining metrics that will align AI policies with company values and goals. Too great a focus on accuracy can lead to the creation of "black box" algorithms in which no one can say for certain why an AI system made the recommendation it did. The ability to explain model outputs to stakeholders is a major lever in ensuring compliance with expanding regulatory and public expectations and in fostering trust to accelerate adoption.

Machine intelligence will never be worth more than the trust managers have in an organization's data practices. Upper management can encourage their organizations to define and apply metrics that best align AI with company values and goals. Not only will AI augment managers' work, but also it will enable managers to interact with intelligent machines in collegial ways, such as through conversations or other intuitive interfaces. AI's role can be leveraged as a contextual, real-time assistant and advisor. Leaders therefore can frame and ensure adoption of a thoughtful process around "trust by design"—first by establishing definitions and metrics for assessing fairness, as described earlier, and then continually challenging data science teams to consider fairness during the full range of their work.

3.5.4 Semantic Drift

What does truth mean when business is reduced to "facts" and figures? Charles Filmore suggested that the primary function of language is communication, we use words, idioms, and expressions to convey meaning in exchanging ideas, products, and services (Clark, 1996). Shared meaning in business communication depends upon the context in which we work: descriptions, opinions, and ideas are woven together using technology (paper, text, video, etc.) to form the setting or background for an event, statement, or idea. *Semantic drift* refers to the evolution of language over time, often to the point in which the current meaning of a concept is radically different from its original usage. How can we communicate with our colleagues and customers if they there is little agreement on the very meaning of the words we use?

Consider the notion of privacy in its relationship to personal identity. Privacy has been defined as an individual's "right to be free from unwarranted intrusion and to keep certain matters from public view" (Law 2015). In this light, the concept of privacy "is an indispensable feature of a democracy ... (that) protects our subjectivity from the pervasive efforts of commercial and government actors to render individual and communities fixed, transparent and predictable" (Cohen, 2012). Today, as internet technologies like our smartphones, personal assistants, and connected devices allow public and private actors to capture and aggregate our communication, actions, and intentions, it may be impossible to build a protective wall around our personal data. As Danny Weitzner concludes, privacy in the digital age may well be an illusion, the best we can hope is to convince organizations to "be transparent about how they use our (personal) information" (Henn, 2014).

Does the concept of "truth" fare any better when data science is employed to perpetuate "fake news"? Oxford Dictionaries' "Word of the Year" in 2016 was post-truth, the post-modernist idea that there is no longer any single version of the truth. Before the internet replaced traditional journalism, editors and publishers played the role of gatekeepers in cautioning what was and wasn't eligible to be considered the truth. When truth depends only on intentions and context, data science is enlisted to influence public opinion with messages that appeal to emotions, beliefs, and prejudices rather than using facts. These tactics are referred to as *bordering*, which is narrative as much as territorial, and is directly linked to current challenges of both US foreign policy and Brexit in the UK (Mathieu, 2019). The current business models of the world-wide web contribute to propagating these practices in business—clickbait attracts "eyeballs" and digital properties are largely evaluated more as a function of the size of their footprint than the value of their products or services.

Behind the notion of "truth" relies the concept of "trust" that has been also subject to semantic drift the last few decades. The 2017 Edelman Trust Barometer reveals that trust is in crisis around the world: the general population's trust in all four key institutions—business, government, NGOs, and media—has declined broadly, a phenomenon not reported since Edelman began tracking trust among this segment in 2012. The nature of consumer trust has evolved considerably over the last few years. Several years ago, Vanessa Hall pointed out that "blind trust" based on faith in organizational leadership and products was a thing of the past (Hall, 2004). Absolute trust has been replaced by "situational trust," where consumers gave credence to experts because of their focused insight and experience. Today, when confronted with a multiplicity of data sources and versions of the truth, situational trust has in turn given way to "referred trust" based on the perception of shared beliefs. The internet has allowed for entirely new kinds of relationships and clusters of communities in which trust must be negotiated and developed in unfamiliar ways with unknown entities who are using our personal data with or without our consent.

3.6 Conclusion

Can machine intelligence improve managerial decision-making? We began our analysis based on the assumption that human decision-making can be analyzed, modeled, and improved. We posited two potential use scenarios for machine intelligence. In the first, machine intelligence is destined to replace some or all managerial decisions. In the second, machine intelligence should be leveraged to help people become better managers at all levels of an organization. What lessons can be learned from our experience and what still needs to be explored?

Decision-making involves the selection of a course of action from among two or more possible alternatives in order to arrive at a solution for a given problem. Rational decision-making is bound by human experience, judgment, and bias. Can machine intelligence replicate human decision-making? Should organizations replace managers with algorithms? If there are situations in which machine learning is preferable, when and where should we rely on machine intelligence and when should we defer to the human touch?

Before improving human decision-making, we would be wise to identify what makes us human. We have argued that there are at least four characteristics that separate humanity from machines: the notion of human agency, human capacity for abstraction and empathy, the multiple forms of human intelligence, and the human desire to decipher right from wrong. Does the introduction of machine learning enhance these qualities or, on the contrary, reduce managerial decision-making to a self-serving tautology of the organizational performance? Will machine intelligence one day be able to mimic these fundamental traits, and if so, how will machine learning need to evolve? Is there a real danger in allowing organizations to be run by algorithms, and if so, how can management adequately address these challenges?

If machine learning is concerned with producing data to improve human decision-making, artificial intelligence is an attempt to mimic human decision-making. Machines learn from the use of data, logic, and algorithms—machine intelligence will unlikely be more effective than the data practices that management builds into their corporate DNA. Of the three potential forms of artificial intelligence, only limited AI has provided useful examples today of machine learning in executing relatively simple decisions and/or tasks. What challenges hinder current approaches to general and super AI? Where will these applications likely find their uses in commerce and industry? What ethical challenges will these applications produce?

If the goal of AI is to enhance human experience, management needs to focus on the context and the conditions in which human and machine intelligence can work together. In the AI Roadmap, we have divided managerial decision-making into a four-step process involving perception, prediction, evaluation, and action. What objectives should management set to encourage both their employees and their customers to explore the eventual use scenarios in each step of the process? What human, technical, and financial resources need to be allocated to encourage the development and adoption of these new technologies? Which ethical framework can be adopted to help organizations benchmark acceptable data practices?

References

Accenture. *The Promise of Artificial Intelligence*. accessed 12/12/2019 at https://www.accenture.com/_acnmedia/PDF-32/AI_in_Management_Report.pdf.

Bandura, A., (2001). Social Cognitive Theory: An Agentic Perspective. *Annual Review of Psychology*, 52(1):1–26.

Bazerman, Max H., (2011). *Blind Spots: Why We Fail to Do What's Right and What to Do about It*, Princeton University Press.

Briggs, W.M., (2016). *The New Religion of Dataism* [blog]. accessed 15/10/2019 at https://wmbriggs.com/post/19677/.

Brown, Dan, (2018). *Origin*, Anchor Publishing.

Camillus, J., (2008). Strategy as a Wicked Problem. *HBR*, 86(5):98–101.

Clark, H.H., (1996). *Using Language*, Cambridge University Press

Cohen, J.E., (2012). What privacy is for (2013). *Harvard Law Review*, 126.

Gigerenzer, G. and R. Selten eds., (2002). *Bounded Rationality: The Adaptive Toolbox*, MIT Press.

Harris, R., (2012). *Introduction to Decision Making*. accessed on 19/10/2019 at https://www.virtualsalt.com/crebook5.htm.

Henn, S., (2014). *If There's Privacy in the Digital Age, It Has A New Definition*. accessed 12/10/2019 at https://www.npr.org/sections/alltechconsidered/2014/03/03/285334820/if-theres-privacy-in-the-digital-age-it-has-a-new-definition.

Kahneman, D., (2011). *Thinking, Fast and Slow*, Macmillan.

Klein, G., (2007). *The Power of Intuition: How to Use Your Gut Feelings to Make Better Decisions at Work*, Crown Publishing Group.

Law, Jonathan, (2015). *A Dictionary of Law*, Oxford University Press.

Liebowitz, J. (ed.), (2019). *Developing Informed Intuition for Decision Making*, Taylor & Francis.

Liebowitz, J., Y. Chan, T. Jenkin, D. Spicker, J. Paliszkiewicz, and F. Babiloni (eds.), (2019). *How Well Do Executives Trust Their Intuition*, Taylor & Francis.

Mathieu, Joseph, (2019). *Technology and Truth in the Digital Age*. accessed 10/19/2018 at https://newsroom.carleton.ca/story/technology-truth-digital-age/.

Neal, L. and C. Spetzler, (2015). An Organization-Wide Approach to Good Decision-Making. *Harvard Business Review*.

Simon, H.A. and J. March, (1976). *Administrative Behavior: A Study of Decision-Making Processes in Administrative Organizations*, Free Press.

The Anatomy of a Great Decision [WWW Document], (2019), Farnam Street. accessed 1/6/2020 at https://fs.blog/2019/04/decision-anatomy/.

Trewatha, R.L. and M.G. Newport, (1976). *Management: Functions and Behavior*, Business Publications, Dallas.

Turing, A.M., (1950). I.—Computing Machinery and Intelligence. *Mind:LIX*, 433–460. doi:10.1093/mind/LIX.236.433.

Chapter 4

Measurement Issues in the Uncanny Valley: The Interaction between Artificial Intelligence and Data Analytics

Douglas A. Samuelson

Contents

4.1 A Momentous Night in the Cold War 54
4.2 Cybersecurity 55
4.3 Measuring AI/ML Performance 56
4.4 Data Input to AI Systems 58
4.5 Defining Objectives 59
4.6 Ethics 60
4.7 Sharing Data—or Not 61
4.8 Developing an AI-Aware Culture 62
4.9 Conclusion 62
References 62

Artificial intelligence (AI) researchers call it "the uncanny valley": numerous studies indicate that people fear and distrust machines that seem nearly human, but not quite. There are many theories about this, but nothing conclusive ("Uncanny Valley," Wikipedia, 2020).

The phenomenon can be extended, admittedly without strong empirical evidence of its existence and extent, to many subject areas relating to AI—or machine learning (ML). The latter term has become more popular than the original among researchers still queasy about the history, over the past 50 years or so, of AI being oversold and over-promised, with disappointing outcomes. In particular, it is worthwhile to address the question of how well we know whether an AI/ML system has performed satisfactorily. If it did not work exactly as its developers predicted, how good was it? How sure are we about that assessment? In short, the performance of AI/ML systems is a subject area that clearly requires better measurement and assessment—which, of course, is exactly what good data analytics is about.

The dependence operates in the opposite direction, as well. There are many efforts, recent and ongoing, to improve data analysis using AI/ML techniques. Reviewing and assessing these efforts is well beyond the scope of this chapter—and the author's expertise. What is relevant, however, is the resulting paradox: if AI/ML methods can quickly solve data analysis problems that defy traditional inference techniques, how sure can we be that the AI/ML solution is correct? How can we better assess whether to trust the AI/ML answer?

These are not merely theoretical issues. AI/ML systems are increasingly in use in a number of application areas, some of which are literally life or death decisions. AI/ML systems are contemplated to direct swarm and counter-swarm warfare involving thousands of supersonic unmanned vehicles. This is a situation in which humans would be incapable of making judgments sufficiently quickly, much less then translating those judgments into thousands of movement and action orders in seconds. Therefore, despite the best intentions and admonitions from the AI/ML research community, we could soon have AI/ML systems making kill decisions. Knowing how much to trust the machines is, therefore, critically important and becoming even more so.

4.1 A Momentous Night in the Cold War

The issue of how much to trust machines is not new. On the night of September 26, 1983, Lieutenant Colonel Stanislav Yefgrafovich Petrov had the watch command in the Soviet air and missile defense system. The shooting down of Korean Airlines Flight 007 had occurred just three weeks before, and Soviet commanders were eager to improve their ability to distinguish true threats from false alarms. They had, therefore, upgraded their primary satellite-based sensor system. Now that system was reporting the launch of five ICBMs from the United States toward the Soviet Union.

All eyes in the command center were on LTC Petrov. He recounted later, "I felt as if I was sitting in a hot frying pan." In a real attack, a few minutes' delay could cost millions of the lives he was there to protect. However, reacting to a false alarm would precipitate an immense catastrophe, literally ending human civilization as we have known it.

Fortunately, he had another warning system, based on ground-based radars, that he could check. He decided to wait for the ground-based radars to confirm the launches. "I just had this intuition," he explained later, "that the U.S. would not launch five missiles. Either they would launch one or two, to show they were serious, and give us an ultimatum, or they would launch all 1,053. So I did—*nothing*. I was afraid that informing my superiors, in accordance with my orders, would start a process that would acquire a momentum of its own" (Petrov obituary, New York Times, September 18, 2017).

LTC Petrov's story has many implications, but one in particular is noteworthy here: he made the right decision *because he acted counter to his orders and refused to trust the machine's conclusion.* His intuition was correct. He had contextual information the machine-based system did not. (The Soviets had analyzed and wargamed what attack profiles the US might employ in various situations.) But suppose the Soviets, or the Americans, or whoever else developed a new detection and warning system, more powerful, more reliable, arguably more trustworthy. How could such a system be taught the intuition on which LTC Petrov relied? How would we know that the system had enough such intuition to be trusted? At this time, these questions are totally unanswered in the AI/ML research.

4.2 Cybersecurity

At least it is possible in kinetic combat to assess some results quickly. In non-kinetic conflict, such as economic and diplomatic confrontations, effects take much longer to appear and are then much harder to link back to causes. In information systems conflicts, the difficulty is even greater. Douglas W. Hubbard, a well-known expert on measurement and risk assessment, declares, "The biggest risk in cybersecurity is not measuring cybersecurity risk correctly" (Hubbard, 2016). What he meant by this is that the threats are mostly events that have never happened, so estimating their probability of occurrence becomes a highly judgmental exercise. The use of Bayesian methods is promising, but then the analyst faces the danger of introducing overly influential biases in the choice of prior probability distributions and in the selection of the presumed process to be modeled. Training analysts to calibrate their estimates of uncertainty—that is, to have a much better understanding of how uncertain they are about their conjectures—improves the resulting risk assessments. In contrast, many popular methods and techniques increase estimators' confidence in their estimates without actual improvement. If, as in cybersecurity, we cannot avoid relying on opinions, we can at least train the people forming those opinions to be more realistic about how likely they are to be right.

It is also useful to get senior decision-makers accustomed to the fact that analyses based on guesses do not produce certainty or even near-certainty. Moreover, analyses based on highly imprecise data cannot produce conclusions any more precise than the least precise input. Better trained analysts can more effectively insist on these principles when senior decision-makers push for unrealistic assurances. This is one of the areas in which better data analytics can drive better AI.

If anything, Hubbard seems to have been optimistic: it is not clear that many organizations with major responsibilities in the field can even *define* cybersecurity risk—or even just what cybersecurity is. Some influential organizations advocate developing and applying a maturity model to information management: if everything is forced into well-defined processes, and those processes are rigorously followed, then perfect security will ensue. This approach has a fundamental flaw. *The most important fact anyone can know about a detection system is what it can't detect.* However, no metrics of observed adherence to defined processes yield any information on this all-important subject. Only challenge testing does. This, in turn, has the limitation that one cannot test the system's response to challenges one never imagined. Still, with metrics depicting the range of challenges the system has detected, it is at least possible to compare systems and rank them in terms of demonstrated responsiveness to these specified types of threats.

4.3 Measuring AI/ML Performance

There are many other ways in which better data analytics, starting with better metrics, can impel improvements in AI. As Hubbard also points out, very few things are truly impossible to measure. The impossibility of certainty should encourage rather than discourage measurement. A measurement, he states, is any piece of information that reduces uncertainty. It follows that the first few measurements of a phenomenon are generally much more valuable than many more measurements where several are already present.

Then we can narrow our uncertainty by simple logic. Does this subject area look like anything else we have seen? Can we make any guesses at all about upper and lower bounds of the number? If we have no idea how many pianos there are in Chicago, we do know the population of Chicago and can conjecture that the number of pianos would be fewer than that. We can also find out the number of people advertising piano lessons in Chicago and guess how many students each would have to have to make a living. We can also find out how many piano tuners there are in Chicago and, again, conjecture how many pianos it would take to keep the tuners in business. In short, we can often construct helpful metrics by relating the subject of interest to other subjects we know more about.

Another method can be inferred from one of the most famous philosophical problems in AI: Searle's Chinese Room (Cole, 2004). He posited an experiment in which two translators are in opaque, soundproof cells, and we pass in Chinese scripts and they pass out English translations. If the two translations seem equally good, to our inexpert view, we conclude that the translators are also equally good. Now, if it turns out that one cell actually contained an expert Chinese translator and the other contained a novice with an excellent Chinese-English dictionary, Searle argues that any translating ability in the second cell was in the dictionary, not the person using it. From this, he argues that AI is a nonsensical concept, as the real intelligence lies in the software, not the machine. This argument has spawned lively debate.

Often lost in the debate is that the setup is what is nonsensical, or at least highly forced and unrealistic. Searle explicitly excludes from the experiment what any reasonable evaluator would do: ask each translator to critique the other's translation! The difference between naively relying on the literal meanings of words and, in contrast, understanding implied context and the use of idiom would readily emerge. For example, in 2009, actress Sharon Stone posed nude for *Paris Match* (Huffington Post, 2009). (Lest any sensibilities be offended, please note that this reference tells the story but does not display the nude photos.) The headline read, "J'ai 50 ans, et – alors!" Some American headline writer with a dictionary and absolutely no knowledge of idiomatic French rendered this as, "I'm 50 years old, and then some!" This version—usually without the photo, in the US—got wide circulation. But the correct meaning is, "I'm 50 years old, and *look here!*"

Having AI systems critique each other to correct errors is also not a new idea. The Space Shuttle had four computers. They had to agree before taking a critical action, such as a course change. If one disagreed with the others some number of times, the other three ignored it and eventually shut it down or advised ground-based control to do so. So an important concept in evaluation is already in practice to some extent: AI/ML systems supporting or advising critical decision-making should be required and designed to critique each other's performance and help human decision-makers understand how solid the AI systems think their recommendations are. (This, of course, is exactly what human decision-makers are also usually advised and trained to do. Somehow, however, this ancient wisdom is sometimes forgotten in the design and use of AI/ML systems.)

Another useful approach is—again—challenge testing. One of the tasks AI systems are often assigned is to reason out the likely behavior of another party, especially an adversary. There has been much research and even more speculation about how to do this. But, to this author's knowledge, nobody has ever implemented what I call the Trogdor Test. Trogdor is a rather simple, silly online game in which a dragon, Trogdor, moves through a landscape stomping on peasants ("Trogdor," 2020). When he stomps on a specified number of peasants, he acquires the power to burn huts. Burning all the huts in a village advances him to the next level. The player moves Trogdor around using the arrow keys on the keyboard.

Trogdor must face deadly attacks from archers shooting arrows at him from the side boundaries, and from two sword-wielding knights who prowl the landscape. Avoiding the arrows is simply a matter of staying alert, seeing them coming, and getting out of the way. But a player needs to know how to move to avoid the knights, or else Trogdor dies by the sword. Simply staying as far as possible from the knights doesn't work, as they eventually converge systematically on Trogdor. A good approach is to recognize occasions, when the knights are some distance apart, when Trogdor can safely move between them from one region to another. This apparently resets the knights' movements to random, halting their more effective search-and-seek movements.

Now, clearly these knights' movements are dictated—entirely and invariably—by a computer program. It is therefore possible to ascertain *exactly* what their behavior is, for all situations. So the test is: can the AI, by playing the game, deduce the knights' behavioral programming? Unlike most situations in real life, we have documented truth against which to compare any conjectures an AI produces. So here is a modest proposal: any AI for which the developers claim an ability to deduce opponents' behavior should be required to pass the Trogdor Test. (The present author is aware that widespread adoption of this proposal could bring huge riches to the company that produced and runs the Trogdor game. The present author hastens to add that he has no financial ties to that company or its owners.)

In the interests of fairness and impartiality, it is also proper to concede that other games could furnish an equally valid test. The point is that such games do exist, and it is simply ludicrous not to require AI systems to demonstrate, by means we have now shown to be readily available, that they can reproduce documented reality for at least one of the rare instances in which it exists.

4.4 Data Input to AI Systems

Data analytics also has much to contribute to AI/ML on the input side. AI/ML systems, whether used for data inference, control, or decision-making, are voracious consumers of data. Indeed, they cannot function without data. More attention is needed to the collection, vetting, and storage of data AI/ML systems use.

IBM's Watson represented a huge triumph of machine learning, winning at the television game *Jeopardy!* against the strongest human opponent. This raised high hopes for applications in more consequential subjects, such as medical diagnosis. How well this worked can be seen from the TV ads IBM has run about Watson: many testimonials about what it can do, but almost none about what it has done. It turns out that in *Jeopardy!*, the category from which the question will come is specified first, and the task is to find a document somewhere in the vast data store that contains the necessary piece of information. But finding the most highly recommended treatment for a specific disorder is much easier than reasoning out, from a few relatively common symptoms, what the diagnosis is.

If you asked a human sixth grader to identify the 16th most populous city in the US, probably the sixth grader would find a list of cities and their populations, rank them, and count down to 16. As of a few years ago, it is my understanding that Watson couldn't deduce that procedure. (Private communication from a friend at IBM, 2016). It needed to find a document stating, "The sixteenth most populous city in the US is..." In short, without quite a bit of structuring of data input, AI/ML systems can prove remarkably lacking in what humans would deem to be simple cognitive tasks.

The difficulties AI/ML systems have with data are compounded by some current practices in data analytics. Many people have had the experience of having a library moved by professional movers. The movers are concerned with which books will pack together tightly in the boxes. Size, not content, matters. The result is that the move goes smoothly, the books arrive undamaged, and the owner may then need weeks to put books of different sizes but related content back together on the bookshelves.

In big data analytics, much efficiency in input processing can be obtained by "sharding" the data, breaking the data into more manageable smaller chunks ("Sharding," 2020). In some cases, this might consist of something sensible, like separating the data set into geographic regions, in which there is little interaction among data elements in different regions. In other cases, however, the process is more like what the movers did, matching the next incoming chunk of data to the storage area closest to it in size. This achieves near-maximum efficiency in the use of storage space at the cost of vast inefficiencies in retrieval (Samuelson, 2014). "The computer is fast, it will find it soon enough" is a recipe for disaster when the data, stripped of all metadata and contextual information, are thus stored willy-nilly—in terabytes. The question of how much metadata to keep, and how much content relationships can or should influence storage locations, looks like a promising area for research. In general, research is called for into many issues of how best to prepare data to be used by AI/ML systems—focusing on facility of use rather than ease of storage.

4.5 Defining Objectives

Another issue too little addressed, in both AI/ML and data analytics, is—as in the discussion of cybersecurity risk, above—defining the objective. One of the more trenchant criticisms that came to be raised about US policy in Vietnam in the 1960s was that nobody seemed sure of how success was defined, hence how it was to be recognized. This was part of why the administration lost credibility by repeatedly assuring the American public that success was near at hand—and then redefining what that meant when the conflict dragged on.

Even at that tender age, many of my contemporaries had learned, some from relying on insight gained from board games such as Avalon Hill "D-Day," "Afrika

Korps," and "Panzer Blitz," that a clear and unambiguous definition of victory conditions is essential to success in any competition. Attempting to construct a game and define victory conditions quickly impresses on the designer the practical necessity of specifying a criterion less than "total victory," whatever that means. The Allies did not need to kill every German soldier in Europe to reclaim the continent from Nazi domination. In any poorly structured debate over policy and strategy, there will always be some fool who insists that nothing short of total victory is acceptable. A cursory overview of history indicates that pursuing this insistence leads to disaster. To cite just one example, Thucydides, in assessing the outcome of the Pelopponesian War, attributed the ultimate defeat of the Athenians to "want of more," the pursuit of additional gain after the major objectives had been mostly won (Thucydides, trans. Strassler, 2008).

Of course, these historical observations are still subject to dispute. The reader will also readily recognize that the appropriate definition of success is complicated, controversial, and most likely unending. But this ambiguity is precisely the point for AI: it is inconceivable that humans can clearly and unarguably define success and teach that definition to a machine, when no such definition can be constructed by humans. Moreover, machines tend to have a much lower tolerance for ambiguity than humans. What humans explain as "feels close enough" calls upon intuition that machines do not have. Even with human subordinates, but especially with machines, much more specificity and detail in instructions are necessary to avoid damaging failures. In particular, we are challenged to develop metrics that characterize the outcomes, including the associated uncertainties, much more precisely than we have been accustomed to doing.

4.6 Ethics

The ethics of constructing, using, limiting, counteracting, and generally trying to live with AI/ML systems constitute a subject area far beyond the scope of this chapter. A few observations seem in order, however.

First, it is widely agreed that machines should not be trusted with a kill decision. One proposed formulation of the principle is, "Never trust a kill decision or recommendation to any entity—whether an individual human, a group of humans, a trained animal, a machine, an organization—that is incapable of remorse." Like Asimov's Laws of Robotics, this seems to encompass all the meaningful situations. Also like the Laws of Robotics, there are many ways to bend this principle, get around it, misuse it, and create chaos and mishaps. Still, it seems useful as a guideline.

One of the problems is, as mentioned earlier, that there are serious capabilities in development, in many advanced countries, to use AI/ML to direct swarms of extremely fast-moving unmanned vehicles against opposing swarms of extremely fast-moving unmanned vehicles, generating a combat decision space far beyond the attention and control span of humans. This raises, among other serious questions, grave ethical concerns about how such combat systems can be properly limited—or perhaps whether they should be prohibited, as poison gas and toxic organisms are, as too dangerous. Such a prohibition, of course, raises new questions about detection of and response to the now-outlawed creation of such systems—with attendant measurement and risk assessment challenges that data analytics can address.

How to evaluate and report uncertainty also has ethical aspects. Decision-makers want to be sure, even when the supporting analysis indicates that certainty is unattainable. When the decision could have grave consequences, "how sure are we really?" becomes more than an analytical disagreement. Add to this the trend of modern science: *as methods and techniques progress, we tend to drive uncertainty from the computation to the assumptions, where it is much more difficult to detect.* Similarly, *as complex systems are designed to drive the probability of minor failures lower and lower, there is an unintended consequence that the only possible failures remaining are big, rare, multiple-cause events that are more likely, when they happen, to overwhelm the respondents.*

This trend has a counterpart in the management of organizations that analyze data and make and support decisions. Management is becoming more and more adept at insisting on what they want and ignoring or marginalizing objections from subordinates. Ironically, the US, both in the government and in the private sector, is spending billions of dollars to teach machines to think like humans, while spending trillions of dollars to teach and incentivize humans to act more like automata.

4.7 Sharing Data—or Not

Speaking of large-scale organizational incentive structures, yet another interesting topic regarding data analytics and AI/ML is the decision-making process about data transparency. US intelligence and national security agencies frequently proclaim that more data sharing would improve national security, and these agencies declare their determination to share data more easily and openly (Samuelson, 2017).

These efforts repeatedly run into a resistant and contrary incentives structure. A custodian of sensitive data risks chastisement for withholding data that should have been shared. Said custodian risks career-ending disaster, possibly including criminal prosecution, for releasing data that should have been withheld.

The issue is additionally complicated by advancing capabilities in data analytics and AI/ML. One of the most daunting considerations in classification/declassification of information is whether a knowledgeable adversary could assemble several pieces of information, each innocuous by itself, into a pattern that reveals something sensitive. A knowledgeable adversary using statistical pattern recognition and/or AI/ML could do more such assembly, so prudence indicates less transparency, not more.

Meanwhile, however, society as a whole is becoming less and less protective of individuals' privacy and confidentiality. Intelligence professionals sometimes joke, "What information the law won't let us collect, we can probably buy from Google or Amazon." This is too true to be funny. Here, too, there is a need for risk-benefits analysis of the balance of desirable features of our information and inference systems, including but not limited to the criteria for sharing information.

4.8 Developing an AI-Aware Culture

Finally, central to all these issues is the question, "Who is going to use these data analytics and AI/ML capabilities, and how?" AI/ML and data analytics take place within a culture. The rapid expansion of these technologies necessitates having more people who can think about how to use them and whether to trust them. The Center for Strategic and International Studies (CSIS), among others, has strongly addressed this need (Hunter et al., 2018). Without the development of what the CSIS study authors called "an AI ecosystem," the benefits of AI/ML will not be attained, the risks will not be properly recognized, and the threats will not be contained. Only knowledgeable, creative people, well versed in the developing capabilities of AI/ML and data analytics, properly incentivized by their employers and other organizations, can move the balance toward better outcomes and away from potential disasters.

4.9 Conclusion

AI/ML and data analytics have much to contribute to each other, especially in evaluating the performance of tools, technologies, and methodologies that support critical decision-making. Data analytics can and should be used much more broadly and creatively to assess the performance and risks of AI/ML systems. AI/ML systems can extend and improve data analytics. These efforts will also support needed analyses of ethical and policy considerations. The development and sustenance of a workforce that can better understand, use, explain, and critique AI/ML and data analytics is critical to our society, as these technologies offer great potential for both good and harm.

References

Cole (2004). https://plato.stanford.edu › entries › chinese-room retrieved January 9, 2020.
Hubbard, D.W, Seierson R. (2016). *How to Measure Anything in Cybersecurity Risk*, New York: Wiley.

Huffington Post (2009). https://www.huffpost.com/entry/sharon-stone-topless-on-p_n_25
    2960?guccounter=1&guce_referrer=aHR0cHM6Ly93d3cuZ29vZ2xlLmNvbS8&g
    uce_referrer_sig=AQAAANnqyxYU4TFYtZYN_4UIK-yynyenIaUE9ND87IcJo7lqYp-
    pViLYu-_9fRxdtDVvd93rGRBzfp1_Gpx8fGZkql9b6wqDwpAoEsFTCjnY9S6ufYd
    HFz3CKMyFNP8-B6FQIRzQ_EM-YwGYmcwE4cuiNt5_4rd5jjrmRegjnI501Fyd-.
    retrieved January 8, 2020.
Hunter, A., Sheppard L., et al. (2018). Artificial Intelligence and National Security: The
    Importance of the AI Ecosystem. Center for Strategic and International Studies,
    November. Downloadable from the site for the discussion event. https://www.csis.
    org/events/artificial-intelligence-and-national-security-importance-ai-ecosystem.
Petrov. http://www.nytimes.com/2017/09/18/world/europe/stanislav-petrov-nuclear-war-
    dead.htML. retrieved January 7, 2020.
Samuelson D. (2014). The Sharding Parable. *OR/MS Today*, April.
Samuelson D. (2017). The CIA's New Transparency: Analytics Plays a Role in Opening
    Access. *Analytics*, February.
Sharding. https://searchoracle.techtarget.com/definition/sharding. retrieved January 7, 2020.
Thucydides, Strassler R. trans. & ed. (2008), *The Landmark Thucydides*, New York, Free Press.
Trogdor. http://homestarrunner.com/trogdor-canvas/index.htML. retrieved January 8, 2020.
Uncanny Valley. https://en.wikipedia.org/wiki/Uncanny_valley. retrieved January 7, 2020.

Chapter 5

An Overview of Deep Learning in Industry

Quan Le, Luis Miralles-Pechuán,
Shridhar Kulkarni, Jing Su, and Oisín Boydell

Contents

5.1 Introduction 66
    5.1.1 An Overview of Deep Learning 66
        5.1.1.1 Deep Learning Architectures 67
    5.1.2 Deep Generative Models 69
    5.1.3 Deep Reinforcement Learning 69
5.2 Applications of Deep Learning 70
    5.2.1 Recognition 70
        5.2.1.1 Recognition in Text 71
        5.2.1.2 Recognition in Audio 72
        5.2.1.3 Recognition in Video and Images 72
    5.2.2 Content Generation 76
        5.2.2.1 Text Generation 76
        5.2.2.2 Audio Generation 78
        5.2.2.3 Image and Video Generation 79
    5.2.3 Decision-Making 81
        5.2.3.1 Autonomous Driving 82
        5.2.3.2 Automatic Game Playing 83
        5.2.3.3 Robotics 85
        5.2.3.4 Energy Consumption 86
        5.2.3.5 Online Advertising 87

5.2.4 Forecasting 88
    5.2.4.1 Forecasting Physical Signals.............................88
    5.2.4.2 Forecasting Financial Data 90
5.3 Conclusion 91
References 92

5.1 Introduction

Applications driven by deep learning are transforming our society. To name but a few examples: Google Assistant supports real-time speech-to-speech translation between 44 languages—helping to break down human communication barriers, Amazon Alexa understands human voice commands and assists in many everyday tasks such as ordering products and interacting with our smart homes, autonomous driving is assessed to be safer than human drivers, and deep learning models are helping us to understand our genome and to develop precision medicine.* Deep learning's ability to learn highly accurate representations of the task at hand, given enough annotated training data, helps it achieve better accuracy than traditional machine learning methods in many cases. This capability has opened up opportunities for its application to many new problems where traditional machine learning methods have fallen short.

In this chapter, we introduce the reader to many important applications of deep learning in industry. To begin, we provide a high-level overview of deep learning and its key architectures. We follow with a survey and discussion of the main applications of deep learning, categorized into four general tasks: recognition; generation; decision-making; and forecasting. We conclude the chapter with a discussion on the strengths and weakness, as well as the future applications of deep learning.

5.1.1 An Overview of Deep Learning

Deep learning models are artificial neural networks which emphasize the use of multiple connected layers (modules) to gradually transform input signals to the desired outputs. Given a sufficiently large data set of input-output pairs, a training algorithm can be used to automatically learn the mapping from the inputs to the outputs by tuning a set of parameters at each layer in the network. The input data is typically left in its raw form—for example, the gray level values for the pixels in an image or the raw readings over time from a set of sensors. Once the optimal values for the parameters at each layer in a network have been learned, we can view the layers as encoding high-level features extracted from the raw input data.

---

* www.forbes.com/sites/insights-intelai/2019/02/11/how-machine-learning-is-crafting-precision-medicine/

As such, deep learning models do two things at the same time: learning an effective feature representation from the raw inputs and learning a model that maps from the feature representation to the outputs. The early layers of the models may only capture simple features calculated from the raw inputs, but the later layers combine these simple features to learn more abstract features which are optimized for the task at hand.

5.1.1.1 Deep Learning Architectures

Many different deep learning architectures or configurations of connected layers and arrangements of connections between layers have been proposed. In this section, we present the main deep learning architectures from the literature (Goodfellow et al. 2016). They are the main components of the deep learning models used in the applications we discuss later on.

■ *Convolutional Neural Network.* Convolutional neural networks layers (CNNs) (LeCun et al. 1989) are neural network layers designed to process data whose features have regular spatial dependency (e.g., the grid-like topology of images, or other multi-dimensional data). CNNs take advantage of these dependencies by applying local *convolutional* filters in specialist layers in the network. A CNN module is typically composed of a succession of convolutional layers. A CNN network typically connects inputs to a CNN module, then to a fully connected feed-forward module that ultimately produces the outputs of the network (Figure 5.1).

The early convolutional layers in a CNN typically learn low-level local features, such as edges and lines in the case of image data, while later layers with bigger receptive fields will combine these local features into more complicated features, such as shapes or even faces (such as in facial recognition). As the same stationary pattern could appear anywhere in the raw input, the same set of filters should be applied everywhere in the input. This feature of CNNs is called *parameter sharing*, helping it avoid the *overfitting* problem. The characteristics of CNNs have made them incredibly effective at image processing tasks, as well as other tasks involving low-level inputs with spatial dependencies with which they can take advantage.

■ *Recurrent Neural Network Modules.* Recurrent neural network modules (RNN modules) (Rumelhart et al. 1986) are a family of neural network architectures designed to process sequential data. RNN modules allow looped connections through which the hidden state calculated from the last input presented to an RNN module is included as the input to the RNN module along with the next set of input values so as to encode sequential relationships in a network.

Theoretically, RNNs can handle long-term dependencies and use information of arbitrary long sequences, but in practice this is not the case due to the gradient vanishing and gradient explosion problems. Long short term

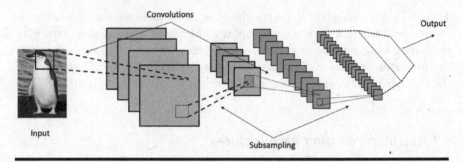

Figure 5.1   A typical convolutional neural network model.

memory (LSTM) networks (Hochreiter and Schmidhuber, 1977) and other gated architectures have been proposed as a way to alleviate the problems with earlier RNN architectures, and have been hugely effective in many applications from speech recognition, to machine translation, to finding machine faults based on sensor data (see Schmidhuber (2015) for a detailed overview of the applications of LSTMs).

■ *Residual Architecture.* Depth in a deep learning model is essential for its expressivity and its generalization performance. For example, from 2012 to 2015, the top-5 error (a classification of an image is considered as an error if the correct label is not in the top 5 predicted categories) in the 1000-class image classification problem of the ImageNet challenge reduced from 16.4% to 3.57% as the depth of the neural networks increased from 8 to 152 layers. While convolutional neural layers are effective in exploiting the correlations between data features to create new useful features, they still face the same problem as other multiple layer networks: having gradients that either explode or diminish after being propagated through multiple layers. The residual network module is designed to address this problem (Kaiming et al. 2015). Residual architectures have since been used extensively for a wide range of applications.

■ *Attention Module.* The attention module arose in the context of the sequence to sequence models (Sutskever et al. 2014) used for machine translation— where an RNN encoder network is used to convert the original text sequence into a context vector, and an RNN decoder network is used to translate the context vector to the piece of text in the target language, one word at a time. Researchers realized that the original sequence to sequence model performs badly for long texts, hence Bahdanau et al. (2014) proposed using the attention module on the hidden state sequence of the encoder to provide context for the decoder at each generation step. Nowadays, deep models using attention (e.g., Transformer (Baltrušaitis et al. 2018), BERT (Devlin et al. 2018)) is the dominant approach in natural language processing, as well as in other sequence learning problems.

5.1.2 Deep Generative Models

Generating new content is an important area of machine learning with applications ranging from conversational artificial intelligence (AI) to knowledge discovery, and generative models are approaches that simulate how the data from the desired distribution are generated. Once a generative model is learned from a data set of samples, it could be used for generating new data as well as for other important inferencing tasks. Deep generative models (Goodfellow et al. 2016) refer to the neural network based generative models; in this section, we will discuss three major classes of deep generative models with many important applications: autoregressive models, a variational autoencoder, and a generative adversarial network.

Deep autoregressive models use neural networks to generate future data given past data in a chosen direction; they have no latent random variables.

Autoencoder is the unsupervised neural network approach to learn how to encode data efficiently in a latent space. An autoencoder includes two neural networks: an encoder that maps data from the input space to the latent space and a decoder to reconstruct the input data from the encoded latent data. A variational autoencoder (VAE) is a class of autoencoder where the encoder module is used to learn the parameter (mean, standard deviation) of a distribution. And the decoder is used to generate examples from samples drawn from the learned distribution.

A generative adversarial network (GAN) includes two components: a generator network and a discriminator network; a data set of examples from the desired source (e.g., the images of dogs) is required to train the GAN. The generator generates a simulated example given as its input a latent variable value drawn from a specified distribution. Both the generated examples and the authentic ones are fed to the discriminator network, whose job is to distinguish between the authentic and the simulated examples. The GAN is trained by updating the weights of the discriminator by gradient descent to increase its discriminative power, while updating the weights of the generator by gradient ascent to improve its ability to mimic the authentic examples and fool the discriminator. Over time the generator will learn to generate new data which simulate well the examples drawn from the target source.

5.1.3 Deep Reinforcement Learning

Reinforcement learning (RL) is a machine learning branch aimed at solving problems in which a set of sequential decisions is needed to maximize a goal. RL has a completely different approach to supervised and unsupervised learning. The goal of supervised learning is to create models that learn patterns from a set of labeled data to generate a function that maps the entries with the output. Whereas the purpose of unsupervised learning is finding hidden structures within unlabeled data. On the other hand, the RL algorithm goal is to learn a set of sequential actions that maximize the cumulative reward based on the experience obtained when interacting with the environment (e.g., playing a game, manipulating a robot, or activating and deactivating the heater). Some examples of RL objectives are playing online games at a human level, driving cars without human intervention, or managing traffic lights to reduce traffic.

RL was developed a few decades ago but, because of some limitations, it was unable to reach its full potential. This situation changed in recent years with the development of deep learning. Deep learning algorithms, for example, the popular deep Q-learning algorithm is able to approximate the Q-Table with an artificial neural network very effectively in terms of memory and processing requirements. The combination of deep learning and RL is called deep reinforcement learning (DRL) and has multiplied the potential of RL, boosting the general interest in RL of the industry and the scientific community.

5.2 Applications of Deep Learning

As the effectiveness of deep learning approaches has become evident, they have become widely applied. In this section, we provide an overview of some notable applications of deep learning. We categorize applications of deep learning as achieving one of four distinct objectives: *recognition*, *generation*, *decision-making*, and *forecasting*. Throughout this section, we will see how applications of deep learning across many different industries and domains rely on a small set of the same core deep learning approaches (Figure 5.2).

5.2.1 Recognition

In the context of machine learning, and specifically deep learning, *recognition* is defined as a task of identifying predefined labels from unannotated inputs—for

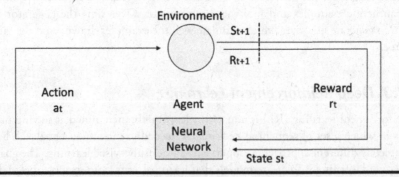

Figure 5.2 In reinforcement learning, there is an agent that takes actions in an environment. The environment gives a reward for that action and the agent moves to the next state.

example, recognizing that an image contains a particular species of flower—and is an example of a *supervised learning* task. Deep learning received much of its early attention because of its success in recognizing objects in images and so we describe this application in detail. Recognition, however, is not confined to image-based applications. Deep learning approaches have improved the accuracy of object recognition in videos, audio, and text as well as other types of data and we describe key applications of those.

5.2.1.1 Recognition in Text

Much of the digital data we collect and analyze is text-based (e.g., scientific literature, news articles, contracts, and medical reports), and the popularity of social media has led to an online text explosion. Deep learning has been applied successfully in natural language processing (Collobert et al. 2011) where deep feedforward neural networks (often with the use of convolution layers) are used to learn features automatically and perform competitively in key tasks along the natural language processing pipeline.

Deep text models are the dominant approach for sentiment analysis, usually a part of any text analytics pipeline. Modern sentiment analysis systems can be decomposed into different subtasks: target detection and polarity classification (Zhang et al. 2018). Li et al. (2017) proposed deep memory networks for both of these tasks. Other text information extraction tasks that have benefited from the application of deep learning include topic classification, semantic role labeling, part of speech tagging, named entity recognition, and chunking (Young et al. 2018).

In the era of *fake news*, important work is being done on using deep neural networks—usually a combination of CNN and RNN models—to detect deceptive opinions (Sharma et al. 2019). In a recent development, Graph CNN was used to detect fake news on social media with high accuracy (Monti et al. 2019). FakeNewsAI* is an example of a commercial news verification service based on a deep learning architecture.

Another commercial application of a deep text model is in the Google search engine, where the attention based BERT model is used to rank results returned from a search query.[†] In an example of a more end-to-end application of deep learning, Amazon's Alexa personal assistant uses LSTM to classify text and recognize the commands of the users (Naik et al. 2018). Apple's Siri[‡] and Google's Assistant[§] also use similar techniques.

---

* www.fakenewsai.com

[†] https://www.blog.google/products/search/search-language-understanding-bert/

[‡] www.apple.com/ios/siri/

[§] assistant.google.com

5.2.1.2 Recognition in Audio

Making sense of audio has long been a focus of the machine learning community, and deep learning has made significant progress in this field which leads to important commercial applications. Conversational speech recognition (CSR) is one of the most important such applications. In 2016, a series of breakthroughs were reported in CSR based on the advances of deep neural networks. For example, IBM researchers (Saon et al. 2016) achieved a 6.6% error rate with a large vocabulary English conversational telephone CSR system using a combination of CNNs and RNNs. In 2016, Microsoft achieved the milestone of reaching human parity in speech recognition for English with a 5.9% error rate on a similar task (Xiong et al. 2016). For commercial use cases, Google uses speech recognition to generate subtitles for videos automatically as well as to carry out voice searches.

Speech recognition is a more challenging task in noisy environments or in conversations. Different from single-speaker speech recognition, a step of vocal source separation is needed. For example, in order to process recordings from a cocktail party, we need to identify the voice from one speaker out of other speakers as well as background noise. Simpson et al. (2015) have applied CNNs to this problem to very good effect.

Moving away from speech, identifying the characteristics of music has been widely studied in machine learning and again deep learning is making inroads here. For music recommendation systems, automatic music genre recognition is a key step and deep learning brings a new approach in this area. Julien Despois demonstrated how to classify the genre of a piece of music or a complete song with CNNs* achieving genre recognition accuracies in the high 90% range. Niland is an important commercial player in the application of deep learning to music and in 2017 was acquired by Spotify.†

5.2.1.3 Recognition in Video and Images

Deep learning approaches, and in particular CNNs, are especially well suited for processing visual data. The large image data set ImageNet Large Scale Visual Recognition Challenge (ILSVRC) (Russakovsky et al. 2015), where the 2012 version includes 1,432,167 images labeled in 1,000 classes through crowd sourcing, has been the driving force for the development of new deep learning architectures in computer vision. Deep learning announced its arrival in computer vision by winning the ILSVRC image classification task in 2012 with the AlexNet CNN model: AlexNet achieved a top-5 error rate of 15.3%, significantly better than the error rate of the best non-deep learning models of 26.5%. After it, CNN models have become the dominant approach for computer vision tasks, and in 2015 the Residual

---

* chatbotslife.com/finding-the-genre-of-a-song-with-deep-learning-da8f59a61194
† www.spotify.com

Network (He et al. 2015) achieved the landmark of performing better than human performance. Figure 5.3 shows an example of image classification on a CNN model trained on the ImageNet data set.

Similar CNN-based approaches have been used for image recognition tasks such as Google photo search for medical application (Hegde et al. 2019), image caption generation, and video frame classification.* Salesforce research arm[†] is an example of a commercial application that uses deep models for textual sentiment analysis, as well as image classification tasks. There are also good examples of deep learning-based image recognition solutions being used to drive revenue in niche areas. For example, Deepomatic[‡] have leveraged deep learning to build commercially successful image tagging services in domains including fashion, security, and interior design.[§] Similarly, Tractable[¶] are using deep learning to estimate the cost of repair for insurance claims by recognizing the amount of damage in images of cars involved in incidents.

Face recognition is a long-standing image processing challenge. Prior to the introduction of deep learning models, state-of-the-art approaches to face recognition in images relied on first recognizing a set of carefully selected hand-crafted features within an image using image processing techniques, and then using these as an input to a machine learning model. CNNs enable very accurate facial recognition in an end-to-end system. For example, the DeepFace system from Facebook (Taigman et al. 2014) is a nine-layer deep CNN-like neural network used for face recognition. The DeepFace system was shown to achieve an accuracy of 97.35% on the Labeled Faces in the Wild (LFW) data set (Huang Erik Learned-Miller, 2014) (a well-known and challenging face recognition benchmark), which is significantly better than the state-of-the-art non deep learning approaches prior to 2014. Subsequent to the release of DeepFace, Google researchers introduced FaceNet (Schroff et al. 2015), which was also based on CNNs and achieved 99.63%

Domestic cat	Classic car	Malayan Tiger	Sunflower
Persian cat	Vintage car	Bengal cat	Marigold
Ocicat	Used car	Leopard	Daffodils

Figure 5.3   Examples of image classification

---

* cs.stanford.edu/people/karpathy/deepvideo/
† https://einstein.ai/
‡ www.deepomatic.com
§ www.deepomatic.com/demos
¶ www.tractable.ai/technology

accuracy on the LFW data set. Face recognition is an active area of research with many new deep learning models being proposed recently; for example, SphereFace and ArcFace (Wang and Deng, 2018). It has also been widely applied in business: from mobile systems that implement the technique to log users in automatically, to many law enforcement agencies who use it to detect criminals.

The success of deep learning models in image classification has translated to many successful applications of deep models in medical images, often through the use of the transfer learning technique. One notable example is the system described by Ciresan et al. (2013) that won the MICCAI 2013 Grand Challenge on Mitosis Detection. The mitosis detection task is particularly interesting as unlike the ILSVRC image classification task (Russakovsky et al. 2015), the goal is not to classify an entire image as belonging to a category, but rather to identify the portions of a large image that belong to a particular category—in this case, examples of mitosis in an image. This is referred to as image segmentation and is at the core of many image processing tasks. In recent years, deep models have attained human expert level performance in multiple tasks, including melanoma screening and detection, identifying diabetic retinopathy, cardiovascular risk analysis, and pneumonia detection on chest X-rays (Esteva et al. 2019).

The vast amounts of aerial imagery enabled by the lowering costs in satellite technology and the prevalence of low-cost aerial drones underpin another area in which deep learning-based image recognition is being widely applied. In 2010, Mnih and Hinton (Mnih and Hinton, 2015) produced a pioneering work in which deep learning methods were used to identify roads in aerial images. This is an example of an image segmentation problem (similar to the medical image recognition problem described previously) as the system not only recognizes that a road is present in an image but also the specific pixels in the image that contain the road. Marcu (Marcu, 2016) used CNNs to very accurately segment portions of aerial images into semantically meaningful categories (e.g., roads, buildings, parks). Recently, Facebook used deep learning to automatically segment roads from satellite images and generate accurate maps.* Their work automates the costly and time-consuming process of annotating maps manually, which will be helpful in many unmapped regions of the world—especially the regions in developing countries.

Aiming for the insurance industry, TensorFlight[†] uses these techniques to analyze aerial images and to provide automatic annotation on construction type, building footprint, and roof characteristics. Terrapattern[‡] is an interesting example of a group adopting similar deep learning-based approaches to build an aerial photo search engine that will find common patterns in massive collections of aerial

---

* ai.facebook.com/blog/mapping-roads-through-deep-learning-and-weakly-supervised-training/
† www.tensorflight.com
‡ www.terrapattern.com/about

imagery. Figure 5.4* shows an example set of search results for wastewater treatment plants.

Extending systems that recognize objects in images to systems that recognize objects in video is an obvious step and modifications to the core deep learning approaches (e.g., CNNs) to work on video have been shown to work well (Girshick, 2015; Ren et al. 2015). Clarifai† is an interesting startup working on automatic object recognition in video using deep learning for a wide range of tasks in industry. They are especially focused on the advertising industry and they use their technology to find appropriate videos in which to place ads.

Deep learning has allowed a step change in the performance of systems built to recognize objects in images and are now the *de facto* standard for that task. CNNs can be used both to classify entire images or to segment objects within images. It is worth noting that object recognition in *non-standard images* remains very challenging. For example, while it is possible (e.g., Valdenegro-Toro, 2016), object recognition in the sonar images collected by autonomous underwater vehicles (AUVs), widely used in the oil and gas industry, remains very difficult for automated systems. Similarly, it is worth noting that almost real-time object recognition is required in certain applications (e.g., autonomous vehicle control). While this can be achieved in some cases (e.g., Iandola et al. [2016] for traffic light recognition), it remains a significant challenge in using deep learning as significant computation is required to use a deep network to make a prediction. GANs are also beginning to become

Figure 5.4 GeoVisual search results for wastewater treatment plants in satellite imagery.

---

* www.medium.com/descartestech/geovisual-search-using-computer-vision-to-explore-the-earth-275d970c60cf

† www.clarifai.com

widely adopted for image recognition tasks but only for specialist applications and CNNs remain much more popular.

5.2.2 Content Generation

Rather than recognizing what is available in the data, in *generation* tasks, the objective is to output novel or additive content based on input data. Examples include generating captions for images, converting a piece of music into a new style (Hadjeres and Pachet, 2016), or composing entire documents. This section surveys key applications of deep learning for generating novel content. The ability to build machine learning systems that generate new content is something that did not really exist before the advent of deep learning approaches and has spurred a renewed interest in the area of *computational creativity*.

5.2.2.1 Text Generation

In terms of using deep learning for generation, text has attracted more attention than any other data format. Deep learning approaches have been successfully applied to many different tasks including generating captions for images, generating conversational responses for chatbots, generating screenplays, novels or speeches, and machine translation. In this section, we describe a selection of interesting examples of this application of deep learning technology.

Image and video captioning techniques are created to address the multimodality challenge of visual data and human language. A good captioning model needs to identify key objects in view and output a fluent sentence showing correct relations between the identified objects. Basically, there are two approaches in the research community including end-to-end pipelines and stepwise captioning models.

The *Show and Tell* caption generator from Google researchers (Vinyals et al. 2016) gives an early example of end-to-end captioning pipelines. A CNN network is employed to *encode* an input image to a fixed-length vector. Thereafter, this vector is taken as the initial hidden state of an RNN network. RNN *decodes* the vector into a sentence. There is no object detection step in this pipeline; loss of caption error is counted from each generation step. The *Show and Tell* model features ease of manipulation and quality of reading experience.

It was the winner of the Microsoft COCO 2015 Image Captioning Challenge.*

The *NeuralTalk* model sets a milestone of stepwise captioning practice (Karpathy and Li, 2015). This model is not a single CNN plus an RNN. Instead, a more complicated module is applied to extract visual features. The authors use a region convolutional neural network (R-CNN) (Girshick et al. 2014) to detect object regions from an input image. This R-CNN was pre-trained on ImageNet. Thereafter, an image-sentence score metric is introduced to find the maximum correspondence

---

* mscoco.org/dataset/#captions-leaderboard

between each object region and a word in caption sequence. In 2016, Karpathy et al. released NeuralTalk2, a revision of the original system capable of more believable captions.* While the current state-of-the-art of these captioning systems is not yet capable of human-level performance, these systems are already being applied in commercial offerings; for example, automatic captioning of images in the Facebook newsfeed.[†]

Going further than simple image caption generation, the movie director Oscar Sharp and the AI researcher Ross Goodwin developed *Benjamin,*[‡] an LSTM-based system that can generate original screenplays automatically. This is achieved by training it with dozens of science fiction screenplays and then asking it to generate its own. Their system was capable of generating long sections of novel movie script—one of which was actually filmed and released as the short film *Sunspring.*[§]

Although most of the text generation systems described so far are commercially interesting, they have not yet seen wide industrial adoption. *Machine translation* of texts from one language to another, on the other hand, is of massive commercial value. Deep learning approaches to the machine translation task, commonly referred to as neural machine translation (NMT), have led to a step change in the performance of automated machine translation systems. Instead of using phrase-level matching between two languages (as is done in older approaches to machine translation), the NMT model works on entire sentences which provide NMT systems with the opportunity to model more contextual information than is possible in other approaches. Google's NMT system is a good example of a modern NMT engine and it has three main components: the *encoder LSTMs*, the *decoder LSTMs*, and an *attention module* (Wu et al. 2016). The encoder LSTMs transforms an input sentence to a list of vector representations with one vector per symbol. The decoder LSTMs takes the vectors from the encoders and generates one language symbol at a time. The attention module regulates the decoders to focus on specific regions during decoding to drive increased accuracy of translations, and their addition was an important step in driving translation accuracy.

NMT systems reach translation error rates significantly below those statistical machine translation (SMT) approaches. As a result, Facebook have moved their entire translation system to an NMT-based solution based on LSTMs which will handle more than 2,000 translation directions and six billion translations per day. Skype by Microsoft has also deployed an NMT-based translation system. In this case, speech is automatically translated from one language to another. The system first performs speech recognition on the original language, then translates the text to the destination language, before finally using a text-to-speech system to generate speech in the destination language, where all of these components rely on deep

---

* cs.stanford.edu/people/karpathy/neuraltalk2/demo.html
[†] www.wired.com/2016/04/facebook-using-ai-write-photo-captions-blind-users/
[‡] bigcloud.io/filming-the-future-how-ai-directed-a-sci-fi-short/
[§] www.arstechnica.com/the-multiverse/2016/06/an-ai-wrote-this-movie-and-its-strangely-moving/

learning models. Skype translator currently supports speech-to-speech translation between ten languages.*

5.2.2.2 Audio Generation

It is also possible to use deep learning approaches to generate audio. Speech synthesis is by far the most studied application but approaches to music composition and sound effect generation have also been proposed. In this section, we describe some of the most interesting applications of deep learning approaches to audio generation.

Generating authentic sounding artificial speech, or *speech synthesis*, has long been a focus of artificial intelligence researchers. Deep neural networks, however, bring new approaches to this long-standing challenge. WaveNet (van den Oord et al. 2016), a deep autoregressive model developed by Google DeepMind, achieves state-of-the-art performance on text-to-speech generation and the generated speech audio is rated as subjectively natural by human raters. This performance is achieved with a dilated CNN model that manages to model long-term temporal dependencies with a much lower computational load than LSTM models.

Recently, text-to-speech synthesis techniques reached a new milestone after the landmark of WaveNet (van den Oord et al. 2016), and Google researchers introduced Tacotron 2 (Shen et al. 2017). This system employs a sequence-to-sequence model to project textual character embeddings to spectrograms in the frequency domain. Then a modified WaveNet model generates time-domain waveform samples from spectrogram features. Compared with WaveNet, Tacotron 2 has a better performance in learning human pronunciations and its model size is significantly smaller.

Beyond text-to-speech (TTS) techniques, speech-to-speech (STS) has drawn attention in recent years. Google researchers introduced a direct STS translation tool, named as Translatotron (Jia et al. 2019). Traditionally, speech-to-speech translation is achieved in three steps (or models) including speech-to-text transcription on the source language, text-to-text translation, and text-to-speech synthesis to generate audio in the target language. This routine is well established with convincing accuracy, also it is widely deployed in commercial applications. Translatotron is the first trial to merge the aforementioned three steps in one model and show its value. Although the benchmark of Translatotron is slightly below a baseline model on the Spanish-to-English translation task, this direct translation approach is able to mimic the voice of the source speaker in the synthesized target speech.

As a side-effect of the advances on TTS, it is now easy to generate a fake voice or speech toward a target person. An AI startup Dessa released a speech synthesis model called RealTalk which creates the human voice perfectly.[†] Currently, details of data set, models, and benchmarks are not publicly available, but people can try to tell the real voice from the fake on this page.[‡]

---

* www.skype.com/en/features/skype-translator/
[†] medium.com/dessa-news/real-talk-speech-synthesis-5dd0897eef7f
[‡] http://fakejoerogan.com/

Rather than generating speech from text, deep learning approaches have also been used to generate sound effects based on video inputs. An artificial foley artist* described by Owens et al. (2015) can reproduce sound effects for simple silent videos based on an ensemble of CNN and LSTM models. A CNN model is trained to extract high-level image features from each video frame. A sequence of these image features (color and motion) is taken as input to an LSTM model, and the LSTM model is trained to create an intermediate sound representation known as a *cochleagram*. In the final step, the *cochleagram* is converted to waveforms through an LSTM-based sound synthesis procedure. Although only applied in very simple environments, the results are impressive.

Deep learning models can also be used to generate original music. DeepBach (Hadjeres and Pachet, 2016), for example, uses an LSTM-based approach to *compose* original chorales in the style of Bach. The model is composed of multiple LSTM and CNN models that are combined in an ensemble which given a melody can produce harmonies for the alto, tenor, and bass voices. Similar systems based on RNNs that generate original music in other styles have also been demonstrated—for example, music in the style of Mozart[†,‡] or traditional Irish music.[§,¶]

5.2.2.3 Image and Video Generation

Deepfake is a buzz word in the recent news press. This word comes from *deep learning* and *fake*. Paul Barrett, adjunct professor of law at New York University, defines deepfake as falsified videos made by means of deep learning. We would like to confine the concept of deepfake as falsified human faces in image or video made by generative adversary networks (GAN) (Goodfellow et al. 2014) or related AI techniques. The general goal of deepfake is to transfer stylistic facial information from reference images or videos to synthetic copies.

Hyperconnect** released MarioNETte, one of the state-of-the-art face reenactment tools in 2019 (Ha et al. 2019). Previous research suffers from identity preservation problems on unseen large poses. MarioNETte integrates image attention block, target feature alignment, and landmark transformer. These modifications lead to better realistic synthetic videos.

Other than research publications, we find face reenactment tools for smartphones. ZAO, a free deepfake face-swapping app, is able to place user's face

---

* vis.csail.mit.edu
† www.wise.io/tech/asking-rnn-and-ltsm-what-would-mozart-write
‡ www.hochart.fr/rnn/
§ highnoongmt.wordpress.com/2015/08/07/the-infinite-irish-trad-session/
¶ highnoongmt.wordpress.com/2015/05/22/lisls-stis-recurrent-neural-networks-for-folk-music-generation/
** https://hyperconnect.com/?lang=en

seamlessly and naturally into scenes from hundreds of movies and TV shows using just a single photograph.*

Deepfake techniques are developing fast and this is becoming a challenge for personal privacy and public security. It is not only humans that cannot tell a faked portrait or video clip from the original, but advanced face recognition software is also being cheated. Korshunov and Marcel (Korshunov and Marcel, 2018) performed a study where the results showed that state-of-the-art recognition systems based on VGG and Facenet neural networks are vulnerable to Deepfake videos, with 85.62% and 95.00% false acceptance rates respectively. The best fake detection method is based on visual quality metrics which shows an 8.97% error rate on high-quality Deepfakes.

In order to improve fake detection techniques, Korshunov and Marcel (2018) released the first public available fake video data set, vidTIMIT. Tech giants also joined this campaign. Recently, Google and collaborators released a deep fake detection data set with over 3,000 manipulated videos (Rössler et al. 2019). Facebook and partner organizations started the Deepfake Detection Challenge (DFDC) and funded over US$10 million to support this industry-wide effort.[†]

Image generation refers to the process of automatically creating new images based on existing information sources. Deep learning has been applied in many image generation tasks, including image (and video) super-resolution, image colorization, image generation from text or other images, and so-called neural art.

Image super-resolution (ISR) is an image generation problem in which the resolution of a digital image is vastly increased through the application of algorithms. In recent years, Microsoft researchers have applied CNNs to this problem and achieved state-of-the-art restoration quality (Dong et al. 2014). Although deep CNNs significantly improve the accuracy and speed of ISR, there still remains a challenge of restoring the finer texture details. Ledig et al. (Ledig et al. 2016) proposed SRGAN for image super-resolution. The SRGAN is capable of restoring photo-realistic natural images for 4× upscaling factors. Recently, a team from ElementAI developed HighRes-net,[‡] a deep learning model capable of stitching multiple low-resolution satellite images to create a super-resolution image. Unlike other super-resolution models which could add fake details to the final image, their model recovers the original details in the super-resolution version after aggregating the information from multiple low-resolution ones. As such, their model has wide applications: from automatic land management to mapping road networks.

While it remains a very challenging task (and performing it at a human level is well beyond the current state-of-the-art), deep learning has led to advances in the ability of systems to automatically generate images based on textual descriptions. Systems that can do this can be helpful in graphic design, animation, and

---

* www.theverge.com/2019/9/2/20844338/zao-deepfake-app-movie-tv-show-face-replace-privacy-policy-concerns

† ai.facebook.com/blog/deepfake-detection-challenge/

‡ www.elementai.com/news/2019/computer-enhance-please

architecture. RNNs are one of the successful approaches to automatically synthesizing images from texts. Mansimov et al. (2015) introduced a seminal approach to image generation. There are two parts in the model by Mansimov et al. A bidirectional RNN is used to learn the sequence (or alignment) of words in input captions. Another generative RNN is used to learn the sequence of image patches from training images. Mansimov's model successfully generates synthesized images from input captions and some of the images are novel from the training set. However, the generated images often look blurry and need further refinement.

More recently, GANs have been demonstrated to be useful for image generation from text. Reed et al. (2016) introduced a text-conditional convolutional GAN architecture to address this challenge. In this design, both the generator network and the discriminator network use convolution layers for text encodings. The GAN generated images tend to look more natural than those produced using other methods.

Slightly different from generating images from text, it is also possible to generate new images from existing ones. For example, there are massive numbers of pictures captured by Google's Street View project, but an image from a required point of view may not be available. To solve this problem, Google researchers proposed DeepStereo (Flynn et al. 2015), in which CNN models are trained to predict new views based on available image sources to a quite good effect.* Similarly, the Irish company Artomatix† uses models based on CNNs to generate realistic looking texture for 3D models based on existing images.

Framing image generation as an image-to-image translation problem, Isola et al. (2016) used conditional adversarial networks to generate photo-realistic images from edge maps or sketches.‡ Zhu et al. (2016) proposed generative visual manipulation methods for similar objectives to create more stylized images.§ Going even further away from photo-realistic images, so called neural art seeks to create stylistic representations of images. For example, Gatys et al. (2015) used CNNs to generate new paintings with template artistic styles. A sample output image is shown in Figure 5.5.

5.2.3 Decision-Making

The recognition and generation systems described in previous sections perform niche tasks that are often embedded in larger systems. It is, however, also possible to build end-to-end control systems using deep learning, in particular, DRL which is, as described in Section 5.1.3, the combination of deep learning and reinforcement learning.

---

* For examples of DeepStereo see www.youtube.com/watch?v=cizgVZ8rjKA
† www.artomatix.com
‡ Christopher Hesse has a demonstration of Isola's model at www.affinelayer.com/pixsrv/
§ A demonstration is available at people.eecs.berkeley.edu/~junyanz/projects/gvm/

Figure 5.5 An example of neural art. (Reproduced from www.instapainting.com.)

In this subsection, we introduced systems mainly based in DRL that make decisions continuously in dynamic and static environments. As it has been described by Yuxi Li (2017), there is a wide range of applications areas where DRL can be effectively applied such as dialogue systems, education, healthcare, or computer vision. In the following sections, we focus on applications in autonomous driving, game playing, robotics, energy consumption, online advertising, and finance.

5.2.3.1 Autonomous Driving

An autonomous car or self-driving car is "a vehicle that is capable of sensing its environment and navigating without any human input" (Hussain, 2016). Deep learning approaches are often used for object recognition as part of an autonomous driving pipeline, and technologies based on these systems dominate the current commercial autonomous driving efforts. Google's self-driving car unit, for example, started in 2009 and in the next seven years drove over two million miles of test journeys on open roads. This car implements deep learning models extensively for object recognition. Similarly, the Tesla Autopilot system incorporates Tesla-developed deep learning systems based on CNNs for the tasks of recognizing objects through vision, sonar, and radar sensors. There are also examples of smaller startup self-driving car companies such as Drive.ai, which created a deep learning-based software for autonomous vehicles, or Tealdrones.com, a startup that equips drones with onboard deep learning modules for image recognition and navigation.

In this section, however, we are more interested in DRL based end-to-end control systems in which deep learning models are used not only for recognition tasks but also to actually make control decisions based on inputs from cameras and other sensors. The use of neural networks for end-to-end autonomous driving control has a history that stretches back to the late 1980s. The ALVINN system (Pomerleau and Pomerleau, 1989) or Nvidia's DAVE-2 system are good examples of a modern deep learning approach to controlling autonomous cars. In the case of the DAVE-2 system, CNN models generate steering commands based on the video input from three cameras placed at the front of the car. To train the model, long segments of recorded video, together with human steering, were used to link the correct steering commands with the camera inputs. The DAVE-2 system has achieved impressive results in simulation and has driven long journeys in a fully autonomous mode. Deep Tesla is another interesting example of an end-to-end autonomous car control system based on CNNs. However, due to some limitations, it is much more likely that, for the moment, deep learning models will be used for developing specific components of self-driving car control systems such as pedestrian detection or road-sign recognition.

As described in Section 5.1.3, RL creates a table that associates states to actions. In such a way that the agent driving the car is constantly looking up the table to see which is the best action for each state. RL cannot be applied in training mode in real scenarios because the agent will take random actions to learn and this can be very dangerous (Sallab et al. 2017). This is a big handicap for real-world applications because it is not possible in real life to have accidents in order to learn. However, there are simulations of the environment in which the car can learn how to behave and once the car learns the right actions, it can be deployed in the real world. For example, in an investigation carried out by Dong Li et al. (2018), neural networks were trained with the images obtained from a car simulator called TORCS (The Open Racing Car Simulator). The implemented model used to drive the car was composed of two modules: one based on multitasking neural networks, which were responsible for taking the driver's vision as an input, and another one based on DRL, which was responsible for making decisions from the extracted features of the neural network. This proposed model was capable of driving the car with great precision and was also able to adapt to new screens (situations) not previously seen by the system. The lack of real-world simulators is one of the main limitations of implementing DRL end-to-end systems in cars, nevertheless, the number of cars driving with multiple cameras makes it much more feasible to create a real-world simulator where DRL can be trained.

5.2.3.2 Automatic Game Playing

In 2015, Google DeepMind received massive publicity for its DRL system that could play Atari 2600 games at a superhuman level (Van Hasselt et al. 2016). This performance was achieved through the use of deep Q-networks (DQNs), which is an approach that combines both deep neural networks and reinforcement learning (Van Hasselt et al. 2016). DQNs incorporate a CNN model trained to predict the action with the highest expected reward based on an image of the current game state. The reward is the mechanism by which RL algorithms learn. For example, in Atari 2600 games, the agent gets a positive reward when it increases the score and a negative reward when the agent loses a game. In the case of the DQNs applied to the Atari 2600 (Van Hasselt et al. 2016), it was notable that it only utilized an image of the game screen as the input. The agent was able to learn by itself and it achieved superhuman levels after playing the game for several hours.

Deep Q-Networks can be distinguished from other deep learning architectures by the fact that they do not require labeled training sets. Rather, training DQNs involves multiple iterations of experimentation, the success of which is measured using an appropriate reward function. For the DeepMind Atari game playing system, the reward function was the score achieved in a round of playing the game. By playing hundreds of thousands of rounds, the system used the reward to modify the parameters of a deep network and to guide it to a version that could achieve superhuman performance at the game.

The DQN algorithm inspired many researchers to develop control systems for other games. For example, MIT researchers developed DeepTraffic, a gamification of highway traffic, Lin applied a DQN to play FlappyBird,* and Tampuu et al. (2015) applied a DQN to a multiagent Pong game where each agent was controlled by a DQN.

It is also worth including board games among the applications discussed here for two reasons: first, the level of difficulty that they entail, and second if a DQN is able to solve difficult problems, it will also be able to solve the easy ones. The problem of making a machine able to play chess or the game of Go better than a human has been a challenge for AI since its beginning (Silver et al. 2018). Some remarkable authors such as Alan Turing and John Von Neumann tried to develop hardware and software to enable computers to play board games. One of the milestones of AI was achieved when the Deep Blue program beat the world chess champion in 1997. However, the development of these programs required great levels of supervision by experts in both chess and coding (Figure 5.6).

The most widely known example of a deep learning approach to play board games is probably that of DeepMind's AlphaGo, which is an autonomous agent for the game of Go. AlphaGo defeated the world Go champion, Lee Sedol, 4-1 in March 2016 (Chouard, 2016) and continues to beat world-class human players. The AlphaGo model uses deep convolutional neural networks and a general tree search algorithm (Silver et al. 2017). The architecture of AlphaGo is especially interesting as it is a hybrid system incorporating Monte Carlo tree search algorithms, supervised learning (SL) policy networks, reinforcement learning policy networks, and value networks (Silver et al. 2016). The first of these components, Monte Carlo tree search, has been a mainstay of automated Go playing systems since the 1990s (Brugmann, 1993). The latter three components are implemented

---

* https://github.com/yenchenlin/DeepLearningFlappyBird

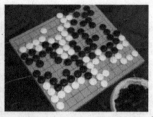

Figure 5.6 Algorithms based on deep reinforcement learning techniques have surpassed human level performance in many games such as chess (left), video games (center), and Go (right).

as CNN models with slightly different objectives. This makes AlphaGo an interesting mix of traditional and cutting edge AI techniques.

AlphaZero, which was developed following on from the work on AlphaGo, leverages RL so that it does not need any human telling the agent what the best movements are or which are the best strategies. Through RL, the agent is able to learn by itself on the basis of trial and error. Playing against itself over many millions of games, the agent is able to learn which are the best moves in many different games, including chess and the game of Go.

5.2.3.3 Robotics

While autonomous vehicles can be thought of as robots, there is a much broader set of robotic systems that also implement deep learning approaches to control their actions. We are primarily interested in systems that use deep learning for end-to-end robot control rather than systems that use deep learning components for specific tasks such as object recognition or speed control. For example, BRETT* from UC Berkeley can learn to perform tasks such as stacking LEGO blocks, putting together a toy plane, and screwing bottle caps onto bottles using deep reinforcement learning (Levine et al. 2015). CNN models are used to process the image input and to convert them into motor control signals. The model is trained using a technique similar to the DQN approach previously described (Levine et al. 2015). Other similar systems include the Google Brain grasping robot (Levine et al. 2016) and the systems developed by Delft Robotics that used deep learning to win the Amazon Picking Challenge.[†]

Moving away from fixed-base grasping robots, Peng et al. (2016) introduced a deep reinforcement learning approach for a robot locomotion control policy in a physical simulation. The objective in this simulation setting was to navigate a simulated robot dog through different types of terrain obstacles, such as gaps, walls, and slopes. This control task shares similar challenges to those faced in the Atari

* https://news.berkeley.edu/2015/05/21/deep-learning-robot-masters-skills-via-trial-and-error/
† http://amazonpickingchallenge.org/

2600 games previously described. The terrain descriptions, as well as the robot state descriptions, are high dimensional, therefore they are not suitable to be used directly for traditional reinforcement learning systems (Figure 5.7).

In this case, a mixture of actor-critic experts (MACE) approach is introduced to learn the right output, the parameterized actions, for complex input data (e.g., leaps or steps) (Peng et al. 2016). The actor-critic approach in RL consists of creating two models: the first takes the actions and the latter evaluates how good the action was, so the agent can learn. The MACE system is a type of CNN in which the inputs are terrain features and the robot state features, and the outputs are the actions and estimated rewards.

As we already said for self-driving cars, it is unlikely that in the short term, end-to-end deep learning systems will be used for the control of autonomous robots that interact closely with humans. Rather, it is more likely that deep learning models will be used as components in these systems for specific tasks such as object recognition or text detection. For robotic applications that do not involve significant interactions with people, however, end-to-end control systems based on deep reinforcement learning are feasible. Another interesting potential for the application to robotics is using simulations to train models that are deployed in real robots (Rusu et al. 2016). This overcomes the complication of performing hundreds of thousands of experiment iterations in a real environment.

5.2.3.4 Energy Consumption

One of the applications that called the attention of many companies has been the reduction by 40% of the cooling bill of Google data centers.* These data centers, which can be seen in Figure 5.9, are in charge of storing all the information collected in Google applications such as emails in Gmail, photos in Google Maps, or

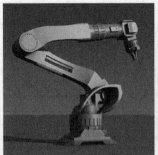

Figure 5.7 Deep reinforcement learning techniques have been successfully used in robotic arms (left) and in drones (right).

---

* https://deepmind.com/blog/article/deepmind-ai-reduces-google-data-centre-cooling-bill-40

the documents in Google Drive. This information is stored in large rooms with around 2.5 million servers, according to the company Gartner Inc. To prevent these servers from overheating, it is necessary to cool them down every so often using a cooling system usually based on pumps, chillers, and cooling towers.

Developing an algorithm to optimize energy consumption to cool down the servers is very complex because each data center has its own characteristics. These include factors such as the local climate, the demand for computing power, and the cost of energy. However, any improvement in the reduction of energy consumption can result in a large economic saving and a potential reduction in energy generation derived carbon emissions.

Google decided to address the problem of maximizing energy consumption by implementing an algorithm based on deep reinforcement learning. The objective of the algorithm is to maximize the power usage effectiveness (PUE), which is a metric obtained by dividing the total energy consumed by the data center by the energy consumed to run the computer infrastructure. Google does not usually give information about the techniques used to achieve their achievements, and the case of maximizing the PUE was not an exception. However, Google itself published information showing that its algorithm was trained with historical data from thousands of sensors that captured information from several factors (temperature, consumption, pump speed, etc.) to create a system able to automatically adapt to dynamic environments by using deep neural networks (Figure 5.8).

5.2.3.5 Online Advertising

Bidding optimally in internet advertising is a very complex task where RL has been successfully applied (Du et al. 2017). In the paper presented by Han Cai et al. (2017), a case is presented of success where an agent is able to bid intelligently for each impression in the real-time bidding (RTB) model. RTB is like a massive worldwide auction where publishers offer visits (from users who access their pages) to advertisers so that they can display their ads. Generally, in online

Figure 5.8 An approach based on reinforcement learning has reduced the electricity bill of Google Data Centers by 40%.

advertising, bids are made by algorithms on behalf of the advertiser because it would be impossible to individually bid on each impression (there could be thousands per second).

Generally, the objective of RTB algorithms is to get the largest number of clicks from a certain budget. However, in other approaches, different metrics are used such as the number of conversions or the revenue generated (Zeff and Aronson, 1999).

Usually, if the bidding price is very high, the budget will be finished quicker, and the number of impressions will be lower. On the other hand, if the bidding price is too low, the number of impressions will be very small because other candidates with a higher price will be selected. Additionally, we have to consider that the market is in constant movement. Advertisers raise and lower the price all the time. And advertisers and publishers come and go. It is, therefore, a very complex problem. To test the performance of RL to address this problem, RL algorithms were compared with linear bidding strategy (LIN) (Perlich et al. 2012), which is the best state-of-the-art algorithm for this problem, with the RL algorithm giving a higher performance.

5.2.4 Forecasting

In this section, we introduce the application of deep learning to forecasting future values of a time series. We distinguish between three main categories of application—forecasting physical signals, forecasting financial data, and forecasting wind speed and power.

5.2.4.1 Forecasting Physical Signals

Physical signals in the real world are complex and inter-correlated. Although the variation of one environmental condition may not affect people's lives if it is not on an extreme level, there is a requirement in many industries to precisely predict the values of one or more physical signals into the near future. For example, forecasts of *solar irradiance* (the power per unit area received from the sun) have long been of interest to the industry. Generally, solar irradiance on a day $t+1$ can be modeled with three types of inputs: the value of solar irradiance on day t or before and the values of other physical factors (e.g., air temperature, humidity, wind speed, wind direction, sunshine duration, or geographical location). Mellit and Pavan (2010) applied a wavelet network deep learning model to predict solar irradiance 24 hours into the future. This model achieves forecasting accuracies in the high 90% range and is at the top end of the current state-of-the-art. Kmet and Kmetova (2015) introduced an application of a specific type of RNN known as an echo state network (ESN) (Jaeger, 2001) for the same problem with similarly impressive results. Cao and Lin (Cao and Lin, 2008) proposed a diagonal recurrent wavelet neural network to forecast global solar irradiance and proved that the model is capable of mapping solar irradiance, which is usually highly non-linear and time changeable, as it combines advantages of recurrent and wavelet neural networks (Figure 5.9).

Another application is in wind forecasting in relation to wind energy production. Wind prediction is complex due to the wind's high degree of volatility and deviation. Therefore, in real electricity markets, system operators have barely begun to factor wind forecast information into their daily operations and reserve determination. However, in terms of academic research, many publications have introduced short-term or long-term wind forecasting technologies and experience based on deep learning approaches. In Kariniotakis et al. (1996), a recurrent higher-order neural network (RHONN) model was developed for wind power forecasting in a wind park. This model can be used to predict wind speed or power in time scales from some seconds to three hours. The work of More and Deo (2003) employs the technique of neural networks (feed-forward and recurrent networks) and statistical time series respectively to forecast daily and monthly wind speeds in India. The results show that the neural networks perform better than the baseline ARIMA models. However, the average of daily and monthly wind speed could be smoother than that of hourly wind speed, which implies that it is not difficult to obtain a more accurate forecasting result for daily and monthly wind speed. In Rohrig and Lange (2006), a method based on artificial neural networks was utilized to predict the average hourly wind speed. A multilayer perceptron neural network with three-layer feed-forward architecture was adopted as their forecasting system. The input selection was determined on the basis of correlation coefficients between previous wind speed observations.

Other authors of deep learning applications to physical system forecasting include: Romeu et al. (2013) who applied *stacked denoising autoencoders* (Vincent et al. 2010) (a specific type of feed-forward network) to the task of indoor temperature forecasting and James et al. (2017) who applied deep learning models to forecast wave conditions. These techniques are also being applied in industry. For

Figure 5.9   Deep learning has been widely applied in both domains, wind speed estimation (left) and forecasting financial data (right).

example, Nervana* leveraged deep learning for extreme weather forecasting and climate change modeling and Descartes Labs[†] applied deep learning over satellite images for predicting crop production.

5.2.4.2 Forecasting Financial Data

Reviewing the application of deep learning to financial forecasting is difficult as commercial players are very secretive about the techniques that they use and how effective they are. There are, however, a smaller number of examples of academic publications illustrating how this can be done. Currency exchange rate forecasting is one that has received attention, and one that is recognized as a challenging problem (Beirne et al. 2007). Chao et al. (2011) used *deep belief networks*, a form of feed-forward network, to accurately predict future exchange rates. Galeshchuk and Mukherjee (2017a, 2017b) report good results applying recurrent neural networks to the same problem.

Not surprisingly, researchers have also focused on attempting to predict stock prices, with some success.

Bao et al. (2017) used a combination of autoencoder networks and recurrent neural networks to predict stock prices with impressive results. Similarly, Fischer and Krauss (2017) demonstrated how recurrent networks can be used effectively for market predictions. Rather than focusing on predicting prices directly, a lot of work focuses on volatility—accurate predictions which are key for devising trading strategies. It has been shown repeatedly that hybrid models including recurrent networks and feed-forward networks can be used to do this effectively (Poklepović et al. 2014; Kristjanpoller et al. 2014; Monfared and Enke, 2015; Lu et al. 2016).

One of the advantages of deep learning approaches is their ability to handle sparse data types. News sources are essential driving forces for stock market activities and may be even more influential than the current and past stock prices (Fama, 1965). Ding et al. (2015) proposed a CNN-based framework to model the influence of news events on stock market prices. The proposed framework has two key features. First, a neural tensor network (NTN) is applied to learn event embeddings from word embeddings in an automatic way. Second, a CNN model covering both short-term and long-term events is used to predict a binary output indicating whether a stock price is rising or falling. This CNN-based architecture is demonstrated to show increased prediction accuracy over state-of-the-art non-deep learning baseline methods (Ding et al. 2015). A later modification to this approach (Ding et al. 2016) integrates knowledge graph information during the learning process of event embeddings to predict stock prices even more accurately.

---

* www.nervanasys.com/
[†] www.descarteslabs.com/

As mentioned previously, detailed reports of how deep learning is being used for commercial applications are difficult to find. However, many new companies are open about the fact that they are trying to perform such actions. Sentient Technologies* led by Babak Hodjat formerly of Apple, for example, is a hedge fund that puts deep learning approaches at the heart of their trading strategies.† Similarly, Man Group,‡ one of the world's largest hedge funds, is utilizing deep learning methods extensively in their trading strategies.§ A recent report by EurekaHedge⁵ analyzed a range of machine learning-based hedge funds and showed that, in general, they are outperforming other types of funds.

Numerai** is a particularly interesting player in the financial forecasting space. Rather than creating their own forecasting models, Numerai has created a platform through which interested data scientists can access data sets and deploy their own forecasting models. The forecasts made by this disparate set of models are then combined into an ensemble on which a hedge fund is based. With a payment system built on top of blockchain technologies, Numerai is an interesting experiment in crowdsourcing investment decisions from deep learning experts that could be worth watching.††

5.3 Conclusion

In this chapter, we have reviewed a broad range of different applications of deep learning, categorized into four general types of task: recognition, generation, decision-making, and forecasting, with a particular focus on relevance to industry. As we have shown, deep learning has produced impressive achievements both in terms of improvements in accuracy, compared with traditional machine learning approaches, as well as enabling completely new AI applications. We are already benefiting from many of these in our everyday lives, and as applications of deep learning continue to improve and expand, we can expect to experience many more benefits in the future.

However, recent applications of deep learning in industry have also raised concerns such as hidden biases in training data, adversarial manipulation of trained models, and the difficulty in understanding the rationale behind decisions made by

---

* www.sentient.ai
† www.bloomberg.com/news/articles/2017-02-06/silicon-valley-hedge-fund-takes-on-wall-street-with-ai-trader
‡ www.man.com/
§ www.bloomberg.com/news/features/2017-09-27/the-massive-hedge-fund-betting-on-ai
⁵ www.eurekahedge.com/Research/News/1639/Quantitative-Hedge-Funds-Strategy-Profile
** www.numer.ai
†† www.wired.com/2017/02/ai-hedge-fund-created-new-currency-make-wall-street-work-like-open-source/

deep learning models due to their black box nature. Further research is needed to make deep learning applications safer and more trustworthy in society.

References

D. Bahdanau, K. Cho and Y. Bengio. "Neural machine translation by jointly learning to align and translate". *arXiv preprint arXiv:1409.0473* (2014).

T. Baltrušaitis, C. Ahuja and L.-P. Morency. "Multimodal machine learning: A survey and taxonomy". In: *IEEE*, 2018.

W. Bao, J. Yue and Y. Rao. "A deep learning framework for financial time series using stacked autoencoders and long-short term memory". *PloS one* 12.7 (2017), e0180944.

J. Beirne, J. Hunter and M. Simpson. "Is the real exchange rate stationary? – A similar sized test approach for the univariate and panel cases". In: *Economics and Finance, Dept of Economics and Finance Research Papers, Brunel University* (2007). url: http://bura.brunel.ac.uk/ handle/2438/1024.

B. Brugmann. *Monte Carlo go*. Tech. rep. Technical report, Physics Department, Syracuse University, Syracuse, NY, 1993.

H. Cai et al. "Real-time bidding by reinforcement learning in display advertising". In: *Proceedings of the Tenth ACM International Conference on Web Search and Data Mining*. ACM, 2017, pp. 661–670.

J. Cao and X. Lin. "Application of the diagonal recurrent wavelet neural network to solar irradiation forecast assisted with fuzzy technique". *Engineering Applications of Artificial Intelligence* 21.8 (2008), pp. 1255–1263.

J. Chao, F. Shen and J. Zhao. "Forecasting exchange rate with deep belief networks". In: *The 2011 International Joint Conference on Neural Networks*. July 2011, pp. 1259–1266. doi: 10.1109/IJCNN. 2011.6033368.

T. Chouard. "The Go Files: AI computer wraps up 4-1 victory against human champion". *Nature News* (2016).

Dan C. Cireşan et al. "Mitosis detection in breast cancer histology images with deep neural networks". In: *D. Image Computing and Computer-Assisted Intervention – MICCAI 2013: 16th International Conference, Nagoya, Japan, September 22–26, 2013, Proceedings, Part II*, Springer, Berlin Heidelberg, 2013, pp. 411–418. isbn: 978-3-642-40763-5. doi: 10.1007/978-3-642-40763-5 51.

R. Collobert et al. "Natural language processing (almost) from scratch". *Journal of Machine Learning Research* 12(Aug 2011), pp. 2493–2537.

J. Devlin et al. "Bert: Pre-training of deep bidirectional transformers for language understanding". *arXiv preprint arXiv:1810.04805* (2018).

X. Ding et al. "Deep learning for event-driven stock prediction". In: *Proceedings of the 24th International Conference on Artificial Intelligence*. IJCAI'15. AAAI Press, Buenos Aires, Argentina, 2015, pp. 2327–2333. isbn: 978-1-57735-738-4. url: http://dl.acm.org/citation.cfm?id=2832415.2832572.

X. Ding et al. "Knowledge-driven event embedding for stock prediction". In: *COLING 2016, 26th International Conference on Computational Linguistics, Proceedings of the Conference: Technical Papers, December 11-16, 2016, Osaka, Japan*. 2016, pp. 2133–2142. url: http://aclweb.org/anthology/ C/C16/C16-1201.pdf.

C. Dong et al. "Learning a deep convolutional network for image super-resolution". In: *Computer Vision – ECCV 2014: 13th European Conference, Zurich, Switzerland, September 6–12, 2014, Proceedings, Part IV.* Ed. by David Fleet et al. Springer International Publishing, Cham, 2014, pp. 184–199. isbn: 978-3-319-10593-2. doi: 10.1007/978-3-319-10593-2 13.

M. Du et al. "Improving real-time bidding using a constrained markov decision process". In: *International Conference on Advanced Data Mining and Applications.* Springer, 2017, pp. 711–726.

A. Esteva et al. "A guide to deep learning in healthcare". *Nature Medicine* 25.1 (2019), pp. 24–29.

E. F. Fama. "The behavior of stock-market prices". *The Journal of Business* 38.1 (1965), pp. 34–105. issn: 00219398, 15375374. url: http://www.jstor.org/stable/2350752.

T. Fischer and C. Krauss. *Deep Learning with Long Short-Term Memory Networks for Financial Market Predictions.* Tech. rep. FAU Discussion Papers in Economics, 2017.

J. Flynn et al. "DeepStereo: Learning to predict new views from the world's imagery". *ArXiv* abs/1506.06825 (2015). url: http://arxiv.org/abs/1506.06825.

S. Galeshchuk and S. Mukherjee. "Deep learning for predictions in emerging currency markets." *ICAART* 2. 2017a, pp. 681–686.

S. Galeshchuk and S. Mukherjee. "Deep networks for predicting direction of change in foreign exchange rates". *Intelligent Systems in Accounting, Finance and Management* 24.4, (2017b), pp. 100–110.

L. A. Gatys, A. S. Ecker and M. Bethge. "A neural algorithm of artistic style". *ArXiv e-prints* (Aug. 2015). arXiv: 1508.06576 cs.CV.

R. B. Girshick. "Fast R-CNN". *arXiv* abs/1504.08083 (2015). url: http://arxiv.org/abs/1504.08083.

R. Girshick et al. "Rich feature hierarchies for accurate object detection and semantic segmentation". In: *Proceedings of the 2014 IEEE Conference on Computer Vision and Pattern Recognition.* CVPR '14. IEEE Computer Society, Washington, DC, 2014, pp. 580–587. isbn: 978-1-4799-51185. doi: 10.1109/CVPR.2014.81.

I. Goodfellow, Y. Bengio and A. Courville. *Deep Learning.* MIT Press, 2016. http://www.deeplearningbook. org.

I. Goodfellow et al. "Generative adversarial nets". In: *Advances in Neural Information Processing Systems 27.* Ed. by Z. Ghahramani et al. Curran Associates, Inc., 2014, pp. 2672–2680. url: http: //papers.nips.cc/paper/5423-generative-adversarial-nets.pdf.

S. Ha et al. "MarioNETte: Few-shot face reenactment preserving identity of unseen targets". *arXiv e-prints* (Nov. 2019), arXiv:1911.08139. arXiv: 1911.08139 cs.CV.

G. Hadjeres and F. Pachet. "DeepBach: A steerable model for bach chorales generation". *ArXiv e-prints* (Dec. 2016). arXiv: 1612.01010 cs.AI.

K. He et al. "Delving deep into rectifiers: Surpassing human-level performance on imagenet classification". In: *The IEEE International Conference on Computer Vision (ICCV).* Dec. 2015.

N. Hegde et al. "Similar image search for histopathology: SMILY". *NPJ Digital Medicine* 2.1 (2019), p. 56.

S. Hochreiter and J. Schmidhuber. "Long Short-Term Memory". *Neural Computation* 9.8 (Nov. 1997), pp. 1735–1780. issn: 0899-7667. doi: 10.1162/neco.1997.9.8.1735. url: http://dx.doi.org/10. 1162/neco.1997.9.8.1735.

G. B. Huang E. Learned-Miller. *Labeled Faces in the Wild: Updates and New Reporting Procedures.* Tech. rep. UM-CS-2014-003. University of Massachusetts, Amherst, May 2014.

M. Hussain. "Security in connected cars". In: *Proceedings of the European Automotive Congress EAEC-ESFA 2015.* Springer International Publishing, Cham, 2016, pp. 267–275. isbn: 978-3-31927276-4. doi: 10.1007/978-3-319-27276-4 24.

F. N. Iandola et al. "SqueezeNet: AlexNet-level accuracy with 50x fewer parameters and ¡1MB model size". *arXiv* abs/1602.07360 (2016). url: http://arxiv.org/abs/1602.07360.

P. Isola et al. "Image-to-image translation with conditional adversarial networks". *ArXiv e-prints* (Nov. 2016). arXiv: 1611.07004 cs.CV.

H. Jaeger. "The "echo state" approach to analysing and training recurrent neural networks with an Erratum note". *German National Research Center for Information Technology* (2001). url: http://www.faculty.jacobs-university.de/hjaeger/pubs/EchoStatesTechRep.pdf.

S. C. James, Yushan Zhang and Fearghal O'Donncha. "A machine learning framework to forecast wave conditions". *arXiv preprint arXiv:1709.08725* (2017).

Y. Jia et al. "Direct speech-to-speech translation with a sequence-to-sequence model". *CoRR* abs/1904.06037 (2019). arXiv: 1904.06037. url: http://arxiv.org/abs/1904.06037.

G. N. Kariniotakis, G. S. Stavrakakis and E. F. Nogaret. "Wind power forecasting using advanced neural networks models". *IEEE transactions on Energy conversion* 11.4 (1996), pp. 762–767.

A. Karpathy and F-F Li. "Deep visual-semantic alignments for generating image descriptions". In: *IEEE Conference on Computer Vision and Pattern Recognition, CVPR 2015, Boston, MA, USA, June 7–12, 2015,* 2015, pp. 3128–3137. doi: 10.1109/CVPR.2015.7298932.

T. Kmet and M. Kmetova. "A 24H forecast of solar irradiance using echo state neural networks". In: *Proceedings of the 16th International Conference on Engineering Applications of Neural Networks (INNS).* EANN '15. ACM, Rhodes, Island, Greece, 2015, 6:1–6:5. isbn: 978-1-4503-3580-5. doi: 10.1145/2797143.2797166.

P. Korshunov and S. Marcel. "DeepFakes: A new threat to face recognition? Assessment and detection". *CoRR* abs/1812.08685 (2018). arXiv: 1812.08685. url: http://arxiv.org/abs/1812. 08685.

W. Kristjanpoller, A. Fadic and M. C. Minutolo. "Volatility forecast using hybrid neural network models". *Expert Systems with Appllication* 41.5 (Apr. 2014), pp. 2437–2442. issn: 0957-4174. doi: 10. 1016/j.eswa.2013.09.043.

Y. LeCun et al. "Generalization and network design strategies". *Connectionism in Perspective* (1989), pp. 143–155.

C. Ledig et al. "Photo-realistic single image super-resolution using a generative adversarial network". *arXiv* abs/1609.04802 (2016). url: http://arxiv.org/abs/1609.04802.

S. Levine, N. Wagener and P. Abbeel. "Learning contact-rich manipulation skills with guided policy search". In: *IEEE International Conference on Robotics and Automation, ICRA 2015, Seattle, WA, USA, 26–30 May, 2015.* 2015, pp. 156–163. doi: 10.1109/ICRA.2015.7138994.

S. Levine et al. "End-to-end training of deep visuomotor policies". *ArXiv* abs/1504.00702 (2015). url: http://arxiv.org/abs/1504.00702.

S. Levine et al. "Learning hand-eye coordination for robotic grasping with deep learning and large-scale data collection". *ArXiv* abs/1603.02199 (2016). url: http://arxiv.org/abs/1603.02199.

Y. Li. "Deep reinforcement learning: An overview". *arXiv preprint arXiv:1701.07274* (2017).

C. Li, X. Guo and Q. Mei. "Deep memory networks for attitude identification". *ArXiv e-prints* (Jan. 2017). arXiv: 1701.04189 cs.CL.

D. Li et al. "Reinforcement learning and deep learning based lateral control for autonomous driving". *arXiv preprint arXiv:1810.12778* (2018).

X. Lu, D. Que and G. Cao. "Volatility forecast based on the hybrid artificial neural network and GARCH-type models". *Procedia Computer Science* 91 (2016), pp. 1044–1049. Promoting Business Analytics and Quantitative Management of Technology: 4th International Conference on Information Technology and Quantitative Management (ITQM 2016).. issn: 1877-0509. doi:10.1016/j.procs.2016.07.145. url: http://www. sciencedirect.com/science/article/pii/ S1877050916313382.

E. Mansimov et al. "Generating images from captions with attention". *CoRR* abs/1511.02793 (2015). url: http://arxiv.org/abs/1511.02793.

A. Marcu. "A local-global approach to semantic segmentation in aerial images". *ArXiv* abs/1607.05620 (2016). url: http://arxiv.org/abs/1607.05620.

A. Mellit and A. Massi Pavan. "A 24-h forecast of solar irradiance using artificial neural network: Application for performance prediction of a grid-connected {PV} plant at Trieste, Italy". *Solar Energy* 84.5 (2010), pp. 807–821. issn: 0038-092X. doi: http:// dx.doi.org/10.1016/j.solener. 2010.02.006. url: http://www.sciencedirect.com/ science/article/pii/S0038092X10000782.

V. Mnih and G. E. Hinton. "Learning to detect roads in high-resolution aerial images". In: *Computer Vision – ECCV 2010: 11th European Conference on Computer Vision, Heraklion, Crete, Greece, September 5–11, 2010, Proceedings, Part VI.* Ed. by Kostas Daniilidis, Petros Maragos and Nikos Paragios, Springer, Berlin, Heidelberg, 2010, pp. 210–223. isbn: 978-3-64215567-3. doi: 10.1007/978-3-642-15567-3 16. url: http://dx.doi.org/10.1007/978-3-642-15567-3 16.

S. A. Monfared and D. Enke. "Noise canceling in volatility forecasting using an adaptive neural network filter". *Procedia Computer Science* 61 (2015), pp. 80–84. issn: 1877-0509. doi:10.1016/j.procs.2015.09.155. url: http://www.sciencedirect.com/science/article/ pii/S1877050915029853.

F. Monti et al. "Fake news detection on social media using geometric deep learning". *rXiv preprint arXiv:1902.06673* (2019).

A. More and M.C. Deo. "Forecasting wind with neural networks". *Marine Structures* 16.1 (2003), pp. 35–49.

C. Naik et al. "Contextual slot carryover for disparate schemas". *arXiv preprint arXiv:1806.01773* (2018).

A. Owens et al. "Visually indicated sounds". *ArXiv e-prints* abs/1512.08512 (2015). url: http://arxiv.org/abs/1512.08512.

X. B. Peng, G. Berseth and M. van de Panne. "Terrain-adaptive locomotion skills using deep reinforcement learning". *ACM Transactions on Graphics (Proc. SIGGRAPH 2016)* 35.4 (2016).

C. Perlich et al. "Bid optimizing and inventory scoring in targeted online advertising". In: *Proceedings of the 18th ACM SIGKDD International Conference on Knowledge Discovery and Data Mining.* ACM, 2012, pp. 804–812.

T. Poklepović, J. Arnerić and Z. Aljinović. "GARCH based artificial neural networks in forecasting conditional variance of stock returns". *Croatian Operational Research Review* 5.2 (2014), pp. 329–343.

D. A. Pomerleau and D. A. Pomerleau. "ALVINN: An autonomous land vehicle in a neural network". *Advances in Neural Information Processing Systems 1* (1989).

S. E. Reed et al. "Generative adversarial text to image synthesis". *ArXiv e-prints* abs/1605.05396 (2016). url: http://arxiv.org/abs/1605.05396.

S. Ren et al. "Faster R-CNN: Towards real-time object detection with region proposal networks". *arXiv* abs/1506.01497 (2015). url: http://arxiv.org/abs/1506.01497.

K. Rohrig and B. Lange. "Application of wind power prediction tools for power system operations". In: *2006 IEEE Power Engineering Society General Meeting.* IEEE. 2006.

P. Romeu et al. "Time-series forecasting of indoor temperature using pre-trained deep neural networks". In: *Proceedings of the 23rd International Conference on Artificial Neural Networks and Machine Learning – ICANN 2013 - Volume 8131,* Springer-Verlag New York, Inc., New York, NY, 2013, pp. 451–458. isbn: 978-3-642-40727-7. doi: 10.1007/978-3-642-40728-4 57.

A. Rössler et al. "FaceForensics++: Learning to detect manipulated facial images". *CoRR* abs/1901.08971 (2019). arXiv: 1901.08971. url: http://arxiv.org/abs/1901.08971.

D. E. Rumelhart, G. E. Hinton and R. J. Williams. "Learning representations by back-propagating errors". *Nature* 323 (Oct. 1986), pp. 533–536. doi: 10.1038/323533a0.

O. Russakovsky et al. "ImageNet large scale visual recognition challenge". *International Journal of Computer Vision (IJCV)* 115.3 (2015), pp. 211–252. doi: 10.1007/s11263-015-0816-y.

A. A. Rusu et al. "Sim-to-real robot learning from pixels with progressive nets". *arXiv preprint arXiv:1610.04286* (2016).

A. E. L. Sallab et al. "Deep reinforcement learning framework for autonomous driving". *Electronic Imaging* 2017.19 (2017), pp. 70–76.

G. Saon et al. "The IBM 2016 english conversational telephone speech recognition system". *ArXiv e-prints* (Apr. 2016). arXiv: 1604.08242 cs.CL.

J. Schmidhuber. "Deep learning in neural networks: An overview". *Neural Networks* 61 (2015), pp. 85–117. Published online 2014; based on TR arXiv:1404.7828 cs.NE. doi:10.1016/j.neunet.2014. 09.003.

F. Schroff, D. Kalenichenko and J. Philbin. "FaceNet: A unified embedding for face recognition and clustering". *arXiv* abs/1503.03832 (2015). url: http://arxiv.org/abs/1503.03832.

K. Sharma et al. "Combating fake news: A survey on identification and mitigation techniques". *ACM Transactions on Intelligent Systems and Technology (TIST)* 10.3 (2019), p. 21.

J. Shen et al. "Natural TTS synthesis by conditioning WaveNet on mel spectrogram predictions". *CoRR* abs/1712.05884 (2017). arXiv: 1712.05884. url: http://arxiv.org/abs/1712.05884.

D. Silver et al. "A general reinforcement learning algorithm that masters chess, shogi, and Go through self-play". *Science* 362.6419 (2018), pp. 1140–1144.

D. Silver et al. "Mastering chess and shogi by self-play with a general reinforcement learning algorithm". *arXiv preprint arXiv:1712.01815* (2017).

D. Silver et al. "Mastering the game of go with deep neural networks and tree search". *Nature* 529.7587 (Jan. 2016), pp. 484–489. doi: 10.1038/nature16961.

A. J. R. Simpson, G. Roma and M. D. Plumbley. "Deep karaoke: Extracting vocals from musical mixtures using a convolutional deep neural network". In: *Latent Variable Analysis and Signal Separation: 12th International Conference, LVA/ICA 2015, Liberec, Czech Republic, August 25–28, 2015, Proceedings.* Ed. by Emmanuel Vincent et al. Springer International Publishing, Cham, 2015, pp. 429–436. isbn: 978-3-319-22482-4. doi: 10.1007/978-3-319-22482-4 50.

I. Sutskever, O. Vinyals and Q. V. Le. "Sequence to sequence learning with neural networks". *ArXiv e-prints* (Sept. 2014). arXiv: 1409.3215 cs.CL.

Y. Taigman et al. "DeepFace: Closing the gap to human-level performance in face verification". In: *Proceedings of the 2014 IEEE Conference on Computer Vision and Pattern Recognition*. CVPR '14. IEEE Computer Society, Washington, DC, 2014, pp. 1701–1708. isbn: 978-1-4799-5118-5. doi: 10.1109/CVPR.2014.220.

A. Tampuu et al. "Multiagent cooperation and competition with deep reinforcement learning". *ArXiv* abs/1511.08779 (2015). url: http://arxiv.org/abs/1511.08779.

M. Valdenegro-Toro. "Objectness scoring and detection proposals in forward-looking sonar images with convolutional neural networks". In: *Artificial Neural Networks in Pattern Recognition: 7th IAPR TC3 Workshop, ANNPR 2016, Ulm, Germany, September 28–30, 2016, Proceedings*. Ed. by Friedhelm Schwenker et al. Springer International Publishing, Cham, 2016, pp. 209–219. isbn: 978-3319-46182-3. doi: 10.1007/978-3-319-46182-3 18.

A. van den Oord et al. "WaveNet: A generative model for raw audio". *ArXiv eprints* abs/1609.03499 (2016). url: http://arxiv.org/abs/1609.03499.

H. Van Hasselt, A. Guez and D. Silver. "Deep reinforcement learning with double qlearning". In: *Thirtieth AAAI Conference on Artificial Intelligence*, 2016.

P. Vincent et al. "Stacked denoising autoencoders: Learning useful representations in a deep network with a local denoising criterion". *Journal of Machine Learning. Research* 11 (Dec. 2010), pp. 3371–3408. issn: 1532-4435. url: http://dl.acm.org/citation.cfm?id=1756006.1953039.

O. Vinyals et al. "Show and tell: Lessons learned from the 2015 mscoco image captioning challenge". In: *IEEE Transactions on Pattern Analysis and Machine Intelligence*, 2016.

M. Wang and W. Deng. "Deep face recognition: A survey". *arXiv preprint arXiv:1804.06655* (2018).

Y. Wu et al. "Google's neural machine translation system: Bridging the gap between human and machine translation". *ArXiv* abs/1609.08144 (2016). url: http://arxiv.org/abs/1609.08144.

W. Xiong et al. "Achieving human parity in conversational speech recognition". *ArXiv e-prints* (Oct. 2016). arXiv: 1610.05256 cs.CL.

T. Young et al. "Recent trends in deep learning based natural language processing". *IEEE Computational intelligenCe Magazine* 13.3 (2018), pp. 55–75.

R. L. Zeff and B. Aronson. *Advertising on the Internet*. John Wiley & Sons, Inc., 1999.

L. Zhang, S. Wang and B. Liu. "Deep learning for sentiment analysis: A survey". *Wiley Interdisciplinary Reviews: Data Mining and Knowledge Discovery* 8.4 (2018), e1253.

J-Y Zhu et al. "Generative visual manipulation on the natural image manifold". In: *Computer Vision – ECCV 2016: 14th European Conference, Amsterdam, The Netherlands, October 11–14, 2016, Proceedings, Part V*. Ed. by Bastian Leibe et al. Springer International Publishing, Cham, 2016, pp. 597–613. isbn: 978-3-319-46454-1. doi: 10.1007/978-3-319-46454-1 36.

Chapter 6

Chinese AI Policy and the Path to Global Leadership: Competition, Protectionism, and Security

Mark Robbins*

Contents

6.1 The Chinese Perspective on Innovation and AI 101
6.2 AI with Chinese Characteristics 103
6.3 National Security in AI 104
6.4 "Security" or "Protection" 106
6.5 A(Eye) 109
6.6 Conclusions..112
Bibliography..113

* A great many thanks to Jared Adams, Executive at the Association of Public Sector Executives (Canada) for his wit, keen eye, and thoughtful support in the drafting of this chapter.

Once viewed as a niche endeavor of digital specialists and researchers, the twin issues of data production and analysis have been vaulted to the forefront of policy in the emerging global "artificial intelligence (AI) race." With the growing significance of data to realms of economic, social, and political endeavor, there has been a commensurate growth in both political and popular attention to data and its downstream applications. Of all those involved, it may well have been Vladimir Putin who did the most to push the idea of a global AI race forward when he stated in 2017 that "whoever leads in (artificial intelligence) will rule the world."[*]

While many have pointed out that alluding to an "AI race"—drawing comparison with the "space race" of the last century—may serve to overstretch the analogy,[†] it is nonetheless remarkable to note how comparative standing in AI has become such a coveted commodity among geopolitical powers. Unlike the space race of the 1950s and 1960s, however, it is not Russia, but China who has done the most to draw the world's attention to state-backed leadership in AI through its challenge to American primacy. China's strategic pursuit of leadership in data and AI may lack the rhetorical flourish of a Vladimir Putin, but it lacks none of the audacity. In 2017, China announced a bold "New Generation Artificial Intelligence Development Plan," which has as its goal positioning the country as the indisputable global leader in artificial intelligence by 2030.[‡]

Certainly, political leaders are accustomed to proclaiming ambitious targets, especially when long-term time horizons provide a degree of insulation from the potential for failure. However, this type of announcement takes on a special significance in a place like China where close adherence to publicly shared plans are held as sacrosanct by the political leadership. As an authoritarian country where continued political rule depends on the regime's ongoing credibility in delivering programs and services, failure to adhere to such a plan has the potential to strike at the core of the government's legitimacy and hold on power. That is to say that such an announcement is not one that is made lightly, and should be taken by observers as a credible statement of China's ambition and self-assessed capacity.[§] China's confidence in its growing AI capacity stems from some fairly linear observations about fields of endeavor which contribute to success in the AI sector.

While historically China has had a weak environment for innovation due to a lack of venture capital, few startups, and a weak tertiary education system, it has been systematically addressing these weaknesses for years. Huge government initiatives to build the university system and attract global talent have had a marked impact on the performance of this sector.[¶] China has also had a great deal of success in supporting a tech startup culture, including through the founding of innovation

---

[*] Meyer, 2017.
[†] Biddle, 2019.
[‡] Notice of the New Generation Artificial Intelligence Development Plan (trans.), 2017.
[§] Lee, 2018.
[¶] Robbins, 2016.

parks and business incubators. Although at the time of writing there appears to be growing softness in the Chinese venture capital market, there has otherwise been significant year-over-year improvement in access to venture capital for the better part of a decade.* Improvements in all of these sectors contribute to the country's strength in AI specifically (and the technology sector more broadly) and work to bolster AI-specific programs that have been launched to support China's AI leadership drive.

This is to say that much of China's leadership declaration for AI is underpinned by improvements in the weakest parts of China's innovation system, in areas that China should have the undebatable capacity to improve. Its global leadership bid is not based on a recent program or policy drive that is specific to AI and viewed to be a silver bullet of sorts. Rather, much of the Chinese story in AI is that of a country which has been frantically pursuing its own development for decades and has concluded more recently that sustained growth will only be supported by an economy that is innovative. Investing in the core drivers of innovation will certainly support China's AI sector along with many others, but having meaningful capacity in AI is viewed by the central government as much more than simply a symptom of wider progress. China views AI as an area worthy of its own dedicated policy approach, much of which is outlined specifically in the "New Generation Artificial Intelligence Development Plan" (AIDP).

6.1 The Chinese Perspective on Innovation and AI

It is important to begin with a recognition that Chinese innovation and development policy is very dissimilar from innovation and development policy in other jurisdictions and political-economic systems. Any investigation of China's AI support strategy should be colored by an understanding that Chinese institutions do not ontologically align with those elsewhere, and this produces a distinctive Chinese approach to innovation policy. For one, China lacks many of the closely held governance conventions of liberal-democratic countries that pertain to the discrete separation of authorities and issue areas, such as the independence of the judiciary, to name an example. When it comes to innovation, this difference in custom is especially clear with the Chinese leadership having a low conceptual tolerance for what is viewed as an artificial separation of political and economic issues.†

Chinese innovation policy as such tends to represent a whole of government policy that includes coordinated and directed actions from institutions ranging

---

* Elstrom, July 9, 2019.
† There are a number of thoughtful pieces pertaining to this issue, not the least of which being the work of Kissinger (2011). A selected works of Xi Jinping was also released in 2014 on the subject of governance in China which, although somewhat one-sided, provides interesting insights into the Chinese perspective (full references in the Bibliography).

from universities, financial institutions, state-owned enterprises (SOEs), entrepreneurs, and even the state itself.* In some cases, this has resulted in awkward interactions between officials and inaccurate comparisons with foreign institutions, which are far from the Chinese experience. One particularly telling example from recent times occurred when the Canadian ministry of foreign affairs sought to inform Chinese diplomats that they had fundamentally misunderstood the relationship between the prime minister and judiciary in their effort to pressure the prime minister in securing the release of Huawei executive Meng Wanzhou.†

The reason for this degree of confusion is that many important Chinese economic institutions follow a corporatist model and cooperate closely with one another in ways that clearly conflict with the political norms of liberal-democratic states. This includes through widespread membership in the Communist Party by those of positions in power, which serves to cross-sect what might otherwise be siloed decision-making structures.‡ In the Chinese financial system, for instance, many of the banks are state-owned (by the central government) and, in turn, provide credit to other, legally separate, levels of government. State-owned financial institutions in China are also in a position of providing credit to state-owned companies, whose private owners are, in turn, members of the ruling political party.§

This context is important, and it should be recognized that there is very little to suggest a radical departure from the status quo of China's overarching governance and social structure in order to address the emerging importance of AI; AI will continue to be governed by such an approach. Yet while the Chinese model has made the country the "workshop of the world," more recent Chinese economic strategy seeks to make China less of a workshop and more of a research park. This shift in industrial policy was captured in the 2015 document *Made in China 2025*, which seeks to pivot China into focusing the creation of higher value products and services, principally in high technology.⁘ This strategy is no longer actively referenced in government announcements, but it does clearly spell out China's ambition to become a technology and innovation powerhouse in the coming decades.

Similar to the AIDP, *Made in China 2025* takes an expansive view to the implications of new and emerging technologies, with specific attention to the inputs of production. While China is quite ambitious in its ability to embrace new technologies such as AI, documents like *Made in China 2025* also indicate how preoccupied the government is with the vulnerability of these industries as a result of their reliance on foreign inputs and firms.** Subsequent strategies and announcements have

* Fu, Woo, and Hou, 2016.
† Blanchfield, Mike. "Chrystia Freeland was urged to tell China to stop the 'inaccurate' talk about Canada's justice system." The National Post. May 28, 2019. https://nationalpost.com/news/politics/canada-calls-out-on-china-at-wto-council-meeting-for-evidence-to-back-canola-ban
‡ Robbins, 2019.
§ Schell and Delury, 2013.
⁘ Zenglin and Holzmann, 2019.
** Zenglin and Holzmann, 2019.

focused on addressing these perceived vulnerabilities by, for instance, supporting the development of the native Chinese superconductor industry or native capacity in the production of electric batteries for cars, that reduces reliance on foreign-made inputs. While the AIDP is focused much more precisely on China's approach to AI, the substance of the AIDP in some senses represents a larger continuation of the status quo in Chinese industrial policy.

6.2 AI with Chinese Characteristics

The AIDP is a key site for probing the Chinese government's perspective on AI. The text of the plan opens by noting the history of research and development in AI that has led to the present day but suggests that recent breakthroughs represent a break with the longer-term trajectory of AI as a research discipline. In the AIDP, AI is viewed to have entered a new stage in its evolution as a subject of inquiry, something the plan ascribes to new methods of data science, improved computing capacity, and the wide proliferation of sensor technology, which, taken as a whole, represent a radical departure from the past.

The clear implication is that AI has become something much more than the niche and siloed area subject of inquiry that it was prior to recent technological advances and requires a different approach in governance. This policy stance was supported by the action of the Chinese leadership as well, with Xi Jinping himself having led a politburo study session on AI in October 2018—a very important symbolic gesture.* With the increased pace of change and the growing significance of AI, the AIDP takes the view that AI now requires an altogether different treatment in policy, industry, and society at large.† This premise is core to the AIDP and to the overarching Chinese perspective on AI.

The AIDP itself describes AI today as being less comparable with a traditional research discipline and more of a node of more general activity that has downstream consequences that cascade through all industry and society at large. In specific terms, it views AI as having evolved into a subject that is at the heart of a "transformative chain reaction" that will be key to the promotion of progress in economic and social fields. Progress in AI research has certainly been rapidly improving in recent years, as the plan notes, the consequences of which are being felt horizontally across a broad cross-section of fields, and not just in its foundational origins in computer science and mathematics.‡

Observations of this type about AI are not revolutionary in and of themselves; many other thinkers have arrived at similar conclusions independently. However, in the context of a policy announcement coming from the government of China, these

---

* Allen, 2019.
† Notice of the New Generation Artificial Development Intelligence Plan, (trans.) 2017.
‡ Notice of the New Generation Artificial Development Intelligence Plan, (trans.) 2017.

statements take on a different significance and merit close attention to the details which indicate an important shift in perspective. With the impact of AI being more broadly felt and widespread than in the past, the AIDP effectively represents a government recognition that AI will have everyday impacts for the Chinese citizenry, a realization that reflects a sort of crossing of the Rubicon in Chinese AI governance. The emerging everyday impact of AI very dramatically increases the importance of the field to the state and in turn, denotes an expansion of the state's role in the governance of AI.

This crucial recognition that AI requires a more comprehensive and active approach from the government signals an end to the status quo which had relegated AI to more or less a niche research area under the purview of siloed experts. The AIDP is, in this sense, explicit in its view of AI as being key to Chinese economic prosperity, which, for a government with a long history of economic interventionism—even at times when laissez-faire economic management has been in vogue—suggests more active state involvement in AI R&D and industrial policy. While the AIDP makes the perspective of there being an explicit connection between AI and overall economic prosperity clear enough, what is perhaps less immediately obvious is the emphasis on the connection between AI and national security.

6.3 National Security in AI

The AIDP clearly and repeatedly establishes an explicit connection between AI for economic development and AI for national security.* This can be confusing to the casual observer. Certainly, there are relevant military applications for AI, as there are relevant applications for AI in most realms of activity, but penetration of AI into military applications is relatively low.† Various forms of data science have featured in the operations of the military for some time, and more sophisticated uses of AI have been key to complex defense platforms as well, such as drones, aircraft, missiles, and the like. Some research suggests that the ability to leverage AI in defense applications might provide players like China an asymmetric advantage in capabilities, which could provide a partial explanation for the emphasis placed on the security implications of AI.‡

Certainly, the impact of technological progress in AI on military affairs cannot be left unstated yet it would be shortsighted to interpret the explicit mention

---

* Notice of the New Generation Artificial Development Intelligence Plan (trans.), 2017.

† By contrast, in the early days of the nuclear age, nearly all activity in nuclear energy was being conducted by the military in one part of the supply chain or another, if for no other reason than that the security imperative crowded-out private R&D. The same cannot be said for AI, where the vast majority of economic activity occurs in the civilian private sector, making AI applications that need to be reconverted to be compatible with military uses (Artificial Intelligence and National Security, 2019).

‡ Artificial Intelligence and National Security, 2019.

of national security as only referring to the military.* While the use of analytics and AI in military systems will continue to be important, the progress being made in these use cases do not encompass the full sea change being described in the AIDP. Many observers have noted that the most significant security concerns for the Chinese political leadership and its hold on power may not be from the external geopolitical threats for which a military prepares so much as the government's ability to retain meaningful political control over the Chinese populous. Indeed, China has had an overriding preoccupation with its territorial integrity and internal security for centuries.†

Given China's longstanding preoccupation with internal stability, it is of little surprise to note that widely spread advancements in AI and proliferation of advanced technologies among the Chinese citizenry are viewed with a degree of caution. In this sense, the stated recognition in the AIDP of AI as having broad-based impacts returns as an important one. One reading of the AIDP's emphasis on national security is to note the potential of AI's proliferation among the citizenry to represent a security concern in the eyes of the Chinese leadership. Indeed, much of the Chinese's leadership's decision-making related to digital technologies has been formed by its experience of the Arab Spring in the Middle East and Color Revolutions in the post-Soviet sphere, whereby the proliferation of new technologies (namely social media) were viewed as the cause of instability, and in some cases even revolution, in these countries.

China's political leadership has been inclined to view these recent waves of political instability as not simply as grassroots uprisings emboldened by open access to digital communications, but as disturbances that were deliberately fostered by rival powers using technology companies as surrogates to advance their geopolitical interests.‡ This again harkens back to the core principle of the Chinese perspective on governance which views political and economic activities as being closely related, if not inseparable. On that basis, China has demonstrated reluctance, and even hostility at times, to Western-originated technology companies that are trying to enter the Chinese market. This reluctance is especially pronounced when these companies have eschewed Chinese political censorship by refusing to adjust their treatment of topics like "human rights" and "free speech."§

China is understandably cautious (if perhaps somewhat paranoid) when it comes to the ability of new technologies like AI to foment domestic unrest, and this tinges its relationship with AI. Complicating matters further is that the line between world-class technology companies and their products, like "AI," is blurred

---

* There are several excellent works on this subject beginning to emerge, and while an important issue, the military application of AI in Chinese falls outside of the scope of this article. For more information, a valuable resource and good starting point can be found in Cory (2019).
† Kissinger, 2011.
‡ Chen, 2010.
§ Tan and Tan, 2012.

and perhaps superficial in many cases, much as are political and economic issues blurred in the Chinese perspective on governance. As technological leadership in the 21st century overlaps greatly with proficiency in AI, so too does being a technology company with an economic footprint in China entail increased political scrutiny from the government of China. In this sense, the security references of the AIDP can be viewed as stating a concern that exists with both the technology itself and the large (and often foreign) firms which employ it.

This can be viewed as a clear continuation and reiteration of Chinese policy toward foreign technology firms and their influence in China, which has been described in terms ranging in tone from measured hesitancy about foreign technology firms to outright persecution of them. As a result of the Chinese government's perspective on AI governance and technology governance more broadly, the relationship between the Chinese government and foreign technology companies has often been a troubled one. China has blocked the entrance of many foreign technology firms, such as Google, Facebook, and Twitter, and produced fatal barriers to success for others, such as Uber and Amazon. At the same time, China has promoted and nourished domestically grown technology mega-firms, such as Baidu, Tencent, and Alibaba, which now hold primacy in the Chinese market and compete in others.*

There are cogent arguments to the effect that China applies a double standard that allows native Chinese technology companies to flourish while preventing multinational firms from competing in the Chinese market. There is certainly some measure of truth to this perceived approach of economic nationalism, but it is far from the whole truth. A more nuanced interpretation notes that the Chinese approach to technology companies demands of them a level of coziness and integration with the Chinese government that proves unacceptable to many multinational firms. Those technology firms that are able to successfully operate in China are thus doing so in a way which is compatible with the very involved approach sought by the Chinese government, one which often requires compromises on issues of liberty, free speech, and human rights for the sake of security—as defined by the government of China.

6.4 "Security" or "Protection"

The relationship between free competition in AI industries and the restrictions placed on competition due to Chinese security concerns is a complicated one. Especially so when considering the clash in viewpoints on political economy between China and liberal-democratic countries. In this light, there are a number of different ways to interpret the explicit statement of the AIDP of connections between national security, AI, and economics. Certainly, it is possible to take

---

* Ferracane and Lee-Makiyama, 2017.

at face value the idea that AI represents a security concern to the government of China, but the very invocation of "security" as an issue raises wider implications for trade and innovation policy.

The reference to security can be understood, for one, as a reiteration of the Chinese government's commitment to economic protectionism.* Rather than being a serious attempt to address security concerns, the "security" references to AI could be interpreted as a way for the government to ensure preferential treatment of Chinese firms, who, given the contours of the Chinese political system, are more receptive to accommodating the demands for censorship and control that may come from the Chinese central government. Firms associated with "security" are given certain privileges in terms of how they report taxes which provides them more insulation from scrutiny. Again, there is certainly some truth to this, as multinational firms' non-compliance with the government of China's restrictions have been used as justifications for their persecution and ejection from the country.

Foreign firms may also be uncomfortable with having such a close relationship with the Chinese government as a basis for operating there because of what it defines as security issues, namely issues of free speech, repression, and censorship. On that basis, foreign firms that are willing to plug their noses on security issues to entertain collaboration with the Chinese government face pressure from their home country to forego such relationships, as Google has over its plans to launch a censored search engine for the Chinese market.† All of this helps to ensure that the Chinese domestic market continues to be captured almost exclusively by Chinese firms

Announcing connections between AI and security also offers additional protections to Chinese AI firms seeking a strong footing to export to foreign markets. A government that gives preferential treatment to domestic firms, whether overtly, covertly, or through systematic advantages in policy treatment, risks legitimate sanction of itself or of those firms in trade negotiations and international economic forums. This is something which could very well present a risk to China. However, as a result of historical circumstances which embed the primacy of state sovereignty in international law, issues deemed by a country to be of importance to "security" are given special treatment in disputes about free trade.

A government declaration that a certain industry constitutes a matter of national security provides a country immunity from World Trade Organization (WTO) challenges that the industry is receiving unfair support from the state or undue protection from foreign competition.‡ These kinds of national security exemptions have been legitimately used to insulate military industries from the pressures of the global marketplace which might otherwise see important industrial components of the defense sector move offshore. Such a move offshore could constitute a very real

---

* Cory, 2019.
† Bastone, June 16th 2019.
‡ Trebilcock, 2011.

threat to national security in the event of a military conflict, and so offering some legalized protectionism in this space helps to ensure the overarching viability of the global trade regime.

It should be clearly stated that this line of argument has yet to be employed in a major trade dispute regarding AI, and while it would be highly abnormal, we live in interesting times. Recent years have seen some very creative interpretations of the national security provision in trade disputes. Perhaps most notable was the invocation of security privileges by the United States, which used it in an attempt to reshore* steel and aluminum production during the United States, Mexico, Canada Agreement (USMCA) negotiations in 2018.† With AI having been declared a security issue in China, ostensibly any Chinese company with a claim to be involved in "AI"—a definition which casts a very wide net as a result of AI's horizontality across industry sectors—could also be afforded protections from international trade law disputes.

This is the theory, at least; it would be quite another thing to see how far this line of argument can be successfully applied in practice. While the security justification for discriminating against foreign steel and aluminum production was widely viewed as a cynical abuse of the security exemption, were China to employ this same security provision for AI industries writ large, it would be a significant escalation in gaming the rules. With the obvious importance of AI to the economic activities of the 21st century, invoking a point of privilege in such a manner might understandably raise some skepticism about how genuine the connection is between "national security" and "AI." It's worth noting that while emerging technologies in the past have a significant overlap with military applications, such as nuclear energy or even aircraft writ large, this same degree of overlap does not exist for AI in the military—at least, not yet.‡

There has nonetheless historically been a close connection between national security issues and cutting-edge emerging technologies. While this is often attributed to the strategic need for the military to have technological supremacy, the truth of the matter is much more complicated, as there is seldom a clear-cut case where national security was invoked in a sector and the motivation for protectionism and

---

* What is often highlighted in this story is how Washington was attempting to reshore these industries to the United States from its allies, Canada and Mexico. While accurate, what can be lost in the details is that this was a threat to Canada and Mexico to persuade those countries to be more restrictive on Chinese steel imports. In some ways it can be better understood as part of an ongoing China–US trade war.

† Globerman, July 18, 2018.

‡ By contrast, in the early days of the nuclear age, nearly all activity in nuclear energy was being conducted by the military in one part of the supply chain or another, if for no other reason than that the security imperative crowded-out private R&D. The same cannot be said for AI, where the vast majority of economic activity occurs in the civilian private sector, making AI applications that need to be reconverted to be compatible with military uses (Artificial Intelligence and National Security, 2019).

state supports was entirely absent, especially when considering the lack of transparency that exists around defense spending practices.* Certainly, emerging technologies are often of military significance, but as they also represent a significant economic interest which may bear much less relation to the security imperative. While the trend is undeniable, the parsing out of economic value from political and security related considerations is a much more challenging task.

6.5 A(Eye)

Trade law and economic policy interpretations of these security declarations aside, it's worth noting the operational connection that exists between the development of domestic Chinese AI industries and the operations of the state security sector, especially with regard to surveillance technologies. China has long employed an extensive state surveillance system, and it has been very proactive in its incorporation of technological solutions to this system. China is today the world's most significant user and producer of public closed circuit television (CCTV) cameras.[†] China at some point began to approach the human limitations of its domestic surveillance system which contained 176 million cameras in 2017, a number projected to increase to 626 million cameras by 2020.[‡]

A clear impediment to these systems is the staggering resource limitations to conduct successful human-only monitoring of the CCTV feeds. Given the bandwidth issue for human-centric observation, there was a clear incentive to support the development of AI technologies which could automate much of the process. This very quickly spilled over into AI software (computer vision) being applied in cameras, making China a global leader in AI-based surveillance today.[§] It really is no coincidence that the country with the highest number of CCTV cameras by very far, also holds a leading edge in AI technologies related to surveillance, namely facial recognition. In fact, the largest acquisition of an AI company in history was the purchase of SenseTime, a Chinese AI that got its start in facial recognition from working with the Chinese government on *Made in China 2025*.[¶]

This lead in AI security surveillance has been networked with other localization technologies, financial records, and other pieces of information, such as purchasing

---

* Robbins, 2015.
[†] There is an interesting conversation to be had about the proliferation of CCTV cameras and what it may signify. China certainly dwarfs all other countries in terms of the sheer number of cameras, but given its population this can be misleading. By cameras per person, and when focusing at the city level, many Chinese cities continue to lead but are in good company with cities like London, UK and Atlanta, USA. That is to say that there is some room for nuanced interpretation (Bishoff, 2019).
[‡] Bishoff, 2019.
[§] Perryer, October 29, 2019.
[¶] Marr, June 17, 2019.

habits, into what is called the "Social Credit System." This system aggregates information about an individual and uses it to assign a moving "social credit score" which increases as a result of socially desirable behaviors and decreases as a result of "undesirable behaviour."* The potential for political censorship in such a system is very significant, and it has already been employed with the greatest enthusiasm in the politically restless regions of Tibet and Xinjiang. As such, there are few AI-based projects of the scope, magnitude, and potential for controversy as the Social Credit System.

The Social Credit System is an initiative of the Chinese government that uses this centralized system as a tool for accomplishing its broader objectives, and the government makes no apologies for doing so. Aside from the political instrumentation for security purposes, it raises objections for clearly violating the norms held in many countries surrounding individual privacy by widely and indiscriminately collecting and analyzing data, including violating the principle of informed consent for data collection and use, limitations on storage and collection, and the right to a private sphere of life more generally. While China offers few natural privacy protections and seems to have light social expectations of privacy, the thought of such an intrusive system is jarring to many elsewhere. At a more visceral level, it raises fears of state control and social engineering, with many observers describing the system as "dystopian" or "Orwellian."†

The system however appears to be quite popular in China itself where it is viewed as a way for re-establishing the potential for trust in strangers against the backdrop of rapid urbanization and creeping social anomie.‡ Indeed, the system is designed not simply to collect information for the state but makes each individual's social credit score openly and transparently available to anyone else who might want to access it. While it is possible to imagine nefarious and questionable uses, some of the common uses of the system are fairly humdrum, such as a reference point for vetting potential dating partners.§ Chinese government officials themselves are often quick to point out that the country has plenty of methods for social control without the Social Credit System, which they insist represents a different endeavor all together.¶

It may be tempting to pass judgement on the ethical or moral worth of such a system, but that is an exercise that will be left for another author. Instead, it is important here to note that the Social Credit System and use of AI in security is closely related to Chinese innovation strategy, governance customs, and many of

---

* There is some nuance to this that is often missed, namely that a universal score does not yet exist in a functional capacity, as much as there are several "scores" being collected and used for different purposes, although policy documents refer to making greater progress in amalgamating this into a single score.
† Campbell, November 21, 2019.
‡ Minter, January 24, 2019.
§ Robbins, 2019.
¶ Creemers, 2018.

China's core competitive advantages in AI, while also representing a divisive wedge issue that has deep seated cultural roots and sensitives elsewhere. Observers have noted that these specific conditions in China give AI researchers a major advantage since successful R&D and testing of AI is fed by access to huge amounts of data. Having the world's largest population, few privacy restrictions, and a supportive government certainly lends to China's competitive advantage as a jurisdiction for AI industries.*

Other leading jurisdictions for AI, such as the United States, are simply unable to offer the same type of beneficial arrangement to AI firms at a structural level; both governance norms and social expectations of privacy forbid it. This is not to say that China has an incontestable advantage in the AI space—that is certainly not the case—however, some of China's most clear and decisive advantages as a jurisdiction are difficult for other political-economic systems to counter or match. In this light, the invocation of "security" in the AIDP and related documents may not only be technically accurate, but also a necessary measure for trying to avoid the penalization of Chinese AI industries in a manner that would ebb away at a purportedly unnatural competitive advantage. Indeed, this is far from a hypothetical concern, as critics and human rights activists have lambasted China and Chinese companies selling surveillance and AI-based facial recognition technology abroad for "exporting authoritarianism."†

Many jurisdictions openly discuss banning facial recognition technology and related surveillance for posing a threat to liberty,‡ privacy, or other closely held values, and some governments are actively pursuing a ban at present.§ Others still, however, suggested that the Chinese approach to AI, particularly those entities which have had a close connection to state surveillance and the Social Credit System, crosses moral and ethical boundaries and needs to be systematically eschewed. The United States government, for one, has imposed stark restrictions on a list of Chinese AI startups (including SenseTime) that have a relationship with the security sector for their involvement in the repression of minorities in Tibet and Xinjiang.¶ Without passing judgement on the issue of whether or not a ban on these technologies should occur, these discussions do represent a move to impose limitations on China's AI specialty and a growing area of national competitive advantage.

---

* Lee, 2018.
† Yang and Murgia, December 9, 2019.
‡ Samuel, November 15, 2019.
§ Lam, December 3, 2019.
¶ Shepardson and Horwitz, October 7, 2019.

6.6 Conclusions

The government of China's strategic objectives, governance conventions, and the cultural norms of the Chinese people closely impact the contours of the economic and technological leadership that China demonstrates in AI today. The free-for-all in data collection in the Chinese "Wild, Wild East" of AI development is only possible due to the country's much more permissive norms surrounding privacy* combined with the Chinese model of governance which permits more integrated collaboration between state institutions and private industry. As China establishes AI as a national priority and stakes important political capital on global leadership in AI, it is clear that the issue will continue to be taken very seriously.

The security sector in China proves to be a central hub of activity in AI for a variety of reasons, and likely will continue to be. Some of this is deeply rooted in Chinese governance practices, such as the perceived need to keep close watch on foreign technology firms or the standing concern about the security risk posed by China's own citizenry. Other reasons are much more pragmatic, such as the ability to mount a legal defense in the event of the sanction of industries of national interest or the opportunity to support innovation in AI in a way that was convenient given other security objectives. This has allowed not only for the rapid development of hard surveillance infrastructure and data collection, but also for these to be integrated with parallel efforts to support AI development in that space.

This strategy has given China a vast gap in leadership in AI applications related to security specifically and related areas like facial recognition more generally. The Chinese approach to AI and security has been a major force in China's overall level of progress with AI and is certainly helping the country's pursuit of global leadership. Kai Fu Lee has famously suggested that this makes the United States and China (as the two leading jurisdictions for AI) natural partners that can find synergies in one another's structural strengths and weakness.[†] This represents a fairly optimistic view, and one which seems increasingly unlikely given the times. The relationship between AI and security is proving not only to be a core part of China's AI strategy, but also one which is deeply divisive in liberal-democratic countries like the United States.

---

* It's worth pointing out that the permissiveness of Chinese privacy law is sometimes contested as the country has released some policies that appear to suggest even higher personal privacy standards than employed by the EU's General Data Protection Regulation (GDPR) which is often viewed as a protective standard. On close examination however, many of these policies seem to be superficial, lacking enforcement mechanisms or much by way of serious commitment. For more see: Sacks, January 29, 2018.

[†] Lee, 2018.

Bibliography

Allen, Gregory C. *Understanding China's AI Strategy: Clues to Chinese Strategic Thinking on Artificial Intelligence and National Security.* Washington, DC: Centre for a New American Security. February 6, 2019.

Bastone, Nick. "Google Executive Finally Confirms That the Tech Giant Is No Longer Working on a Censored Internet Search Engine for China." *Business Insider.* June 16, 2019. https://www.businessinsider.com/google-kills-censored-search-engine-for-china-2019-7.

Biddle, Sam. "An 'AI Race' Between the US and China Is a Terrible, Terrible Idea." *The Intercept.* July 21, 2019. https://theintercept.com/2019/07/21/ai-race-china-artificial-intelligence/.

Bishoff, Paul. "The World's Most Surveilled Cities." *Comparitec.* August 15, 2019. https://www.comparitech.com/vpn-privacy/the-worlds-most-surveilled-cities/.

Blanchfield, Mike. "Chrystia Freeland Was Urged to Tell China to Stop the 'Inaccurate' Talk about Canada's Justice System." *The National Post.* May 28, 2019. https://nationalpost.com/news/politics/canada-calls-out-on-china-at-wto-council-meeting-for-evidence-to-back-canola-ban.

Campbell, Charlie. "'The Entire System Is Designed to Suppress Us.' What the Chinese Surveillance State Means for the Rest of the World." *Time.* November 21, 2019. https://time.com/5735411/china-surveillance-privacy-issues/.

Castro, Daniel, McLaughlin, Michael and Chivot, Eline. *Who Is Winning the AI Race: China, the EU or the United States?* Washington, DC: The Centre for Data Innovation. August 19 2019.

Chen, Titus. "China's Reaction to the Colour Revolutions: Adaptive Authoritarianism in Full Swing." *Asian Perspective* 34(2) 5–51. 2010.

Cory, Nigel. *The Ten Worst Protectionism and Mercantilist Innovation Policies of 2019.* Washington, DC: The Information Technology and Innovation Foundation. 2019.

Creemers, Rogier. *China's Social Credit Score System: An Evolving Practice of Control.* Leiden: Leiden University. May 9, 2018. https://papers.ssrn.com/sol3/papers.cfm?abstract_id=3175792.

Elstrom, Peter. "China's Venture Capital Boom Shows Signs of Turning into a Bust" *Bloomberg.* July 9, 2019. https://www.bloomberg.com/news/articles/2019-07-09/china-s-venture-capital-boom-shows-signs-of-turning-into-a-bust.

Ferracane, Martina and Lee-Makiyama, Hosuk. *China's Technology Protectionism and It's Non-Negotiable Rationales.* Brussels: European Centre for International Political Economy. 2017.

Fu, Xiaolan, Woo, Wing Thye and Hou, Jun. "Technological Innovation Policy in China: The Lessons and the Necessary Changes Ahead." *Economic Change and Restructuring* 49(2–3) 139–157. 2016.

Globerman, Steven. *Trump Administration Summons 'National Security' to Justify Tariffs.* Vancouver: The Fraser Institute. July 18, 2018.

Jinping, Xi. *Governance in China.* Beijing: Foreign Languages Press. 2014.

Kissinger, Henry. *On China.* New York: Penguin Books. 2011.

Lam, Kristin. "Portland, the Largest City in Oregon, Plans to Propose First Facial Recognition Ban Affecting Private Companies." *USA Today.* December 3, 2019. https://www.usatoday.com/story/tech/2019/12/03/facial-recognition-portland-oregon-ban/2601966001/.

Lee, Kai-Fu. *AI Superpowers: China, Silicon Valley and the New World Order.* Boston: Houghton Mifflin Harcourt. 2018.

Marr, Bernard. "Meet the World's Most Valuable Startup: China's SenseTime." *Forbes.* June 17, 2019. https://www.forbes.com/sites/bernardmarr/2019/06/17/meet-the-worlds-most-valuable-ai-startup-chinas-sensetime/#341320c0309f.

Meyer, David. "Vladimir Putin Says Whoever Leads in Artificial Intelligence Will Rule the World." *Fortune.* September 4, 2017. http://fortune.com/2017/09/04/ai-artificial-intelligence-putin-rule-world/.

Minter, Adam. "Why Big Brother doesn't bother most Chinese." *Bloomberg.* January 24, 2019. https://www.bloomberg.com/opinion/articles/2019-01-24/why-china-s-social-credit-systems-are-surprisingly-popular.

N.s. *Artificial Intelligence and National Security,* Congressional Research Service. November 21, 2019. https://fas.org/sgp/crs/natsec/R45178.pdf.

N.s. *Notice of the New Generation Artificial Intelligence Development Plan.* (trans.). State Council of the People's Republic of China. July 8, 2017. http://www.gov.cn/zhengce/content/2017-07/20/content_5211996.htm.

(PDF) Here Be Dragons: Lessons from China's AI Strategy. https://www.researchgate.net/publication/330937827_Here_Be_Dragons_Lessons_from_China.s_AI_Strategy [Accessed December 12, 2019].

Perryer, Sophie. "Surveillance Cameras Have Become One of China's Most Valuable Exports- Heres Why." *World Finance.* October 29, 2019. https://www.worldfinance.com/featured/surveillance-cameras-have-become-one-of-chinas-most-valuable-exports-heres-why.

Robbins, Mark. *Here Be Dragons: Lessons from China's AI Strategy.* Ottawa: The Institute on Governance. 2019.

Robbins, Mark. *The Thousand Talents Program: Lesson From China About Faculty Recruitment and Retention.* Ottawa: The Conference Board of Canada. 2016.

Robbins, Mark. *Towards a Political Economy of Military Spending.* Dissertation. Carleton University. 2015.

Sacks, Samm. *New China Data Privacy Standard Looks More Far Reaching than GDPR.* Washington, DC: Center for Strategic and International Studies. January 29, 2018. https://www.csis.org/analysis/new-china-data-privacy-standard-looks-more-far-reaching-gdpr.

Samuel, Sigal. "Activists want Congress to ban facial recognition. So they scanned lawmakers' faces." *Vox.* November 15, 2019. https://www.vox.com/future-perfect/2019/11/15/20965325/facial-recognition-ban-congress-activism.

Schell, Orville and Delury, John. *Wealth and Power: China's Long March to the Twenty-First Century.* New York: Random House. 2013.

Shepardson, David and Horwitz, Josh. "U.S. Expands Blacklist to Include China's Top AI Startups Ahead of Trade Talks." *Reuters.* October 7, 2019. https://www.reuters.com/article/us-usa-trade-china-exclusive/u-s-expands-blacklist-to-include-chinas-top-ai-startups-ahead-of-trade-talks-idUSKBN1WM25M.

Tan, Justin and Tan, Anna E. "Business Under Threat, Technology Under Attack, Ethics Under Fire: The Experience of Google in China." *Journal of Business Ethics* 110(4) 469–479. 2012.

Trebilcock, Michael. *Understanding Trade Law.* Cheltenham: Edward Elgar Publications. 2011.

Yang, Yuan and Murgia, Madhumita. "How China Cornered the Facial Recognition Market." *The Los Angeles Times*. December 9, 2019. https://www.latimes.com/business/story/2019-12-09/china-facial-recognition-surveillance.

Zenglin, Max and Holzmann, Anna. *Evolving Made in China 2025: China's Industrial Policy in the Quest for Global Leadership*. Washington, DC: Mercator Institute for China Studies. July 2, 2019.

Chapter 7

Natural Language Processing in Data Analytics

Yudong Liu

Contents

7.1 Background and Introduction: Era of Big Data.......................................118
    7.1.1 Use Cases of Unstructured Data..118
    7.1.2 The Challenge of Unstructured Data...119
    7.1.3 Big Data and Artificial Intelligence..120
7.2 Data Analytics and AI..121
    7.2.1 Data Analytics: Descriptive vs. Predictive vs. Prescriptive.............121
    7.2.2 Advanced Analytics toward Machine Learning and Artificial
        Intelligence...122
        7.2.2.1 Machine Learning Approaches 122
7.3 Natural Language Processing in Data Analytics 124
    7.3.1 Introduction to Natural Language Processing 124
    7.3.2 Sentiment Analysis 125
    7.3.3 Information Extraction..127
    7.3.4 Other NLP Applications in Data Analytics 128
    7.3.5 NLP Text Preprocessing 129
    7.3.6 Basic NLP Text Enrichment Techniques 130
7.4 Summary 130
References 131

7.1 Background and Introduction: Era of Big Data

We are fast approaching an era of big data. According to a forecast by the International Data Corporation (IDC) in 2018, by 2025, global data will grow 61% to 175 zettabytes (this is 175 trillion gigabytes). By most estimates, 80% or more of the overall datasphere is unstructured data, and it is expected that this number will increase to 93% by 2022. Unstructured data is data that either does not have a predefined data model or is not organized in a predefined manner (Wikipedia). Some of the most common examples of unstructured data include emails, text files, social media data, webpages and blog posts, presentations, call center transcripts/recordings, open-ended survey responses, images, audio, and videos. Since the bulk of data generated every day is unstructured and it can help answer the most pressing questions faced by organizations, organizations must find ways to manage, analyze, and derive actionable insights from the data so that they can make more informed decisions.

7.1.1 Use Cases of Unstructured Data

There are many business use cases for unstructured data such as log analytics, automated candidate placement in recruiting, insurance fraud detection, and others.* In the following, we will elaborate on three of them.

- *Customer review analytics.* According to a survey released by BrightLocal[†] in 2019, 82% of consumers read online reviews for local businesses, with 52% of 18–54 years old customers saying they "always" read reviews. Nearly 50% of people would not consider using a business with fewer than four stars. Among the customers that read reviews, 97% read businesses' responses to reviews. The number of consumers writing reviews is increasing, with two-thirds of consumers now having written reviews for local businesses. Reviews are important. Monitoring and understanding the customers' needs and sentiments expressed in review content has become critically important for the success of any business. The information that is derived from the review data can be translated into smart business decisions and strategic actions.
- *Reputation management.* Data related to a company's reputation, for example, how they are perceived by their customers, investors, partners, competitors, and thought leaders is critical in today's business environment. Online customer reviews can help provide a view but are far from complete. In the financial domain, such information will rapidly exert a large influence on major market indexes. This requires companies be alerted to any new change as soon as the information becomes available and be prepared to respond

---

* https://www.searchtechnologies.com/blog/big-data-use-cases-for-business
† https://www.brightlocal.com/research/local-consumer-review-survey/

accordingly. Here is where an information extraction (IE) tool comes into play. An IE tool can automatically extract relevant information from various information sources, such as names of organizations and people, the relationship between names, and events that have taken place among names, in unstructured data and put the extracted information into a structured format to be utilized.

▪ *Personalized e-commerce.* Online shopping is growing so fast that the global e-commerce sales are predicted to reach US$4 trillion in 2020 and this number will continue to grow. So far, 69% of the US population has shopped online, and the average revenue per online shopper is US$1,804.* The percentage of online shoppers is expected to increase from 69% to 91% in 2023! Thus, it is important for e-commerce companies to create personalized interactions and shopping experience for customers. To do this, they have to know the users' behaviors (type of devices they use, time, duration and location on site, recently viewed products and categories, and items from abandoned carts), purchase history (past purchases, past customer service record, membership), and others. The data, if obtained and analyzed smartly, will open up enormous opportunities for e-commerce companies.

7.1.2 The Challenge of Unstructured Data

Though unstructured data has become a tremendous source of untapped value for businesses, it doesn't easily lend itself to older models of data storage and analytical processes. The following introduces two of the many challenges around unstructured data today.

▪ *Quality.* The value of data requires a high-quality data source. Unstructured data comes from various sources, in various formats, and with various uses. For example, comments gathered through online forums or social media sites may have issues of *reliability* in that some comments are simply not facts but made-up information by users. The data may also present *inconsistency* during a certain time which makes it hard to be trusted and used. Business goals should be set before data is collected and analyzed, but the amount of data that is gathered does not necessarily guarantee the *relevancy* or *completeness*. It may only be relevant to one but not all aspects of the goal. The deficiency of one component may impact the use, accuracy, and integrity of the data. As unstructured data, *readability* is a persisting issue. Transforming it to a clean and usable format is not a standardized process and always presents as the first challenge in analyzing it.

---

* https://www.statista.com/statistics/278890/us-apparel-and-accessories-retail-e-commerce-re venue/

■ *Volume.* Large volumes of data continue to be generated every second, and it offers different kinds of value to different people in different ways. Building an infrastructure that is able to continuously scale to the ever-growing data has become a challenge faced by many organizations today. For many businesses, due to the lack of techniques and tools for managing and analyzing the amount of data they collect, the data is simply lying around and consuming storage capacity without adding any value. And even worse, if no management watches over what's stored, the organizations may end up losing track of what data they have and what's in the data. Some data may contain sensitive information such as credit card information, social security numbers, or other personally identifiable information. Without encryption, data lays bare and vulnerable, which will raise data privacy and security issues, such as identity theft, financial resources theft, and fraud, and therefore will present huge risks to organizations.

7.1.3 Big Data and Artificial Intelligence

We have a lot of unstructured data. But without effective processing and analyzing tools and technologies, data, no matter how much we have, would not add any value to businesses. Today, thanks to the new advancement of artificial intelligence (AI) algorithms and computer power, extracting valuable insights from such a big volume of data is becoming a reality. The intersection of big data and AI is rapidly changing the way that businesses operate and make decisions. If we look at today's most innovative and valuable tech giants like Google, Microsoft, and Amazon, all of them are dedicated to the mastery at the intersection of AI and big data. Advanced AI-based solutions have been developed in various fields including healthcare, autonomous vehicles, cybersecurity, robotics, and more. The new development of AI algorithms and technologies have created many new opportunities of using big data. For example, unstructured data in the form of pictures, audio, and video were usually costly to store and difficult to process so people tried to avoid them or minimally use them in analytics. But today they are becoming an important source for subfields of AI such as computer vision and speech recognition.

Artificial intelligence was a term coined by John McCarthy, an American computer and cognitive scientist of Dartmouth College, back in 1956 that refers to intelligent machines that behave, think, and solve problems like humans. Early AI research explored topics like problem solving (e.g., chess playing) and symbolic methods (e.g., expert systems). With the breakthrough of machine learning techniques in the past 10–15 years, AI has also embraced its major advances over the past 60 years. As an application of AI, machine learning (ML) works around the idea of automatically learning from the given data and iteratively improve from what has been learned. The reward of big data to the revival of machine learning mainly lies in the virtuous cycle between the data and the ML models. In general, the more data we feed into a machine learning model, the better the model gets.

In the following, we will focus on how cutting-edge AI technology that is centered around machine learning can help advance data analytics. In particular, we will focus on the applications of a subfield of AI, natural language processing (NLP), in the domain of text analytics.

7.2 Data Analytics and AI

7.2.1 Data Analytics: Descriptive vs. Predictive vs. Prescriptive

The term "Data Analytics" has been used in the business world for decades. It refers to the use of various techniques and processes that find meaningful patterns in data. It can be as simple as extracting statistics such as the average age of customers. It may also involve applying advanced AI algorithms to extract from humongous data for making predictions about business trends. Data analytics tools enable us to describe what happened in the past, draw insights about the present, and make predictions about the future.

The type of data analytics that allows us to describe what happened is called "Descriptive Analytics." It can consolidate data in a form that enables appropriate reporting and analysis. As the simplest class of analytics, it usually takes place as the first step in a data analysis process. For example, it helps to answer the questions such as "What is our sales growth this month from last month? What customers have required the most customer service help? What is the total revenue per subscriber?" Such initial questions must be answered regardless of others advanced analytics capabilities. And it establishes a common ground for applying other types of analytics. Presenting the findings from descriptive analytics is frequently through data visualization via reports, dashboards, and scorecards.

Predictive analytics utilizes statistical modeling and machine learning techniques to make predictions about future outcomes based on the patterns found in the existing data. For example, a predictive churn model basically looks at data from customers that have already churned (that is, active users stopped using the service) and their characteristics/behaviors to identify customers who are likely to churn. This method requires data about customers from various sources and statistical modeling techniques to estimate the probability of a user's churn. With some technology, it can also probabilistically identify the steps and stages when a customer is leaving.

Prescriptive analytics makes use of the results obtained from descriptive and predictive analysis to make prescriptions (or recommendations) around the optimal actions to achieve business objective such as customer service, profits, and operation efficiency. It goes beyond predicting future outcomes by suggesting actions to benefit from the predictions and showing the implications of each decision option.[*]

---

[*] https://en.wikipedia.org/wiki/Prescriptive_analytics#cite_note-6

Optimization and decision modeling technologies are used to solve complex decisions with millions of decision variables, constraints, and tradeoffs.*

As the starting step in data analytics, descriptive analytics has been the major form in traditional business intelligence. However, with the availability of big volume data and advanced analysis techniques, more effort is going toward predictive and prescriptive analytics.

7.2.2 Advanced Analytics toward Machine Learning and Artificial Intelligence

If say traditional analytics is important to help answer "what happened?", advanced analytics focuses more on predicting the future and finding patterns and insights that aim to transform the future. Advanced analytics refers to the set of sophisticated analytical tools, techniques, and methods designed to uncover deep trends, patterns, and insights that are hidden within data, predict the future, and drive change using data-driven information. It offers organizations far more control and educated perspective when it comes to making business-critical decisions. It encompasses predictive analytics, prescriptive analytics, and other analytics that involve high-level analytical methods.

The development of advanced analytics has greatly benefited from the advancement of applications of machine learning algorithms which is an intersection of statistics and computer science. As a subset of artificial intelligence, machine learning deals with large-scale statistical models on large data sets and enables computers to automatically self-learn from data and improve from experience. Nowadays, machine learning, especially deep learning, along with big data, is becoming the main driver to advance the applications of artificial intelligence in different fields.

7.2.2.1 Machine Learning Approaches

General speaking, there are four categories of machine learning algorithms.

- *Supervised Learning.* Supervised learning aims to find patterns in data that can be used for predictive analytics. In order to do that, a "well-understood" data set is first established. For example, there could be millions of emails of spam and non-spam types. By labeling each email message with the type it belongs to and defining what features can contribute to distinguishing between the two types, you have a well-understood data set with which a supervised machine learning algorithm can work with. Such a data set is called a "training data set" in the setting of supervised learning. If the label is a discrete value such as "Yes" (or 1) or "No" (or 0), this task is known as "Classification." If the label is continuous, the task is known as "Regression."

---

* https://www.ibm.com/analytics/prescriptive-analytics

Classification has been one of the most common machine learning tasks. A supervised machine learning algorithm is "trained" using the training data set, which means a statistical model is built through modeling the "correlation" among the label and features. The model will be evaluated with a "test" data set. A good test data set should contain a sufficient number of "unseen" examples (data points that did not occur in the training data set) to avoid an "overfitting" issue. This way can make the model built more generalizable.

Some of the most widely used supervised learning methods include linear regression, decision trees, random forests, naive Bayes, logistic regression, and support vector machines (SVM), and have broadly applied to a variety of business applications, including fraud detection, recommendation system, risk analysis, and sentiment analysis.

■ *Unsupervised Learning.* Unsupervised learning applies when not enough labeled data is available. In other words, no well-understood data set is available or labeling a new data set is just too costly. By applying some well-designed distance metrics, an unsupervised learning algorithm can strategically group the data into clusters. Data points within the distance threshold will be grouped together. This process iterates until the number of clusters converges or no more change takes place to each cluster. Some of the widely used clustering algorithms include k-means and k-nearest neighbors (KNN).

■ *Reinforcement Learning.* Unlike supervised learning where the labeled data is given to "teach" or "train" the system to learn, in reinforcement learning, learning takes place as a result of an interaction between an agent and the environment through trial and error. This learning process fundamentally mimics how humans (and animals) learn. As humans, we perform actions and observe the results of these actions on the environment. The idea is commonly known as "cause and effect" which can be translated into the following steps in reinforcement learning:*

1) The agent observes a state in the environment.
2) An action is selected using a decision-making function (policy).
3) The action is performed.
4) The agent receives a scalar reward (reinforcement) or penalty from the environment.
5) The policy is updated/fine-tuned for that particular state accordingly (learning step).
6) The above steps are iterated until an optimal policy is found.

Reinforcement learning has been widely applied in robotics and game playing. It is also used for complex tasks such as autonomous vehicles.

■ *Neural Networks and Deep Learning.* Neural networks and deep learning currently provide the cutting-edge solutions to many problems in traditional AI fields such image recognition and speech recognition. Neural networks

---

* https://www.cse.unsw.edu.au/~cs9417ml/RL1/introduction.html

were developed in the 1950s. Its interconnected structures were designed to attempt to emulate how the human brain works so computers can learn and make decisions in a human-like manner. A neural network consists of an input layer, one or more hidden layers, and an output layer. Due to its high demand for computation resources, there was only one to three hidden layers in a conventional neural network. The term "deep learning" refers to using a neural network when there are more hidden layers within the network. Nowadays, a typical deep neural network may consist of thousands or even millions of nodes that are densely interconnected. Powerful programming tools and computing power are in place to support the computations required on such a big network. Compared with supervised learning where features need to be carefully selected for learning, deep learning can automatically learn features and model high-level representations of data with the multiple processing layers and the non-linear transformations that take place through those layers. Data is often high-dimensional and too complicated to be represented by a simple model. In that sense, deep neural networks can provide simpler but more descriptive models for many problems.

7.3 Natural Language Processing in Data Analytics

As aforementioned, unstructured data is mainly presented in the form of text and multimedia. Textual data such as social media comments, online reviews, medical documents, and legal documents, etc. are becoming major sources of unstructured data. For this reason, text analytics has increasingly become a critical part of data analytics.

Text analytics (also known as "text mining") is the process of turning unstructured textual data into high-quality information through the application of statistics, machine learning, and linguistics. To be more specific, today's text analytics is largely empowered by NLP.

7.3.1 Introduction to Natural Language Processing

As a discipline drawn from computer science, linguistics, information theory, and mathematics, Natural Language Processing (also referred to as "computational linguistics") has been considered as one of the most fundamental and important subfields of Artificial Intelligence. It aims to make computers understand human languages so they can communicate with humans in natural languages. Broadly speaking, NLP studies any form of natural human communication method such as text, speech, sign language, etc. However, a distinction sometimes is made between speech processing and NLP where the term NLP is specifically referred to as processing on text.

NLP has been around for over six decades. The earliest success was in automatic translation, demonstrated by the work of Georgetown University and IBM on translating 60 Russian sentences into English in 1954. With the idea and interest of AI emerging, the NLP work from the late 1960s to late 1970s moved into a new phase of more sophistication, with more emphasis on the representation and manipulation of world knowledge and the construction of a knowledge base. Stimulated by the development of computational grammar theory in linguistics and the use of logic in knowledge representation and reasoning in AI, NLP moved to be more practically motivated from failing to build practical systems in the 1980s. In the 1990s, statistical NLP (Manning & Schütze, 1999) started flourishing due to the arrival of a large amount of data on the internet and the computing power of handling it. Corpus data, together with machine learning, has greatly driven the development of statistical parsing, which is one of the core NLP tasks, whereby NLP has made significant progress during this period in other subtasks such as machine translation and information extraction. Presently, NLP research and development have entered another new and exciting era due to the availability of rich computational resources, vast quantities of data, rapid development of machine learning techniques and tools, and the emergence of many new application opportunities and challenges. From IBM's "Watson"* (2006) to Apple's "Siri"† (2011), from Amazon's "Alexa"‡ (2014) to Google's "Google Assistant"§ (2016), powered by Natural Language Processing and other technologies, AI has gradually become part of our daily life and will continue to transform our lives in every conceivable field. The applications of NLP today are incredibly diverse. It spreads in various fields such as machine translation (e.g., Google Translate), question answering (e.g., Apple Siri), information extraction, natural language generation (document summarization, chatbot), writing assistance, video scripting, text categorization, sentiment analysis, speech technologies (speech recognition and synthesis), hate speech detection, fake news detection, etc. In the following, we will introduce some NLP applications in data analytics.

7.3.2 Sentiment Analysis

Sentiment analysis (SA, also named opinion mining, opinion extraction, subjectivity analysis) focuses on the extraction of people's sentiments, opinions, emotions, and attitudes toward entities such as services, products, organizations, individuals, issues, events, topics, and their attributes (Liu, 2015). With the rapid growth of social media data on the web, the amount of opinionated data in digital form has become unprecedentedly available. Since early 2000, sentiment analysis has grown to be one of the most active research areas in NLP. Due to its important role in decision-making, its applications have been widely spread across fields such as

---

* https://en.wikipedia.org/wiki/Watson_(computer)
† https://en.wikipedia.org/wiki/Siri
‡ https://en.wikipedia.org/wiki/Amazon_Alexa
§ https://en.wikipedia.org/wiki/Google_Assistant

marketing, finance, political science and health science. Many big corporations as well as small startups are dedicated to providing sentiment analysis services.

Sentiment analysis can be performed at three levels: document-level, sentence-level, and aspect-level. Document-level SA assumes each document expresses either a positive or a negative opinion on a single aspect and aims to determine the overall opinion of the document. Sentence-level SA aims to extract sentiment expressed in each sentence. There is no fundamental difference between document and sentence-level SA because a sentence can be viewed as a short document. Aspect-level SA* aims to answer the question of "What aspects of the entity do people love/hate." This requires extracting aspects (attributes) of an object and allocating each aspect a sentiment (positive or negative). This task is particularly useful for a customer review report generation.

Document- and sentence-level SA is usually formulated into a binary classification task. Supervised and unsupervised techniques are applied. Common supervised learning methods include SVM, naive Bayes, maximum entropy, and so on. And the common features that are used include n-grams (n = 1, 2, 3) and their frequencies, part-of-speech tags, opinion words (or sentiment words) and phrases, negotiations, and syntactic dependencies. Opinion words/phrases are the words/phrases that carry commendatory or derogatory senses themselves. For instance, *good, fantastic, amazing*, and *excellent* are commendatory terms and *bad, slow, flimsy, worst*, and *poor* are derogatory words. Although most opinion words are adjective or adverbs, nouns ("*rubbish*") and verbs ("*hate*," "*like*") can also often indicate opinion. Negations are undoubtedly important in SA because the sentiment of a sentence can be completely reversed due to their presence. Syntactic dependency features are useful when multiple opinion words exist in text thus the interactions among these words need to be taken into account. Unsupervised methods use the (co)occurrences of positive and negative words in the sentence/document to calculate their weighted sum/average, respectively. The one with the higher score will be the final sentiment of the text.

Sentiment lexicon plays an important role in SA, so the construction of sentiment lexicon has also been studied extensively in NLP. In general, there are three methods: manual construction, corpus-based methods, and dictionary-based methods. Manual construction is time-consuming and costly which is rarely used or used only when combined with other methods. Both corpus-based methods and dictionary-based method use an initial seed set of opinion words. Corpus-based methods use co-occurrence metrics to iteratively gather more opinion words and dictionary-based methods construct the lexicon by propagating the seed words through the WordNet† synonym/antonym graph until a threshold is reached.

---

* http://alt.qcri.org/semeval2016/task5/
† https://wordnet.princeton.edu

7.3.3 Information Extraction

IE is the process of extracting useful information from unstructured or semi-structured text. The extracted information is either readily usable or requires some additional processing and analyses. Although there is no strict rule on what information an IE system should extract, there are three types of information that are commonly extracted by most IE systems. They are named entities, relations, and events.

■ Named Entity Recognition

As the simplest but most commonly performed IE subtask, named entity recognition (NER) aims to identify the named entities and their types: person, organization, location, etc. Named entities carry important information about the text itself and it can help build a common ground for other analytics tasks such as relation and event exaction, document summarization, question answering, semantic search, etc.

NER is usually formulated as a multi-class classification or sequence labeling task in the supervised learning setting. Word-level features (e.g., case, suffixes, prefixes, shape, and part-of-speech tag), contextual features (e.g., following token(s), preceding token(s), and their past-of-speech tags), and external knowledge (e.g., word clustering, phrasal clustering, and Wikipedia gazetteer) have been widely used in various supervised NER systems. It requires a considerable amount of engineering skill and domain expertise on feature selection.

In recent years, deep learning (DL) based NER models (Li et al. 2018) have become dominant and have achieved state-of-the-art results. As aforementioned, compared with feature-based approaches, the key advantage of deep learning is the capability of automatically discovering latent, potentially complex, representations. As a well-studied topic in NLP, the NER component on languages such as English, Chinese, French, etc. have been readily built in many IE systems. Nowadays, more focus is on building NER systems on low-resource languages (Cotterell and Duh, 2017).

■ Relation Extraction

With named entities identified in text, a further step is to determine how they are related. Consider the following example (Eisenstein, 2019, p387) *George Bush traveled to France on Thursday for a summit.*

This sentence introduces a relation between the entities referenced by *George Bush* and *France*. In the automatic content extraction (ACE) ontology,* the type of this relation is PHYSICAL, and the subtype is LOCATED. This relation would be written as follows:

PHSICAL.LOCATED(GEORGE BUSH, FRANCE)

---

* https://www.ldc.upenn.edu/collaborations/past-projects/ace

Early work on relation extraction focused on handcrafted patterns (Hearst, 1992). In a supervised learning setting, relation extraction is formulated as a classification task. In recent years, the DL models that use Recurrent Neural Networks have been developed that can simultaneously detect entities and then extract their relations (Miwa and Sasaki, 2014).

Not as in classical relation extraction where the set of relations is pre-defined, a relation in open information extraction (OpenIE) can be any tuple (a subject, a relation, an object) of text. Extracting such tuples can be viewed as a lightweight version of semantic role labeling (Christensen et al. 2010).

■ Event Extraction

Relation extraction links pairs of entities, but many real-world situations involve more than two entities. In event detection, a schema is provided for each event type (e.g., ELECTION, CRIME, or BANKRUPTCY), indicating all the possible properties of the event. The system is then required to fill in as many of these properties as possible. Event extraction generally involves finding 1) named entities; 2) the event trigger which is usually a verb or noun that clearly expresses the occurrence of the event, for example, the trigger word "conviction" in an event of "CONVICT"; and 3) event argument(s) which is the participant or general attributes (such as place and time) of the event. As a downstream task of Named Entity Recognition, the performance of event extraction heavily depends on NER performance. More recent work has tried to formulate NER and event extraction as a joint task (Yang and Mitchell, 2016).

7.3.4 Other NLP Applications in Data Analytics

■ *Text summarization*. It is the automatic process of shortening one or multiple documents into a summary that preserves the key information of the original text that is intended to be kept. It's a task that falls under the scope of "natural language generation (NLG)." There are two types of summarization: extractive and abstractive. The former extracts and reuses important nuggets (words, phrases, or sentences) from the original document(s) to create a summary. The latter paraphrases the intent of the original text in a new way. Most of the current summarization systems are extractive in that they are focused on identifying important pieces of information to produce a coherent summary text. Text summarization covers a wide range of tasks such as headline generation, meeting minutes generation, search results presentation by search engines, customer feedback summarization, etc. With the advancement of NLP and machine learning, the methods and applications on text summarization are also evolving.

■ *Chatbots in customer service*. Chatbots for customer service have been utilized to remove repetitions from workflows and provide 24/7 instant support for a number of years. The newer ones have demonstrated a better understanding of language and are more interactive due to the application of NLP techniques. Compared with a traditional rule-based chatbot, an NLP-based chatbot can continue to learn from every interaction and automatically evolves to improve the quality of the support they offer in the future. A social chatbot such as Microsoft Xiaoice (Zhou L. et al., 2018) involves far more sophisticated and advanced NLP techniques, among many other techniques, and represents the highest-level achievement of a chatbot in this generation.

7.3.5 NLP Text Preprocessing

Because of the noisy nature of unstructured text, text preprocessing is usually the first step in the pipeline of an NLP system. There are different ways to preprocess a text. And the steps of preprocessing a text may vary from task to task. In the following, we list some of the common preprocessing steps in NLP.

- *Tokenization.* It is the process of breaking a text into linguistically meaningful units (LMU) called tokens, which are mostly words but could be phrases, symbols, and so on. The output of a tokenizer can then be fed as input for further processing such as NER, document classification, text summarization, etc. Challenges in tokenization depend on the type of language and the domain of the text. For example, English is a space-delimited language, but Chinese is not. Biomedical text contains many special symbols and punctuations which makes it different to tokenize it from tokenizing news text. For an agglutinative language such as Turkish, the tokenizer would require additional lexical and morphological knowledge.
- *Stopword removal.* Stopwords are the words that occur frequently but do not contribute to the content of text. Due to their high frequency in text, their presence may introduce noise and confusion to the downstream steps. This is especially true for an Information Retrieval system.* Examples of stopwords in English are "this," "is," "the," "an," etc. Depending on the specific task, a stopword list can be preestablished or generated on the fly.
- *Normalization.* It is the process of transforming tokens into a single canonical form, so they are consistent when taken as input for further analyzing. Common normalization techniques include:
  - Lowercasing. A text may contain multiple variations of a word like "USA," "usa," and "Usa." Lowercasing is to convert all such occurrences into lowercase. Though lowercasing is very useful in searching because it makes the system not sensitive to the case of the input keywords, it would not be a good practice for a task such as NER where uppercase/capitalization is an important feature for a named entity.

---

* https://bitbucket.org/kganes2/text-mining-resources/downloads/A%20Brief%20Note%20on%20Stop%20Words%20for%20Text%20Mining%20and%20Retrieval.pdf

- Stemming and lemmatization. Both aim to reduce the inflected form of a word to its base form (e.g., from *produce, produces, producing, product, products, production* to *produce*). The only difference is the former does not necessarily return a dictionary word, but the latter does. Stemming uses a crude heuristic process that chops off the inflected part at the end of a word, but lemmatization uses a dictionary to map a word from its inflected form to its original form. Stemming has been shown to be helpful in improving search accuracy in some high-inflected languages such as Finnish but not as much for the English language.
- Spell correction. Spelling mistakes, as commonly seen in social media text, can present an obstacle for processing it. Spell correction has become a necessary step in text preprocessing. Minimal edit distance* is a widely used technique which measures the number of edit steps ("Deletion," "Insertion," "Substitution") that it takes to transform one string to the other.

7.3.6 Basic NLP Text Enrichment Techniques

Latent information such as parts-of-speech of words or structural dependencies among words can be added to plain text through some basic text enrichment techniques.

- *Part-of-Speech (POS) Tagging.* It is the process of assigning parts-of-speech (such as noun, verb, adjective, etc.) to each token in text. As one of the most well-studied NLP tasks, a state-of-the-art English POS tagger can achieve over 97% accuracy on all tokens. The main challenge lies in tagging the words that are never seen. It can still achieve over 90% accuracy on such words.
- *Syntactic Parsing.* It is the process of analyzing and constructing the syntactic structure of a given sentence. Without it, it would be very difficult to determine the order and syntactic dependencies among words in a sentence and comprehend the sentence. Therefore, it has been deemed to be one of the most important NLP tasks for a long time. A lot of theoretical and practical work has been done around this topic. SyntaxNet, released by Google in 2016,[†] has been announced to be the most accurate English parser so far.

7.4 Summary

As described in this chapter, due to the availability of big data, computational resources, and the advancement of machine learning techniques, there are many remarkable uses of NLP in data analytics today. As NLP continues to make data

---

* https://en.wikipedia.org/wiki/Edit_distance
† https://ai.googleblog.com/2016/05/announcing-syntaxnet-worlds-most.html

more "user-friendly" and "insightful," it will be more and more widely adopted in all types of data analytics platforms. In spite of its wide application, NLP is still in its infancy compared with people's expectations for AI. Languages are complex, subtle, and ambiguous. Processing natural language itself is an extremely challenging task. No matter it is a low-level processing step such as tokenization or a high-level task such as machine translation, the existing NLP systems are still far from perfect. Though there is still a long way to go, NLP is rapidly advancing today along with deep learning techniques and revolutionizing the way people interact with computers and data. Looking to the future, it is clear that NLP-empowered applications will become even more capable, and the improvement will continue to take place. As NLP is embracing a new renaissance that is unprecedented, NLP will play an indispensable part in the next generation of AI-empowered applications and NLP applications will become ubiquitous in our lives.

References

Christensen, J. et al. (2010). *Semantic Role Labeling for Open Information Extraction.* Proceedings of the NAACL HLT 2010 First International Workshop on Formalisms and Methodology for Learning by Reading, pp. 52–61.

Cotterell, R., Duh, K. (2017). *Low-Resource Named Entity Recognition with Cross-Lingual, Character-Level Neural Conditional Random Fields.* Proceedings of the Eighth International Joint Conference on Natural Language Processing (Volume 2: Short Papers), pp. 91–96.

Eisenstein, J. (2019). *Introduction to Natural Language Processing.* Cambridge, MA: The MIT Press.

Hearst, M.A. (1992). *Automatic Acquisition of Hyponyms from Large Text Corpora.* Proceedings of the 14th Conference on Computational Linguistics, vol. 2; pp. 539–545.

Li, J. et al. (2018). *A Survey on Deep Learning for Named Entity Recognition.* arXiv preprint arXiv:1812.09449, 2018.

Liu, B. (2015). *Sentiment Analysis: Mining Opinions, Sentiments, and Emotions.* Cambridge, UK: Cambridge University Press.

Manning, C.D., Schütze, H. (1999). *Foundations of Statistical Natural LanguageProcessing.* Cambridge, MA: The MIT Press.

Miwa, M., Sasaki, Y. (2014). *Modeling Joint Entity and Relation Extraction with Table Representation.* Proceedings of the 2014 Conference on Empirical Methods in Natural Language Processing, pp. 1858–1869. Doha, Qatar: Association for Computational Linguistics.

Yang, B., Mitchell, T. (2016). *Joint Extraction of Events and Entities within a Document Context.* Proceedings of the 2016 Conference of the North American Chapter of the Association for Computational Linguistics: Human Language Technologies, pp. 289–299.

Zhou, Li. et al. (2018). *The Design and Implementation of Xiaoice, an Empathetic Social Chatbot.* arXiv preprint arXiv:1812.08989, 2018.

Chapter 8

AI in Smart Cities Development: A Perspective of Strategic Risk Management

Eduardo Rodriguez and John S. Edwards

Contents

8.1 Introduction 134
8.2 Concepts and Definitions...134
    8.2.1 How Are AI, Smart Cities, and Strategic Risk Connected?...........137
8.3 Methodology and Approach 137
8.4 Examples of Creating KPIs and KRIs Based on Open Data....................141
    8.4.1 Stakeholder Perspective..142
    8.4.2 Financial Resources Management Perspective....................................145
    8.4.3 Internal Process Perspective 146
    8.4.4 Trained Public Servant Perspective 146
8.5 Discussion 147
8.6 Conclusion 148
References 148

8.1 Introduction

This chapter is about the creation of artificial intelligence (AI) systems to support the management of strategic risk in smart cities. The use of AI in smart cities is growing and the applications to several sectors are booming: from analyzing data from sensors in bridges for the maintenance process to health care at home or security and safety of the citizenry.

Some events affecting the performance of cities can be predicted and controlled. However, there exist events that we will call "Black Swans" after Taleb (2007) that cannot be accurately predicted or controlled. For predictable events, societies can take proactive measures to mitigate and control their risks. The prediction of possible results allows the realization of the range of random variables, identification of groups by impact levels/areas in the city, resources used, and time of occurrence. It also enables the administration of the city to proactively intervene to improve the indicators they would like to manage. For non-predictable events, the actions must instead revolve around preparedness to react when the event appears. Nevertheless, possible analytics-based observations and risk management attributes can provide clues to help be prepared.

In this chapter, we present examples of various events affecting a city's performance and show how, with AI use, it is possible to provide a better understanding of the impact of decisions in managing strategic risk. In a city's performance, the allocation of budget is related to protection, hedging, mitigation, and control of risks related to crime, accidents, healthcare, education, and so on. Proactive risk control helps balance the costs of pre-event, event, and after-event actions, thereby reducing them. Natural disasters such as flooding, hurricanes, and other Black Swan events often have the highest impact in societies, but preparedness can reduce the severity of the event's impact.

The analysis of the performance of a city can follow several types of framework. In this chapter, the organization of the performance measurement and strategic objectives set is based on an adaptation of the balanced scorecard (BSC) to municipal administrations. The factors under a city's control are similar to those of for-profit organizations but with a different main purpose, the benefit/satisfaction of citizens rather than financial performance. We will use the stakeholders' quality of life as the driver to align financial, public servant, and services perspectives. The next section presents a brief explanation of the terms that we use in this chapter, and then we describe how to use analytics tools to develop an AI system that can dynamically and continuously guide the city administration. Finally, we offer some examples by way of illustration, but we can only hint at the possibilities in the space available here.

8.2 Concepts and Definitions

For AI, we use a slightly modified version of the definition from Krishnamoorthy and Rajeev (1996) "Artificial Intelligence (AI) is the science of making machines or systems do things that would require intelligence if done by *humans*" [our change in italics: the original said "men"]. This is developed in the context of smart cities by Agarwal et al. (2015) providing us with the aspects to consider in AI applications: "The main objective of the AI system is to create intelligent machines and through this, to understand the principles of intelligence." In the context of this chapter, we consider AI application as part of the process of creating knowledge from data and developing the systems to maintain a continuous analysis of data that can drive actions in the solution, prevention, and orientation of problems in a city.

The concept of a *smart city* is evolving, as the use of technology emerges to connect citizens and their city's administration. Musa (2016) provides a detailed definition:

> A smart city is defined as a city that engages its citizens and connects its infrastructure electronically. A smart city has the ability to integrate multiple technological solutions, in a secure fashion, to manage the city's assets—the city's assets include, but not limited to, local departments' information systems, schools, libraries, transportation systems, hospitals, power plants, law enforcement, and other community services.

The technologies that might provide these solutions are described in a report from the International Standards Organization (ISO/IEC JTC 1 Information Technology, 2015): "Smart Cities is a new concept and a new model, which applies the new generation of information technologies, such as the internet of things, cloud computing, big data and space/geographical information integration, to facilitate the planning, construction, management and smart services of cities." Furthermore, the SmartCitiesWorld/Phillips Lighting survey (Simpson, 2017) identifies the three most important requirements as open/sharing data, citizen engagement, and enhanced services for citizens. Sodhi, Flatt, and Landry (2018) observe that "The path to creating smart cities should be through a culture of openness, co-creation, and shared resources."

As Frigo and Anderson (2011) explained, "*Strategic risks* [our italics] are those risks that are most consequential to the organization's ability to execute its strategies and achieve its business objectives." There are many variables that might be used as KPIs (key performance indicators) and KRIs (key risk indicators) for a smart city. Albino, Beardi, and Dangelico (2015) identify aspects related to the environment, finance, people, administration, living, and so on. Whatever factors a city chooses to consider become strategic in the sense of defining the path for the city administration to follow. The aggregated risk related to those factors is then the strategic risk.

The measurement process is crucial for managing the city and keeping stakeholders satisfied. Measurement generates metrics and indicators. These are potentially affected by uncertainty, and the variation of the expected results is what strategic risk management is looking to assess, mitigate, and control.

Many *types of risk* can affect citizens' lives. There are financial risks associated with the city's capacity to cover its obligations through resources such as taxes. Moody's (2019) indicated risk mitigation actions and allocation of the budget resources that smart cities are taking: credit risk control is one of the areas of concern in a city's risk management. Other types of risk are related to external factors and conditions of the environment that can affect the performance of the city, for example:

Possible controllable risks

1. Changes in KPIs for cities related to changes in industry composition, employment, population composition, housing, cost of doing business, cost of living, family income, and business environment/bankruptcies.
2. Financial risk. Infrastructure maintenance costs are growing. When cities invest in infrastructure, it is not just a capital cost, the maintenance cost is a priority in terms of sustainability.
3. Quality of data. Data can be incorrect or outdated, reducing its use as a source to create knowledge and to develop AI solutions. Data has another strategic risk—it can be an asset, but the step of monetizing data means a continuous trade-off with open data. The interest in municipal data is growing because of the potential value it has for for-profit organizations in marketing, politics, healthcare, etc.
4. Risks of using technology: criminal hacking, systems failures, employee errors, non-compliance with legislation, etc.
5. Sustainability itself. A good example is based on civil engineering projects (Dasgupta and Tam 2005) where the main aspects to consider are regulatory indicators, project-specific indicators, environmental indicators, and technical indicators (materials used).

Possible Black Swans

1. Climate events: "Roughly 60% of the cities' reported climate mitigation or adaptation projects are aimed at managing flood risks. The figure increases to 83% when including projects intended for mitigating multiple climate risks, including flooding. Drought, storms, and heat account for a combined 17% of climate mitigation projects" (Moody's, 2019).
2. Trade wars' impact on finances and employment.

This chapter is about the identification of means to mitigate or control risk by organizing the strategy of the municipal administration using AI. We do not have room to consider other approaches such as insurance policies or put options. Risk mitigation can be organized by the three phases of management control in municipal administration proposed by McNichols (1977). Pre-control refers to gap analysis capabilities, capacity, and opportunities/threats. Continuous control refers to the organization, monitoring, and adaptation to the new socio-economic-environmental conditions. Post-control is the evaluation of the results and feedback to the municipal administration. The concept of the BSC, introduced by Kaplan and Norton (1992) and adapted to non-profit organizations, helps to direct the control process. The analytics process, as the creator of knowledge, provides clues to develop the control systems that mitigate strategic risks.

8.2.1 How Are AI, Smart Cities, and Strategic Risk Connected?

A smart city aims to use technology to connect citizens and city administration. This chapter focuses on the analytics process that supports the AI system in creating knowledge from data to help improve risk mitigation and control, and thus citizens' quality of life. Strategic risk relates to the capacity to respond to the citizens' needs in the presence of hazards or potential risks. AI acts as a vehicle to mitigate the strategic risk by generating early warning systems, awareness, and guides for action.

The McKinsey Global Institute (2018) presented the performance of smart cities based on metrics related to the quality of life and use of technology: time, safety, cost of living, jobs, social connectedness, environment, health. Their analysis indicated that disease burden could be reduced by 8–15%, commuting time by 15–20%, crime incidents 30–40%, citizen expenditures 1–3%, time interacting with the government 45–65%, and emissions, water consumption, and unrecycled waste more than 10%.

The earliest practical AI successes were "expert systems," developed by acquiring knowledge from experts and representing it in algorithms and code. Today, statistical and machine learning methods enable AI systems to generate knowledge based on data analytics. An AI system can create a dynamic dashboard that contains the components of a scorecard for the city administration to use for mitigating and controlling strategic risk.

In this chapter, we present examples of pattern recognition that can guide the design of actions by the city as a means to reduce the variability of the outcomes and hence strategic risk. AI has been used in smart cities in several areas (Allam and Dhunny 2019): energy with maps for supply and consumption planning, as well as climate change impact observation in communities that helps to manage policies, education, and healthcare. However, the concept of risk control and mitigation has not yet been considered. Most importantly, nor has the aggregation of risk as strategic risk in order to maintain the KPIs of the municipal performance in good standing.

8.3 Methodology and Approach

The overall research approach taken is one of action research (Eden and Huxham, 1996) or design science (Van Aken and Romme 2012; Baloh, De Souza and Hackney 2012). We study the process of building the systems by attempting to do it and learning as we go. We use open data from three cities (Baltimore, Toronto, and Chicago) to represent performance aspects where risk events can exist. We illustrate potential components of an AI system by indicating possible KPIs, KRIs, and models. There is a selection of outputs related to crime, traffic management/accidents, budgeting, education, and customer service.

Figure 8.1 represents our proposed process of building an AI system for a smart city. The first component of the system is the definition of KPIs and KRIs. They are the set of goals that the AI for the smart city must help achieve.

Suppose the city intends a strategic initiative to develop programs educating families for awareness and protection. A suitable KPI might be to increase citizen satisfaction by 2%. A potential risk is that the community does not want to engage with such a top-down initiative, so a KRI might be the change in the number of people participating compared with local crime rates. A risk-mitigating strategic response would be to develop local leaders and support the community's activities.

Once the KPIs and KRIs are selected, the next step is to gather data for the analytics of the specific target. The source of data is expected to be the open data that the smart city is building. Data quality is crucial; open data must be seen as more than just generating raw data for citizens' consultation. Table 8.1 indicates general KPIs and KRIs in the domains of the examples in this chapter. They are divided into the four perspectives of the modified BSC: Stakeholder (the driver), Financial Resources Management, Internal Process, and Trained Public Servants. The logic is that influential systems to offer good results to citizens are based on trained people dealing with municipal administration, processes in place that are effective and efficient, and the use of financial resources according to the defined

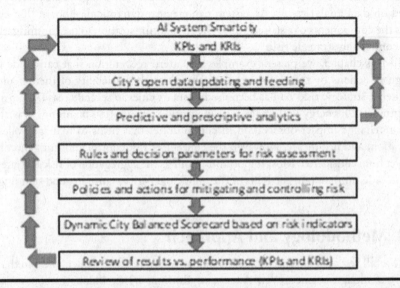

Figure 8.1   The process to design an AI System for strategic risk management.

Table 8.1   Examples of KPIs and KRIs According to BSC Perspectives

Perspective vs. actions in smart cities	Crime control	Traffic management/accidents	Customer service requests	Education
Stakeholder perspective				
KPI	Time to respond to inquiries	Ratio pedestrian volume/accidents	Ratio calls/emergency level	Ratio expenses/graduated students
KRI	Variability of time for attention	Time to repair traffic signs	Changes in level of cases solved	Changes in the number of students graduating: churn analysis
	Variation of appropriate resources	Location: intersections with high accident probability	Time for closing cases with solutions	Changes in expenditure by enrolment
Financial resources management perspective				
KPI	Reduce operational cost	Investment per sign type	Investment in automation and communication	Support for students
KRI	Level of effectiveness	Changes in trend in accidents	Goal achievement variation of the solutions	Changes in number and amounts of benefits
	Level of satisfaction	Level of areas with high accident rate	Cases closed with a good evaluation per dollar invested	Compensation education providers/quality level

(Continued)

Table 8.1 (Continued)   Examples of KPIs and KRIs According to BSC Perspectives

Perspective vs. actions in smart cities	Crime control	Traffic management/ accidents	Customer service requests	Education
Internal process perspective				
KPI	Reduction in process steps	Number of cases to dollars invested	Ratio number of cases to dollars of public resources	Number of schools/ number of students/ investment
KRI	Changes in investment/ time of the process	Variation in the ratio cases to dollar	Changes in the ratio cases to dollars	Change in enrolment/ teaching resources
Trained public servant perspective				
KPI	Hours training per year	Training and incentives	Growth in cases served	Amount of m² areas for education
KRI	Permeability/retention/ practice of good techniques	Evaluation of accidents by human resources	Number of claims	Changes forecast vs. current

strategic priorities for risk and expected performance. Figure 8.2 shows how cause and effect flows from the fourth perspective through to the first.

The third step uses models to provide actionable knowledge in the administration of the city. The examples provided in Section 8.4 indicate possible more detailed KPIs and KRIs, which can be studied with statistical and machine learning algorithms. The process of selecting models that fit and provide better value to prediction and prescription will feed the creation of rules for action, and in parallel, there is feedback to review if the KPIs and KRIs are the ones the city administration should use in future.

The fourth step brings in risk, creating rules, parameters, and thresholds to guide actions such as budgeting and use of resources, and providing awareness and warning systems. AI benchmarking with other smart cities will help "tune up" the KPIs and KRIs.

In the fifth step, the analytics results are translated into policies and actions to manage strategic risk. Human input from management is essential at this stage. No AI model can ever be complete.

The dynamic BSC review then represents the preparedness and orientation to take action based on changes in KPIs and KRIs, finally reviewing the results of those actions and also considering changing the KPIs and KRIs if appropriate.

8.4 Examples of Creating KPIs and KRIs Based on Open Data

As illustration, we present results from various different algorithms and tools. Given the variety of tools in the market, the city administration must choose carefully according to the type of problem. Again, feedback on the use of algorithms, tools, and techniques, and whether or not the raw data can be converted into usable data, is essential.

We have used statistical and machine learning techniques to build predictive models that will generate the risk control scorecard. Techniques include logistic regression, forecasting, descriptive tables, and decision/classification trees; software tools were Excel, R, and KNIME. This chapter does not have room to illustrate the process of fitting the best model to different types of problems and available data, but we have chosen a range of output formats to illustrate some of the possibilities.

Figure 8.2   Cause-effect modified BSC for a smart city.

From Table 8.1, we present examples to show the interaction between KPI, KRI, Model, and Outcome. We give the most examples for the top-level Stakeholder perspective.

8.4.1 Stakeholder Perspective

Crime. The analysis is based on training a model to detect law enforcement resources' capacity to attend events and be proactive in reducing/controlling expected events, based on patterns over time and severity measured by number of arrests. Data from Chicago.

KPI Time to respond to inquiries
KRI Variability of time to attend

Time of day/week, arrest or not, domestic or not, type of crime, and city area are all factors relating to the use of law enforcement resources. Risk appears as the change in probability of an event's occurrence. Expected higher probabilities could lead changes in available resources and training. Figure 8.3 shows, perhaps surprisingly, that arrests for theft peak around 4 pm and that there is little variation between days of the week. Figure 8.4 displays a forecast with a confidence interval, showing results are not limited to a single value. A fuller analysis, including seasonality (again we have no room for this) would suggest possible law enforcement attributes to consider in scheduling and training resources for operational planning.

Traffic management/accidents.

KPI Ratio pedestrian volume/accidents
KRI Time to repair damaged/faulty traffic signs

Changes in accident rates because of traffic signs is just one example of how infrastructure can affect the occurrence of events. The risk assessment is based on the changes in the expected probabilities of occurrence of accidents. Cities' open data sources can include such variables as age, car type, hour, road conditions, cell phone use, light, number of passengers, alcohol/drug use, and so on. The risk assessment is based on the changes of the probability of accidents at the main points of control in the city. (Data from Toronto and Chicago.)

The outcome measure is based on accident severity using categories of incapacity or fatality. Analysis suggests that traffic signage is in fact only a second level contributory factor, whereas "cell phone use other than texting" is a top-level factor, as is "distraction from inside vehicle." Driver (and passenger?) education may be more important than traffic signage.

Education.

KPI Ratio expenses/graduated students
KRI Changes in number of students graduating successfully

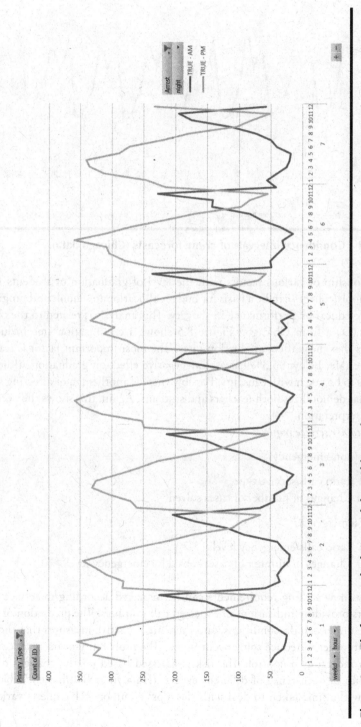

Figure 8.3 Theft arrests by hour and day (Chicago data).

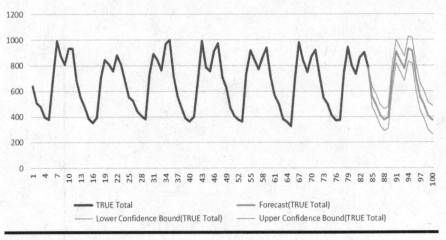

Figure 8.4 Confidence intervals of crime forecasts (Chicago data).

The relationship of various factors with the level of graduation of students from public schools/colleges can be a basis for budget allocation to schools and programs to improve education performance in the city. This analysis is related to the churn situation. (Data from Chicago.) Figure 8.5 shows a classification tree including the factors that most affect graduation rates. The most important factor is teacher attendance rate. Below 95.3% has a clear negative effect on graduation, although care needs to be taken with causality. Possibly there is another factor affecting some schools that demoralizes both teachers and students. Again, this shows the need for human interpretation.

Customer service requests.

311 (non-emergency)

KPI Ratio calls/service type
KRI Changes in number of cases solved

911 (emergency)

KPI Ratio calls/emergency levels
KRI Changes in number of cases solved by emergency level

This shows how staffing requirements can be managed according to service type and factors providing indications of expected call numbers. The prediction of calls is possible under certain conditions, and there are proactive measures that the city can take in order to reduce some occurrences. The probability of occurrence generates the indicator to control. The risk is assessed based on the changes of the probabilities of occurrence of different events. (Data from Baltimore.) Table 8.2 shows how the time taken to deal with the most common 311 requests varies by

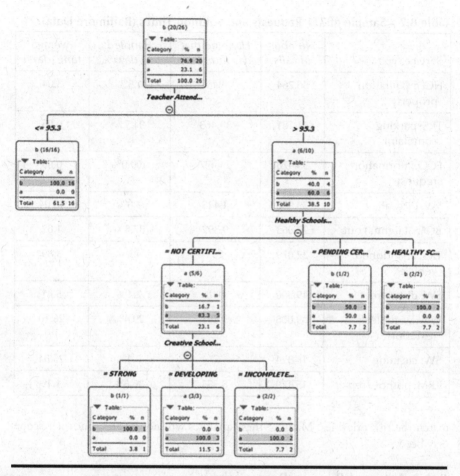

Figure 8.5 Classification tree—key factors affecting graduation rates (Chicago data).

type, from quick-to-handle information requests (what was the "odd one out"?) to harder-to-solve water leaks.

8.4.2 Financial Resources Management Perspective

> KPI Ratio of expenses on the variables related to events to total financial resources allocated
>
> KRI Variation of the level of allocation according to priorities, weight of the relationship to the events

From this perspective, the concept is how resources are used to support the plan and modify the risk level. For example, the budget allocation (Table 8.3) should

Table 8.2 Sample of 311 Requests and Solution Times (Baltimore Data)

Service type	Number of calls	Handled that day (number)	Handled that day (%)	Average time (days)
HCD: sanitation property	56,264	848	1.5%	3.04
TRS: parking complaint	41,781	39,463	94.5%	0.06
ECC: information request	33,478	33,477	100.0%	0.00
SW: dirty alley	29,958	1,425	4.8%	15.04
BGE: St light(s) out	25,063	9,392	37.5%	1.82
TRS: abandoned vehicle	22,079	993	4.5%	3.89
SW: dirty street	19,900	418	2.1%	5.81
WW: water leak (exterior)	19,006	5,583	29.4%	26.10
SW: cleaning	16,324	67	0.4%	25.84
TRM: pothole repair	15,179	5,555	36.6%	1.16

match the risk priorities. Many of these analyses will not be new, but their scope may be.

8.4.3 Internal Process Perspective

KPI Capacity increase to 10% of power generation using non-fossil-fuel based methods
KRI Delays in these substitution projects

This analysis helps prepare the city's administration to maintain the risk indicators under control at the level of financial and stakeholders' requirements.

8.4.4 Trained Public Servant Perspective

KPI Average number of specialized emergency people over the year
KRI Changes in the priorities of human resources demand

People, technology, and processes (Edwards, 2005) need to work together to deliver the city's services. Control of risk based on knowledge and development of people's

Table 8.3 Budget Allocation (Chicago Data)

Areas using resources (HR)	Total budgeted amount
Grand total	$3,017,197,588
Local	$2,887,830,967
Chicago Police Department	$1,253,490,141
Chicago Fire Department	$509,776,763
Department of Water Management	$202,205,966
Department of Streets and Sanitation	$165,932,801
Chicago Department of Aviation	$135,007,976
Chicago Department of Transportation	$119,122,410
Grant	$99,372,723
Office of Emergency Management and Communications	$96,843,426

capabilities is crucial to city operations. Training of public servants in pre-control, continuous control, and post-control is part of the development of strategic risk management for the smart city.

8.5 Discussion

Based on our necessarily brief review, the following are the key aspects of the components of an AI system for a smart city and their integration:

1. Progressing from just providing data and information for citizens to the prediction and review of possible actions to serve citizens better.
2. Embracing the analysis of the smart city under the strategic risk review of what the city needs to accomplish, according to a BSC. Moving from KPIs to KRIs to actions to implement municipal strategies, working on the bases of multiple risks, multiple indicators, and multiple models to create components of the AI system.
3. Moving from fixed rules to dynamic rules in the development and use of BSC, and actions to assess, monitor, and control risks. Use of a Strategic Risk Management Dashboard—an extension of what Kourtit and Nijkamp (2018) describe—that includes current performance and an early warning system element.
4. Defining and providing details of each area of performance in the city using statistical and machine learning models to incorporate the outcomes as components of the AI system.

5. Supporting and maintaining a benchmarking method with other smart cities.
6. Improving the quality of the "food" of the system: data. Generation of data to meet standards of quality in updating, accuracy, and organization, with a connection to risk indicators and models to mitigate and control risks.
7. Operating the AI system in a continuous feedback mode to update parameters, rules, and even components, and recommend appropriate actions. However, humans still need to oversee all actions.

8.6 Conclusion

We have presented illustrative examples of the uses of AI systems to support the management of a smart city. The design of the systems follows an iterative seven-step approach, driven by a focus on strategic risks as represented in a balanced scorecard.

We believe these serve as a proof of concept for using the proposed approach to develop an integrated set of AI systems supporting all aspects of the city's strategic management, though this is still some time away.

References

Agarwal, P.K., Gurjar, J., Agarwal, A.K. and Birla, R. (2015) "Application of Artificial Intelligence for Development of Intelligent Transport System in Smart Cities", *International Journal of Transportation Engineering and Traffic Systems*, 1(1).

Albino, V., Beardi, U. and Dangelico, R.M. (2015) "Smart Cities: Definitions, Performance, and Initiatives", *Journal of Urban Technology*, 22(1), pp 3–21.

Allam, Z. and Dhunny, Z.A. (2019) "On Big Data, Artificial Intelligence and Smart Cities", *Cities*, 89(June), pp 80–91.

Baloh, P., Desouza, K.C. and Hackney, R. (2012) "Contextualizing Organizational Interventions of Knowledge Management Systems: A Design Science Perspective", *Journal of the American Society for Information Science and Technology*, 63(5), pp 948–966.

Dasgupta, S. and Tam, E. (2005) "Indicators and Framework for Assessing Sustainable Infrastructure", *Canadian Journal of Civil Engineering*, 32(1), pp 30–44.

Eden, C. and Huxham, C. (1996) "Action Research for Management Research", *British Journal of Management*, 7(1), pp 75–86.

Edwards, J.S. (2005) "Business Processes and Knowledge Management". In: M. Khosrow-Pour (Ed.), *Encyclopedia of Information Science and Technology* (Vol. I, pp. 350-355), Idea Group, Hershey, PA.

Frigo, M.L. and Anderson, R.J. (2011) "Strategic Risk Management: A Foundation for Improving Enterprise Risk Management and Governance", *The Journal of Corporate Accounting and Finance*, 22(3), pp 81–88.

ISO/IEC JTC 1 Information Technology (2015) *Smart Cities – Preliminary Report 2014*, ISO, Geneva, Switzerland.

Kaplan, R.S. and Norton, D.P. (1992) "The Balanced Scorecard—Measures That Drive Performance", *Harvard Business Review*, 70(1), pp 71–79.

Kourtit, K. and Nijkamp, P. (2018) "Big Data Dashboards as Smart Decision Support Tools for I-Cities – An Experiment on Stockholm", *Land Use Policy*, 71, pp 24–35.

Krishnamoorthy, C.S. and Rajeev, S. (1996) *Artificial Intelligence and Expert Systems for Engineers*, CRC Press/Taylor & Francis, Boca Raton, FL.

McKinsey Global Institute (2018), *Smart Cities: Digital Solutions for a More Livable Future*, McKinsey Global Institute, Brussels, San Francisco and Shanghai.

McNichols, T.J. (1977) *Executive Policy and Strategic Planning*, McGraw Hill, New York.

Moody's (2019) *Largest US Cities Take Proactive Steps to Mitigate Credit Risk from Climate Change* [Online], https://www.moodys.com/research/Moodys-Largest-US-cities-take-proactive-steps-to-mitigate-credit--PBM_1158519.

Musa, S. (2016) "Smart City Roadmap" [Online], http://www.academia.edu/21181336/Smart_City_Roadmap.

Ng, K.-S., Hung, W.-T.. and Wong, W.-G. (2002) "An Algorithm for Assessing the Risk of Traffic Accidents", *Journal of Safety Research*, 33(3), pp 387–410.

Simpson, P. (2017) "Smart Cities: Understanding the Challenges and Opportunities" [Online] *SmartCitiesWorld/Philips Lighting*, https://smartcitiesworld.net/AcuCustom/Sitename/DAM/012/Understanding_the_Challenges_and_Opportunities_of_Smart_Citi.pdf.

Sodhi, Z., Flatt, J. and Landry, J.N. (2018) *Getting to the Open Smart City* [Online] Evergreen and Open North for Future Cities Canada. https://futurecitiescanada.ca/downloads/2018/Getting_to_Open_Smart_City.pdf.

Taleb, N. (2007) *The Black Swan: The Impact of the Highly Improbable*, Random House, New York.

Ullah, I., Fayaz, M. and Kim, D.-H. (2018) "Analytical Modeling for Underground Risk Assessment in Smart Cities", *Applied Sciences*, 8(6), pp 921–939.

Van Aken, J.E. and Romme, A.G.L. (2012) "A Design Science Approach to Evidence-Based Management". In: D.M. Rousseau (Ed.), *The Oxford Handbook of Evidence-Based Management* (pp. 43–57), Oxford University Press, Oxford.

Chapter 9

Predicting Patient Missed Appointments in the Academic Dental Clinic

Aundrea L. Price and Gopikrishnan Chandrasekharan

Contents

9.1 Introduction... 152
9.2 Electronic Dental Records and Analytics 153
9.3 Impact of Missed Dental Appointments.. 155
9.4 Patient Responses to Fear and Pain 157
    9.4.1 Dental Anxiety 157
    9.4.2 Dental Avoidance 158
9.5 Potential Data Sources 160
    9.5.1 Dental Anxiety Assessments 160
    9.5.2 Clinical Notes... 161
    9.5.3 Staff and Patient Reporting... 161
9.6 Conclusions... 162
References 163

9.1 Introduction

The use of information technology (IT) and electronic dental record (EDR) systems has produced a sea change in how dentists are trained and how dentistry is practiced in dental schools. Since the 1980s, dental schools across the United States have seen the incremental introduction of IT in various functional areas. Initially, the focus of IT implementation was on dental billing systems and insurance processing. Adoption of EDRs in dental schools has increased as technology administrators, faculty, and clinicians realize the value of using information technology in additional areas such as dental practice and student progress tracking.

EDRs provide administrators, clinical faculty, and others involved in dental education with several capabilities (Schleyer et al., 2012; Schleyer, 2004). These systems can help link patient data with evidence-based resources to provide recommendations with the help of clinical decision support systems. The patient data can be analyzed to identify errors in medical decision-making and highlight inefficiencies in clinical operations thereby reducing the cost of providing care. Electronic health data can be exchanged much more easily with other care providers compared with paper records and can potentially reduce the need for repeated tests and dental imaging studies such as radiographs (Stewart et al., 2010). EDR data can be reused by researchers to identify therapies and treatments that work in real life and modify treatments that do not work outside of lab settings (Schleyer et al., 2012). This secondary analysis and data mining of healthcare data is one of the biggest drivers for the adoption of electronic health records (EHRs) and EDRs in healthcare organizations.

Analytics in medicine and healthcare generally falls into three main categories: descriptive, diagnostic, and predictive (others have a fourth category dealing with prescriptive to bring in optimization techniques). Descriptive analytics tools and methods are used to depict an event or outcome in a way that helps document anything that may be known about the underlying data. This type of analytics generally tries to answer simply *what* is occurring. For example, EDR data can be used to analyze patient care utilization patterns, such as preventive dental services, across various demographic groups. Diagnostic analytics tools and methods try to resolve *why* certain events occur to uncover the cause of observed outcomes. For example, self-reported patient data could be tracked at specific intervals and analyzed to identify why certain patients are unhappy with the treatment. These and other sources of data could be used together to implement measures that improve overall patient engagement and satisfaction.

The greatest value of any healthcare analytics project involves trying to answer *when* a future event is likely to occur using patterns in historical data. Proactively identifying patients who have the highest risk of poor outcomes and will benefit from clinical intervention is a prime example of the use of predictive analytics in healthcare (Thyvalikakath et al., 2015).

Data mining and text analytics of EDR data, combined with other sources, can help the dental school become more proactive and anticipate outcomes based on data. This allows faculty, students, and staff to take appropriate actions before a negative outcome occurs. Risk scores are commonly used in dental practice. These denote the future risk of an outcome such as periodontal disease which helps the dentist take aggressive measures to prevent further aggravation of the disease. Data from the EDR can be used to predict other medical issues as well, provided the dental and medical data sets can be linked in a meaningful manner (Acharya et al., 2018).

Predictive analytics is also used to identify patients who have the highest risk of treatment failures, such as patients who need dental implants or dental prosthesis (Chuang et al., 2002). It also is used to improve and enhance clinical decision support tools that personalize the treatment for each patient and recommend treatments that can provide the greatest benefit. Furthermore, these three main analytical approaches are used in tandem to target the same problem from different perspectives. In a dental school setting, descriptive analytics can be used to identify current spending patterns and resource utilization. Diagnostic analytics might identify areas where resource utilization can be optimized and make recommendations to improve the efficiency of providing dental care. Predictive analytics can be used to predict resource requirements and allocating resources proactively.

Identifying patients who have a history of missed appointments and reliably flagging patients with a future risk is a key use case for analytics in the dental school environment. Using analytics to identify patients at risk of missing appointments and creating predictive models from EHR data has been attempted in other domains (Lenzi et al., 2019). However, few studies have been done to systematically identify and predict patients who are at risk of missing appointments in a dental school setting (Gustafsson et al., 2010).

The goal of this chapter is to present a broad overview of the reasons for and impact of missed dental appointments in the academic dental clinic, and how certain approaches might be used to reduce missed dental appointments. Features of EDRs will be discussed, particularly regarding the capture of data for analytic purposes and inherent challenges regarding data collection and data quality. An exploration of the research on dental avoidance serves to identify valuable potential risk factors that may not currently be captured consistently in dental school EDRs. Future directions must necessarily be based upon the current ability of dental schools to leverage the functionality of information systems; however, students, faculty, staff, and patients all might play a role in identifying potentially effective interventions to reduce missed appointments.

9.2 Electronic Dental Records and Analytics

Certain features of EDR systems designed for private dental practitioners are also relevant to the dental school, such as capabilities for patient registration, appointment scheduling, a comprehensive dental health history form, and a clinical charting system. EDR systems designed for the dental school also include tools that allow trainers and faculty to track the progress of dental students.

EDRs contain detailed patient data covering all aspects of dental care. For long-term patients of the dental school, this results in valuable longitudinal data to track issues and treatments across many years. If the dental school is part of a Health Information Exchange (HIE), researchers, analysts, and health informaticians can combine this data with EHR data from other hospitals and medical practices to obtain a complete medical and dental overview of the patient's health (Burris, 2017). Some dental schools have developed EDR systems in-house, in some cases with their medical counterparts if they are integrated into a larger health system. Other dental schools have adopted commercial systems from vendors such as Exan, Dentrix, and Epic. The dental software from Exan, axiUm, is currently in use in over 75% of the 66 accredited dental schools in the United States (Schleyer et al., 2012).

Since good quality data is key to a proper analytics project, the essential best practice is to ensure data quality at the source of data. Data quality can be impaired due to several reasons including missing data and incorrect or incomplete data introduced at the time of data entry (Strome & Liefer, 2013). Data errors occur in EHR and EDR systems largely during the input stage when the clinician or dental students enter data into the system and no validation mechanism is present (Weir et al., 2003). Inconsistent entry of data and unstructured fields that permit ill-defined free entry of text exacerbate the issue of data quality. User interfaces that allow users to select the appropriate diagnosis or treatments from a prepopulated list can help to ensure data quality at data entry (Shimpi et al., 2018). However, these interfaces are not universally implemented.

When performing diagnostic and predictive analytics for missed appointments, important data might not be collected consistently for all patients. In some dental schools, only part of the dental record is available in an electronic format. This unavailability of good quality raw data can hinder an analytics project and bias the results. For example, patients with a prior history of missed appointments have a higher likelihood of missing appointments again (Chariatte et al., 2008). If the patient is new to the dental school and the patient's previous records are in other dental or medical organizations where there is no viable linking of data, a previous pattern of missed appointments in other care settings may go undetected. Thus, only an incomplete analysis can be done based on part of a patient profile.

Healthcare data interoperability is a major challenge facing all healthcare organizations. Healthcare data is available in a wide variety of formats isolated in separate information silos using different informatics standards to store and annotate their data. Recent efforts made to harmonize the different dental terminology standards show promise and can help improve dental interoperability in the long run, however, these terminologies have seen limited adoption among dental schools to date (Ramoni et al., 2017). De-identified oral health databases such as the BigMouth Dental Data Repository (https://bigmouth.uth.edu) integrate data from different dental schools into a single data set after mapping data to a common reference terminology (Walji et al., 2014). This helps analysts and researchers query data across a wide variety of sources and create predictive models that are valid across different dental schools. An accurate data set that links diagnosis and treatments with standardized terminologies or ontologies can help a dental school identify the type of patients and procedures where patients are at a high risk of missing appointments.

9.3 Impact of Missed Dental Appointments

Dentistry training at the dental school comprises a mix of didactic and clinical training. During clinical training, students are exposed to scenarios and cases they will encounter in dental clinics. This clinical training reinforces the knowledge obtained through lectures and practical sessions in lab settings. Through clinical rotations, students gain valuable experience in diagnosis treatment planning, patient management, patient education, and professional communication. Patient management and communication is an essential part of clinical training in most dental schools. For example, students learn how to manage medically compromised patients, how to address medical/dental emergencies, and how to assist patients who have dental phobia. Patient communication training may involve developing the skill of establishing a trusting dentist-patient relationship and identifying and addressing communication issues in the dental clinic (Safi et al., 2015).

Dental schools have a varied approach to dealing with scheduling appointments for patients. In some dental schools, the students are actively engaged in scheduling or otherwise required to manage dental appointments as part of their training. In other dental schools, trained office staff manage appointment scheduling and liaise with the dental student to find a time and allocate a dental chair as appropriate (Teich et al., 2012).

Problems with appointments and patient communication are a leading cause of patient dissatisfaction at the dental school (Sachdeo et al., 2012). Some patients, particularly pediatric and geriatric populations, rely upon caregivers to remember follow-up instructions and keep track of upcoming appointments. Depending on how the dental school manages appointment reminders (for example, by asking for a reconfirmation in advance), patients may or may not notify providers that an appointment will be missed. Furthermore, if an appointment is missed and the patient does not initiate contact to reschedule, providers may not know whether the patient intends to return.

Patients who miss appointments are a phenomenon observed in all healthcare systems. Missed appointments are associated with reduced productivity and loss of revenue for the healthcare institution (Guzek et al., 2015). Studies have shown that in some dental schools around 17–19% of appointments have been classified as missed appointments and resulted in significant loss of clinical productivity (Teich et al., 2012; Trenouth, 2003). Missed appointments are particularly prevalent among children and adolescents. Some studies have shown that nearly 38% of the children in the six- to eight-year age group had one or more missed appointments during a three- to six-year period (Wogelius & Poulsen, 2005).

Patients have indicated several reasons for canceling or missing dental appointments. Reasons for canceling appointments include inconvenient timing or the inability to secure transportation. The most common reasons identified for missing dental appointments are forgetfulness and the inability to get time off from work or school (George et al., 2007; Shabbir et al., 2018).

Missed appointments harm dental outcomes because when treatment is disrupted, it may be difficult to continue an established treatment plan. This is particularly problematic when the patient must be seen later (after missing one or more appointments) due to an exacerbation of symptoms. A history of previously missed appointments and frequently missing appointments during treatment are both good indicators of discontinuing treatment. In dental treatments such as orthodontics, patient compliance is a crucial factor that determines the success of treatment. If patients miss appointments and subsequently decide to discontinue treatment, more harm may result than not having the treatment initiated in the first place (Trenouth, 2003). Missed appointments can sometimes add a month to the overall duration of treatment and are a leading cause of increased treatment duration (Beckwith et al., 1999).

From a revenue and operational standpoint, dental clinics and dental schools (regardless of size) face a potential loss of income and productivity due to missed appointments. Missed appointments have additional negative outcomes in a dental school setting compared with a non-academic clinic. When a patient is scheduled for an appointment at the dental school, even routine processes are part of student training to ensure safe and effective dental treatment. Student dentists learn the fundamentals of how a clinic operates and their role in maintaining patient flow throughout the various steps of the patient visit. Because a dental chair is assigned in advance to the patient and the dental student for each expected encounter, high rates of missed appointments can lead dental clinics to overbook dental chairs and undertake other inefficient practice management techniques (Holtshousen & Coetzee, 2012).

Diagnosis and treatment procedures generally take longer in the dental school compared with a private dental clinic due to the focus on clinical training. Therefore, appointments could last between 45 minutes and several hours depending on the complexity of the procedure. Each step of the procedure must be signed off by clinical faculty who oversee the dental students. Dental equipment must be sterilized and prepared beforehand and made ready for the patient. Therefore, if the patient misses an appointment, the result is underutilization of dental chairs, loss of faculty time, loss of time and effort needed to prepare dental instruments, and disruption of dental student training.

Some procedures such as dental prosthetic placement involve multiple phases; each phase involves several steps that must be completed before the next phase of treatment can proceed. Since each phase of dental treatment can occur across multiple appointments, a missed appointment disrupts not only patient care but the phased dental student training process. In cases where the missed appointment results in the patient discontinuing care altogether, the student must find another patient with a similar treatment plan to complete the required number of cases of each type. Some dental schools have adopted a comprehensive care model where the student is assessed on competency exams and the successful and timely completion of all dental procedures based on the patient's needs rather than completing a required number of procedures (Holmes et al., 2000). Nevertheless, high missed appointment rates can negatively impact the educational experience of dental students (Teich et al., 2012).

The type of dental treatment may play a role in patient compliance. Orthodontic treatments may take between 12 and 36 months (Moresca, 2018). Appointments are normally scheduled once a month, which means the patient must sustain motivation to attend over an extended period to complete treatment. External factors such as an inability to find time off school, difficulty arranging transportation, adverse weather, or other types of illness might play a role in increasing the likelihood of a missed appointment. Some (but not all) dental treatments involve pain or uncomfortable clinical procedures. Patients with a low pain tolerance may find it difficult to overcome their fear of the dental procedure in order to attend the subsequent appointments needed to complete the treatment.

Loss of revenue combined with reduced productivity, potential negative impact on patient outcomes, and disruption of dental student training all result from missed appointments. By identifying patients who are at an increased risk of missing appointments, educational interventions might be implemented that can motivate the patient to improve compliance. The dental school can establish measures to seek out non-behavioral factors such as weather or inability to take time off from obligations and schedule appointments accordingly. If the patient is considered at high risk of missing appointments and has shown symptoms of dental fear and anxiety, then additional measures to mitigate these factors can be considered.

9.4 Patient Responses to Fear and Pain

9.4.1 Dental Anxiety

Dental anxiety is a fear of dentists and dental treatments. The anxiety can range from mild anxiety for certain dental procedures to severe anxiety that can seriously affect normal life. In severe cases, dental anxiety can manifest as dental phobia, also known as odontophobia. Dental anxiety is a phenomenon that has been studied since the 1960s (Smith & Heaton, 2003). Dentists have been introducing new treatments, tools, and techniques to help manage or reduce pain experienced during a dental procedure. These new treatment modalities combined with improved pain-reducing medication have benefited patients. Several behavioral and pharmacological interventions have also been developed to help patients better manage their anxiety and fear of dental treatments (Appukuttan, 2016). While general anxiety levels have increased in the United States, studies across several decades have shown that levels of dental anxiety have remained relatively stable (Smith & Heaton, 2003). Research has shown that approximately 10–20% of the adult population has a moderate to high degree of dental anxiety (Armfield et al., 2006; Ragnarsson, 1998; Schwarz & Birn, 1995).

Dental anxiety can vary depending on the type of dental procedure being performed. Invasive procedures such as extraction of teeth, drilling, periodontal therapy, and dental injections tend to invoke greater anxiety (Moore et al.,1993; Stabholz & Peretz, 1999). Dental anxiety can vary based on age group, gender, socio-economic status, and educational levels. Age is associated with increased dental anxiety, with anxiety increasing across age groups (Armfield et al., 2007) and middle-aged patients showing a higher prevalence of dental anxiety (Armfield et al., 2006).

Women tend to have higher anxiety levels when compared with men (Armfield et al., 2006; Moore et al., 1993). Low education and income levels are correlated with moderate levels of dental anxiety (Moore et al., 1993), with the highest prevalence of dental fear found among unemployed people (Armfield et al., 2006; Armfield et al., 2007). The behavior of the dentist toward the patient plays a major role in increased anxiety levels, especially when patients are faced with a dentist that displays hostile behavior such as condescension (Moore et al., 1993).

9.4.2 Dental Avoidance

Low income, lack of dental insurance, and lack of access to dental care are some of the major barriers that prevent patients from receiving the dental care that they require. However, even when these barriers are not a primary factor in accessing dental care, a significant proportion of the population avoids accessing dental services. Dental anxiety is considered to play a key role in contributing to this dental avoidance behavior (Armfield et al., 2007; Moore et al., 1993; Skaret et al., 2003).

The presence of pain may cause a patient to seek emergency dental treatment to alleviate the discomfort (Armfield et al., 2007). This motivation to stop pain may be the primary driver in the short term. However, once the pain and other symptoms such as swelling subside, the fear of sitting through multiple appointments of complex dental procedures can result in dental avoidance behavior. This behavior includes a delay in making dental appointments, missing appointments, canceling appointments without rescheduling, or avoiding some or all recommended dental treatments. Patients with high dental anxiety avoid visiting the dentist for several years (Moore et al., 1993; Schuller et al., 2003). These individuals have a significantly higher number of decayed and missing teeth and a significantly lower number of teeth that have been filled and are functional (Armfield et al., 2007; Schuller et al., 2003).

Only a small proportion (1.5–2%) of adult patients report fear of treatment as a reason for canceling or missing dental appointments (Shabbir et al., 2018). Studies with younger patients have shown that children with dental anxiety are more likely to have two or more missed appointments (Wogelius & Poulsen, 2005). The presence of general anxiety and dental fear among parents or caregivers may make it harder for parents to motivate, educate, and persuade their child to attend a dental appointment (Gustafsson et al., 2010). In particular, the dental anxiety of mothers is strongly correlated with dental anxiety in children (Wigen et al., 2009).

Moderate to high levels of dental anxiety lead to a pattern of behavior that can further exacerbate existing dental problems. If increased levels of dental anxiety lead to children or adults missing or canceling appointments, it may further deteriorate their existing dental condition and result in poor treatment outcomes. A poor treatment outcome can result in a further need for corrective measures to rectify the problem. For example, preventive measures such as frequent oral prophylaxis appointments and application of dental sealants where necessary can prevent the occurrence of gum problems or tooth decay, especially in children. A fear of dental treatment brought on by previous negative dental experiences such as pain may result in the patient avoiding the dental appointment to receive preventive measures. Since patient dental education is part of the treatment process in most dental clinics, the patient is therefore deprived of both the preventive dental treatment and the educational reinforcement required to maintain proper oral health status.

Missing or canceling appointments can prevent dentists and dental students from identifying pathology in the early stages. For example, early-stage dental caries (tooth decay) can be treated using conservative dental restoration techniques. These procedures normally result in very little pain and removal of dental tissues. In some cases, a dental anesthetic may not be required. However, patients with high anxiety are associated with an increased average time between visits (Armfield et al., 2007). Therefore, a problem that could have been rectified easily becomes a bigger issue between visits. If the dental decay extends deep into the tooth, then injecting a dental anesthetic and considerable drilling is required to remove decayed tooth tissue. If the decay extends to the pulp, then removal of the pulp and filling of the root canals will be required. All these procedures are expensive, more complex, and potentially more painful. Studies have shown that patients with most dental fear have significantly more missing teeth than patients with little or no fear (Armfield et al., 2007). Although it has been hypothesized that the fear of dental treatment can motivate patients to maintain good oral health status, studies have shown that this is not the case (Schuller et al., 2003).

9.5 Potential Data Sources

9.5.1 Dental Anxiety Assessments

Dental anxiety scales are questionnaires administered by the dentist before the dental procedure to ascertain relative levels of dental anxiety. The most well-known dental anxiety scale used in dental schools and clinics for adult patients is Corah's Dental Anxiety Scale (Corah, 1969). This short questionnaire is used to determine the patient's level of anxiety concerning different dental situations. Each of the four questions are scored from one (not anxious) to five (extremely anxious). Patients may have a total score that ranges from four to 20. A score of 13 or 14 is a good indicator of an anxious patient. A score above 15 indicates a high level of anxiety in the patient that requires further steps to mitigate (Corah et al., 1978). The original scale was later modified and certain essential factors contributing to increased fear among patients, such as dental injections, were added in an instrument named the Modified Dental Anxiety Scale (Humphris et al., 1995). The Modified Dental Anxiety Scale is one of the most administered dental anxiety scales (Dailey et al., 2001).

The Children's Fear Survey Schedule-Dental Subscale (CFSS-DS) questionnaire is a dental anxiety tool used to measure anxiety in child and adolescent patients (Aartman et al., 1998). Fifteen questions are scored from one (not afraid) to five (very afraid). A total score of 45 or higher represents high levels of anxiety.

Dental anxiety measures have demonstrated high validity and reliability across the years (Corah et al., 1978). However, they have found limited use in clinical routines mainly due to time constraints and certain questions that are asked in the survey. Studies have shown low adoption even among dentists with a special interest in managing dental anxiety (Dailey et al., 2001). A study of the adoption of dental anxiety scales in the United Kingdom showed only 20% of the dental practitioners used adult anxiety scales and only 17% used child dental anxiety scales (Dailey et al., 2001). The study also found low awareness among dentists about dental anxiety scales.

While dental anxiety may seem like a good predictor for missed appointments, there are several issues using self-reported dental anxiety measures alone as a measure to predict the tendency to miss or cancel appointments. Corah's Dental Anxiety Scale is a reliable and useful predictor of the levels of anxiety in the patient in a dental clinic. This anxiety has been tested and used in dental clinics worldwide for several decades (Corah et al., 1978; Ilgüy et al., 2005). However, studies have shown that there may not be a strong correlation between missed appointments and dental anxiety levels (Lin, 2009). Dental anxiety scale scores can be used to predict the anxiety levels which can be combined with other self-reported measures such as "feeling depressed or moody" or prior history of appointment avoidance due to fear. This can be a much more accurate tool for predicting missed appointments than anxiety levels alone (Lin, 2009).

9.5.2 Clinical Notes

Since it has been established that EDR features and appointment scheduling processes differ among dental schools, and that academic EDRs may differ in functionality from those in other dental clinics, it is reasonable to expect that dental students may not encounter a consistent format to enter clinical notes during their training. In this way, EDR systems reflect the challenges faced with entering valuable clinical data into EHRs (Strome & Liefer, 2013). Defined fields may exist but may be inconsistently used (Weir et al., 2003). If fields do not exist, capturing qualitative data in clinical notes—even in unstructured text form—remains valuable for predicting potential future missed appointments. Enhanced student EDR training regarding clinical documentation could emphasize where delineators or notes templates should be used in a consistent manner. This enhances data quality on the structured data in the EDR and improves the ability to use artificial intelligence techniques such as natural language processing (NLP) on unstructured data.

In an academic dental clinic, faculty concurrently oversee multiple students. This presents a unique opportunity for student-faculty communication and faculty-patient communication that may not be available in a conventional dental clinic or primary care setting. These encounters may be natural places to add data collection points to the clinical workflow and enhance the dental record with additional clinical observations that can be used as factors for risk modeling. For example, several students may report to a faculty member that they have seen an increase in the number of missed appointments for a specific reason. Students may not see this as a trend across a certain patient population, and they may not document the findings in clinical notes in a way that would reveal a pattern if researched. Faculty may identify the need to enter the occurrences into the EDR. Furthermore, if faculty regularly interact with multiple patients in the course of supervising many students, they serve as additional clinical resources that could detect predictors of future missed appointments and document accordingly.

9.5.3 Staff and Patient Reporting

As discussed by Goffman et al. (2017) and Lenzi et al. (2019), relevant information about the causes of missed appointments may already be intuitively or anecdotally known to dental patient support staff. Simple yet effective process improvement techniques can be used to collect more relevant and accurate data for the purpose of predicting missed appointments. For example, patients might interact with clinic staff to update contact information, complete a name change, add or remove family members to insurance coverage, and provide medical records from other providers. Any of these could indicate that a patient or caregiver may experience changes in the ability to keep appointments in the future. Additional data collection opportunities might make sense within a currently operational workflow or easily introduced into a workflow, depending on how such changes are usually documented across the clinic.

Composite reports based on patient satisfaction surveys or other quality measures may already be used for operational and financial purposes in the dental school. Even if these reports are maintained in a system outside the EDR, their raw data might be used as a source to compare outcomes of patients who successfully complete appointments compared with those who miss or reschedule appointments. Over time, patient satisfaction surveys might be enhanced with additional questions about the relative level of difficulty involved in keeping appointments, the top reasons patients give for needing to reschedule or cancel appointments, and the ease with which they remember or track future appointments.

Other methods to improve data collection include simple operational changes that focus on a few proven techniques for improving the process of appointment rescheduling, reminder management tools, and missed appointment reason tracking. An additional contact from dental school students or support staff may increase patient appointment compliance, although some methods are more effective than others, particularly when a long appointment lead time is a factor (Goffman et al., 2017).

If the dental school has already implemented a patient portal (such as PatientAccess by Exan), the capability may already exist for patients to contribute data to their dental records. For example, if patients can cancel or reschedule through a self-service tool, the system might provide a list of reason codes before the new appointment can be confirmed or the original appointment canceled. Identifying patients who tend to reschedule presents an opportunity to intervene before the appointment is missed altogether, while gathering data about the difficulties faced by patients to adhere to their dental treatment plans. Finally, if the patient portal includes features for messaging to providers or clinic staff, the text transmitted by the patient could be as valuable as the text found in clinical notes.

9.6 Conclusions

Examining causes of appointment avoidance behavior in the academic dental clinic is an opportunity to improve health outcomes while building on analytic successes in other healthcare settings. From a provider and operational perspective, there are important similarities between dental health clinics that serve a cross-section of the community and primary care clinics (Chariatte et al., 2008; Schmalzried & Liszak, 2012). From the patient perspective, the primary drivers of missed appointments for dental care may have the same root causes as missed appointments for other kinds of medical care.

Since EDR and EMR systems have yet to reach a practical level of interoperability, a complete patient profile across all sites of care remains difficult to maintain

(Burris, 2017). Ideally, the dental student would know causes of missed appointments or the risk of future missed appointments and develop intervention strategies to limit the negative impact to their own training and their patients' dental health outcomes. In practice, oral health providers often only see part of the full patient picture.

Even where information is limited due to missing or inconsistent data, dental schools can still leverage existing systems to collect likely factors to include in predictive modeling. Such analytic methods might combine known sociodemographic factors such as employment status, age, and caregiving status with common assessments used to measure dental avoidance. If a dental school is in the earliest phases of using an EDR to enhance data collection, perhaps the most practical way to begin is with a basic set of scenarios that illustrate a few likely variables that would lead to the increased risk of missed appointments. Then, it might consider the methods that work best for staff, students, and faculty to maintain consistently high data quality when capturing data that can be used to test these scenarios. Once processes are in place to reinforce the importance of including such data in the patient's dental record, other quantitative and qualitative data that can aid in predictive modeling may become more readily apparent.

References

Aartman, I. H., van Everdingen, T., Hoogstraten, J., & Schuurs, A. H. (1998). Self-report measurements of dental anxiety and fear in children: A critical assessment. *ASDC Journal of Dentistry for Children, 65*(4), 252–230.

Acharya, A., Cheng, B., Koralkar, R., Olson, B., Lamster, I. B., Kunzel, C., & Lalla, E. (2018). Screening for diabetes risk using integrated dental and medical electronic health record data. *JDR Clinical and Translational Research, 3*(2), 188–194. doi:10.1177/2380084418759496

Appukuttan, D. P. (2016). Strategies to manage patients with dental anxiety and dental phobia: Literature review. *Clinical, Cosmetic and Investigational Dentistry, 8,* 35–50. doi:10.2147/CCIDE.S63626

Armfield, J. M., Spencer, A. J., & Stewart, J. F. (2006). Dental fear in Australia: Who's afraid of the dentist? *Australian Dental Journal, 51*(1), 78–85. doi:10.1111/j.1834-7819.2006. tb00405.x

Armfield, J. M., Stewart, J. F., & Spencer, A. J. (2007). The vicious cycle of dental fear: Exploring the interplay between oral health, service utilization and dental fear. *BMC Oral Health, 7,* 1. doi:10.1186/1472-6831-7-1

Beckwith, F. R., Ackerman, R. J., Cobb, C. M., & Tira, D. E. (1999). An evaluation of factors affecting duration of orthodontic treatment. *American Journal of Orthodontics and Dentofacial Orthopedics: Official Publication of the American Association of Orthodontists, its Constituent Societies, and the American Board of Orthodontics, 115*(4), 439–447. doi:10.1016/s0889-5406(99)70265-9

Burris, C. (2017). Connecting oral and physical health via the health information exchange. *North Carolina Medical Journal, 78*(6), 410–412. doi:10.18043/ncm.78.6.410

Chariatte, V., Berchtold, A., Akré, C., Michaud, P., & Suris, J. (2008). Missed appointments in an outpatient clinic for adolescents, an approach to predict the risk of missing. *The Journal of Adolescent Health: Official Publication of the Society for Adolescent Medicine, 43*(1), 38–45. doi:10.1016/j.jadohealth.2007.12.017

Chuang, S. K., Tian, L., Wei, L. J., & Dodson, T. B. (2002). Predicting dental implant survival by use of the marginal approach of the semi-parametric survival methods for clustered observations. *Journal of Dental Research, 81*(12), 851–855. doi:10.1177/154405910208101211

Corah, N. L. (1969). Development of a dental anxiety scale. *Journal of Dental Research, 48*(4), 596. doi:10.1177/00220345690480041801

Corah, N. L., Gale, E. N., & Illig, S. J. (1978). Assessment of a dental anxiety scale. *Journal of the American Dental Association (1939), 97*(5), 816–819. doi:10.14219/jada. archive.1978.0394

Dailey, Y. M., Humphris, G. M., & Lennon, M. A. (2001). The use of dental anxiety questionnaires: A survey of a group of UK dental practitioners. *British Dental Journal, 190*(8), 450–453. doi:10.1038/sj.bdj.4801000

George, A. C., Hoshing, A., & Joshi, N. V. (2007). A study of the reasons for irregular dental attendance in a private dental college in a rural setup. *Indian Journal of Dental Research: Official Publication of Indian Society for Dental Research, 18*(2), 78–81. doi:10.4103/0970-9290.32425

Goffman, R. M., Harris, S. L., May, J. H., Milicevic, A. S., Monte, R. J., Myaskovsky, L., ... Vargas, D. L. (2017). Modeling patient no-show history and predicting future outpatient appointment behavior in the Veterans health administration. *Military Medicine, 182*(5). doi:10.7205/milmed-d-16-00345

Gustafsson, A., Broberg, A. G., Bodin, L., Berggren, U., & Arnrup, K. (2010). Possible predictors of discontinuation of specialized dental treatment among children and adolescents with dental behaviour management problems. *European Journal of Oral Sciences, 118*(3), 270–277. doi:10.1111/j.1600-0722.2010.00734.x

Guzek, L. M., Gentry, S. D., & Golomb, M. R. (2015). The estimated cost of "no-shows" in an academic pediatric neurology clinic. *Pediatric Neurology, 52*(2), 198–201. doi:10.1016/j.pediatrneurol.2014.10.020

Holmes, D. C., Trombly, R. M., Garcia, L. T., Kluender, R. L., & Keith, C. R. (2000). Student productivity in a comprehensive care program without numeric requirements. *Journal of Dental Education, 64*(11), 745–754. Retrieved from http://www.jdentaled.org/content/64/11/745.abstract

Holtshousen, W. S. J., & Coetzee, E. (2012). The effect of overbooking on idle dental chair capacity in the pretoria region of the gauteng oral health services. *SADJ: Journal of the South African Dental Association = Tydskrif Van Die Suid-Afrikaanse Tandheelkundige Vereniging, 67*(8), 460–464.

Humphris, G. M., Morrison, T., & Lindsay, S. J. (1995). The modified dental anxiety scale: Validation and United Kingdom norms. *Community Dental Health, 12*(3), 143–150.

Ilgüy, D., Ilgüy, M., Dinçer, S., & Bayirli, G. (2005). Reliability and validity of the modified dental anxiety scale in Turkish patients. *The Journal of International Medical Research, 33*(2), 252–259. doi:10.1177/147323000503300214

Lenzi, H., Ben, Â J., & Stein, A. T. (2019). Development and validation of a patient no-show predictive model at a primary care setting in southern Brazil. *PLoS ONE, 14*(4). doi:10.1371/journal.pone.0214869

Lin, K. C. (2009). Behavior-associated self-report items in patient charts as predictors of dental appointment avoidance. *Journal of Dental Education, 73*(2), 218–224.

Moore, R., Birn, H., Kirkegaard, E., Brødsgaard, I., & Scheutz, F. (1993). Prevalence and characteristics of dental anxiety in Danish adults. *Community Dentistry and Oral Epidemiology, 21*(5), 292–296. doi:10.1111/j.1600-0528.1993.tb00777.x

Moresca, R. (2018). Orthodontic treatment time: Can it be shortened? *Dental Press Journal of Orthodontics, 23*(6), 90–105. doi:10.1590/2177-6709.23.6.090-105.sar

Ragnarsson, E. (1998). Dental fear and anxiety in an adult Icelandic population. *Acta Odontologica Scandinavica, 56*(2), 100–104. doi:10.1080/00016359850136067

Ramoni, R. B., Etolue, J., Tokede, O., McClellan, L., Simmons, K., Yansane, A., … Kalenderian, E. (2017). Adoption of dental innovations: The case of a standardized dental diagnostic terminology. *Journal of the American Dental Association (1939), 148*(5), 319–327. doi:10.1016/j.adaj.2017.01.024

Sachdeo, A., Konfino, S., Icyda, R. U., Finkelman, M. D., Gulati, H., Arsenault, P., & Hanley, J. B. (2012). An analysis of patient grievances in a dental school clinical environment. *Journal of Dental Education, 76*(10), 1317–1322.

Safi, Y., Khami, M. R., Razeghi, S., Shamloo, N., Soroush, M., Akhgari, E., & Moscowchi, A. (2015). Designing and implementation of a course on successful dental practice for dentists. *Journal of Dentistry (Tehran, Iran), 12*(6), 447–455. Retrieved from https://www.ncbi.nlm.nih.gov/pmc/articles/PMC4754571/

Schwarz, E., & Birn, H. (1995). Dental anxiety in Danish and Chinese adults--a cross-cultural perspective. *Social Science & Medicine (1982), 41*(1), 123–130. doi:10.1016/0277-9536(94)00288-5

Schleyer, T. K. L. (2004). Should dentistry be part of the national health information infrastructure? *Journal of the American Dental Association (1939), 135*(12), 1687–1695. doi:10.14219/jada.archive.2004.0120

Schleyer, T. K., Thyvalikakath, T. P., Spallek, H., Dziabiak, M. P., & Johnson, L. A. (2012). From information technology to informatics: The information revolution in dental education. *Journal of Dental Education, 76*(1), 142–153.

Schmalzried, H. D., & Liszak, J. (2012). A model program to reduce patient failure to keep scheduled medical appointments. *Journal of Community Health, 37*(3), 715–718. doi:10.1007/s10900-011-9505-0

Schuller, A. A., Willumsen, T., & Holst, D. (2003). Are there differences in oral health and oral health behavior between individuals with high and low dental fear? *Community Dentistry and Oral Epidemiology, 31*(2), 116–121. doi:10.1034/j.1600-0528.2003.00026.x

Shabbir, A., Alzahrani, M., & Abu Khalid, A. (2018). Why do patients miss dental appointments in eastern province military hospitals, kingdom of Saudi Arabia? *Cureus, 10*(3), e2355. doi:10.7759/cureus.2355

Shimpi, N., Ye, Z., Koralkar, R., Glurich, I., & Acharya, A. (2018). Need for a diagnostic centric care in dentistry: A case study from Marshfield clinic health system. *Journal of the American Dental Association (1939), 149*(2), 122–131. doi:10.1016/j.adaj.2017.09.030

Smith, T. A., & Heaton, L. J. (2003). Fear of dental care: Are we making any progress? *Journal of the American Dental Association (1939), 134*(8), 1101–1108. doi:10.14219/jada.archive.2003.0326

Skaret, E., Raadal, M., Kvale, G., & Berg, E. (2003). Gender-based differences in factors related to non-utilization of dental care in young Norwegians: A longitudinal study. *European Journal of Oral Sciences, 111*(5), 377–382. doi:10.1034/j.1600-0722.2003.00072.x

Stabholz, A., & Peretz, B. (1999). Dental anxiety among patients prior to different dental treatments. *International Dental Journal, 49*(2), 90–94. doi:10.1111/j.1875-595x.1999.tb00514.x

Stewart, B. A., Fernandes, S., Rodriguez-Huertas, E., & Landzberg, M. (2010). A preliminary look at duplicate testing associated with lack of electronic health record interoperability for transferred patients. *Journal of the American Medical Informatics Association: JAMIA, 17*(3), 341–344. doi:10.1136/jamia.2009.001750

Strome, T. L., & Liefer, A. (2013). *Healthcare analytics for quality and performance improvement.* Wiley: Hoboken, NJ.

Teich, S. T., Wan, Z., & Faddoul, F. F. (2012). Relationship between broken appointments and dental students' clinical experience level. *Journal of Dental Education, 76*(9), 1167–1174.

Thyvalikakath, T. P., Padman, R., Vyawahare, K., Darade, P., & Paranjape, R. (2015). Utilizing dental electronic health records data to predict risk for periodontal disease. *Studies in Health Technology and Informatics, 216*, 1081.

Trenouth, M. J. (2003). Do failed appointments lead to discontinuation of orthodontic treatment? *The Angle Orthodontist, 73*(1), 51–55. doi:10.1043/0003-3219(2003)073<0051:DFALTD>2.0.CO;2

Walji, M. F., Kalenderian, E., Stark, P. C., White, J. M., Kookal, K. K., Phan, D., ... Ramoni, R. (2014). BigMouth: A multi-institutional dental data repository. *Journal of the American Medical Informatics Association: JAMIA, 21*(6), 1136–1140. doi:10.1136/amiajnl-2013-002230

Weir, C. R., Hurdle, J. F., Felgar, M. A., Hoffman, J. M., Roth, B., & Nebeker, J. R. (2003). Direct text entry in electronic progress notes: An evaluation of input errors. *Methods of Information in Medicine, 42*(1), 61–67.

Wigen, T. I., Skaret, E., & Wang, N. J. (2009). Dental avoidance behaviour in parent and child as risk indicators for caries in 5-year-old children. *International Journal of Paediatric Dentistry, 19*(6), 431–437. doi:10.1111/j.1365-263X.2009.01014.x

Wogelius, P., & Poulsen, S. (2005). Associations between dental anxiety, dental treatment due to toothache, and missed dental appointments among six to eight-year-old Danish children: A cross-sectional study. *Acta Odontologica Scandinavica, 63*(3), 179–182. doi:10.1080/00016350510019829

Chapter 10

Machine Learning in Cognitive Neuroimaging

Siamak Aram, Denis Kornev, Ye Han,
Mina Ekramnia, Roozbeh Sadeghian,
Saeed Esmaili Sardari, Hadis Dashtestani,
Sagar Kora Venu, and Amir Gandjbakhche

Contents

10.1 Introduction 168
    10.1.1 Overview of AI, Machine Learning, and Deep Learning in
         Neuroimaging..168
    10.1.2 Cognitive Neuroimaging...170
    10.1.3 Functional Near-Infrared Spectroscopy..................................171
10.2 Machine Learning and Cognitive Neuroimaging 172
    10.2.1 Challenges...173
10.3 Identifying Functional Biomarkers in Traumatic Brain Injury
    Patients Using fNIRS and Machine Learning 173
10.4 Finding the Correlation between Addiction Behavior in Gaming and
    Brain Activation Using fNIRS 174
10.5 Current Research on Machine Learning Applications in
    Neuroimaging 176
10.6 Summary...178
References 179

10.1 Introduction

In this chapter, we will review how neuroimaging models have used predictive models to ask new questions and uncover brand new aspects of organization in cognition. This chapter will provide an overview of current, up-to-date information on how these approaches can be used for brain disorders. This includes two different brain applications:

- Identifying functional biomarkers in the human prefrontal cortex for individuals with traumatic brain injuries using functional near-infrared spectroscopy
- Finding the correlation between addiction behavior in gaming and brain activation using functional near-infrared spectroscopy

Neuroimaging applications using machine learning in regard to identifying biomarkers that are functional within the prefrontal cortex of individuals with game addiction and traumatic brain injuries are discussed and presented. We will discuss the usage of various tasks, such as Iowa gambling and moral judgment, as well as working memory with the usage of functional near-infrared spectroscopy.

10.1.1 Overview of AI, Machine Learning, and Deep Learning in Neuroimaging

Artificial intelligence (AI) is the science of making intelligent computer programs to complete tasks such as pattern recognition and learning from experience (McCarthy, 2017). Machine learning and deep learning, both branches of artificial intelligence, have been used in brain image analysis for classification, diagnosis, and detection of abnormalities. In addition, deep learning has shown potential in helping with image acquisition and enhancement (Zhu et al., 2019). Machine learning is a group of algorithms where the computer program can learn from provided data and perform tasks without an explicit set of rules (Mazurowski et al., 2018). It has shown its crucial values in diagnosing, treating, and predicting outcomes and complications in neurological diseases such as strokes, epilepsy, and psychiatric disorders (Kamal et al., 2018). Classical machine learning includes decision trees, naive Bayes, support vector machine (SVM), nearest neighbor, logistic regression, random forest, and neural networks (Jiang et al., 2017). One of the most widely used classic machine learning models used in medical imaging is the SVM, which generally consists of supervised-based algorithms used for classification. SVMs map the input data vectors to "a high dimensional feature space" and try to set the best possible boundary ("hyperplane") between classes by optimizing the space between the boundary and data points on each side ("margin"), so as to optimize the prediction of classes of new data (Cortes & Vapnik, 1995). SVMs have been applied to neuroimaging data to classify groups of patients based on their neuroimage patterns to detect lesions or diseases. Rehme et al. (2015) applied multivariate

SVMs to resting-state functional magnetic resonance imaging (fMRI) data to classify patients with a disability versus without a disability and to find biomarkers of the impairment. SVM was also used to identify patients with Parkinson's disease by using diffusion tensor imaging (DTI) data in a combination with tract-based spatial statistics preprocessing, which achieved a 97% accuracy on the individual level (Haller et al., 2019). Other classic machine learning methods such as random forest and naive Bayes classification have also been used to classify schizophrenia patients and identify stroke lesions (Rehme et al., 2015; Griffis et al., 2016).

Deep learning, a branch of machine learning, has gained pre-eminence over the classic machine learning framework in recent years (Zhu et al., 2019). As a special type of artificial neural network (ANN), it depends on networks of simple units that form multiple layers to generate high level representations of increasing input (Mazurowski et al., 2018). Compared with the classic machine learning framework, deep learning, or deep neural networks (DNNs), can combine feature selection and classification into an integrated and trainable process. Therefore, DNNs do not require manual feature selection, which is sometimes arbitrary (Mazurowski et al., 2018). However, they need a large amount of training data to be able to optimize feature selection (Chow, 2018; Mazurowski et al., 2018). One of the most common types of DNNs is convolutional neural networks (CNNs), which are widely used in visual recognition. What distinguishes CNN from others are the convolutional layers, where a filter matrix with weights convolved through the input data applies algebraic calculations with each data point and returns an output matrix. This step transforms the image and detects patterns. Each layer passes the output to the next layer for another filter to detect another pattern. CNN architecture also includes pooling layers and fully connected layers ("convolutional neural networks"). Different from a regular neural network, CNN is deeper with typically 10–30 layers, but it can exceed 1,000 layers (Mazurowski et al., 2018).

In addition to interpretation and analysis of neuroimaging data, deep learning has also gained momentum in the production and acquisition of neuroimaging. Magnetic resonance imaging (MRI) and computed tomography (CT) images of diagnostic quality can be extracted from lower-quality images generated with lower parameters using CNNs (Chen et al., 2017; Kang et al., 2017; Schlemper et al., 2017). This can help reduce health risks associated with neuroimaging like the side effects of contrast agents and ionizing radiation exposure (Zhu et al., 2019).

Deep learning based reconstruction approaches can also enhance image data and generate quality images from under-sampled MRI data acquired with shorter periods of sampling times, potentially saving the time and cost involved with taking MRIs (Zhu et al., 2019).

Also, deep learning has been used to incorporate images of different modalities. As an example, a fully convolutional network (FCN) has been leveraged to create CT images using MRIs (Nie et al., 2016); CNNs have also been used to predict positron emission tomographic (PET) patterns from MRIs to help Alzheimer's disease diagnosis (Li et al., 2014). The ability to produce images of the desired modality from existing data without performing actual scans can help avoid radiation (Zhu et al., 2019).

10.1.2 Cognitive Neuroimaging

Cognitive neuroimaging is the science that studies the relationship between human brain activity and other perspectives of the nervous system with cognitive processes and behavior. It uses common approaches and methods of visualization of the structure, function, and biochemical characteristics of the brain. As a study about the human brain, cognitive neuroimaging is the co-discipline of neurology, neurosurgery, and psychiatry on one hand, and as a branch of both neuroscience and psychology intersecting with cognitive psychology and neuropsychology on the other. Since ancient times, people have tried to penetrate into the depths of consciousness, and Hippocrates was one of the first thinkers who claimed that thinking was carried out in the brain (O'Shea, 2013). The modern history of neuroimaging began in the 19th century from a hypothesis Italian neuroscientist Angelo Mosso had that "an attentional or cognitive task can locally increase cerebral blood flow" (Sandrone et al., 2013). Based on this theory, Mosso developed the "Mosso method" (Mosso, 1881) and "human circulation balance" (Mosso, 1882).

Nowadays, in the realm of cognitive neuroimaging, different studies about various forms of cognitive disorders have been provided and the methods of structural and functional neuroimaging are an essential part of these studies (Odinak et al., 2012). These methods are functional near-infrared spectroscopy (fNIRS), fMRI, electroencephalogram (EEG), PET, and magnetoencephalography (MEG), which could be used by researchers for the investigation of the hemodynamic response patterns in a cognitive disorder characterized by memory impairment (Li et al., 2018), vascular dementia diagnosis (Van Straaten, Scheltens, & Barkhof, 2004; O'Brien, 2007), evaluating, classifying, and following some of the cognitive disorders (De Medeiros Kanda et al., 2009), as a marker of the early stage of Alzheimer's disease (Alexander et al., 2002), and as a method for measuring neuronal events in a direct and non-invasive way (Uhlhaas et al., 2017) respectively.

At the same time, affordability and ability empirically predict the result allowing cognitive scientists to use neuroimaging methods to build test models for experiments in spoken word production and research into episodic memory (De Zubicaray, 2006). Based on the current stage of cognitive neuroimaging development, researchers have discussed the present and future perspectives of brain imaging (Dolan, 2008). Now they have the opportunity to address unbelievable challenges in human brain study, scientists can operate, monitor, and predict performance in the human brain without direct impact. They can set questions and provide responses about the reaction of brain regions for external manipulations in terms of correlation with different disorders, such as addictive behavior in gaming using fNIRS, which is one of the reviewed projects in this chapter.

10.1.3 Functional Near-Infrared Spectroscopy

fNIRS is an emerging technology in neuroimaging (see Figure 10.1). Since the first studies in 1993 (Quaresima & Ferrari, 2019), brain activation studies using this technology have been conducted on the sensory systems of vision, hearing, language, motor abilities, and cognition (Bunce et al., 2006). Moreover, fNIRS has had applications in the fields of psychology, education, social sciences, medicine, and beyond (Quaresima & Ferrari, 2019).

fNIRS is portable, non-invasive, safe, relatively inexpensive, nd it can be wireless, enabling it to approximate real-world settings in studies (Bunce et al., 2006). fNIRS is made possible by the following principles:

> *Neurovascular coupling.* Glucose metabolism provides the oxygen needed in brain activity. Consumption of glucose and oxygen triggers the brain to increase cerebral blood volume (CBV), local cerebral blood flow (CBF), and a mechanism recognized as neurovascular coupling—in other words, the synchronization of neural activity and blood flow. The increased blood flow in the activated area often brings more oxygen than needed through oxygenated

Figure 10.1 The fNIRS device was used to find the correlation between addiction behavior in gaming and brain activation.

hemoglobin (oxy-Hb); therefore, causing the oxy-Hb concentration to go up and the deoxygenated hemoglobin (deoxy-Hb) concentration to go down. This change leads to the magnetic electric fields of the area to change (Bunce et al., 2006).

Changing the optical properties of functioning tissues. Other than magnetic fields, the oxygen level of the active area also changes the optical properties. Tissues, where the photons pass by, are going to either scatter or absorb the particles. Water, the main component of most tissues, does not absorb much energy in 700–900 nm light, but oxy-Hb and deoxy-Hb do, so this wavelength range is called the "optical window" for assessing brain activity. In addition, oxy-Hb and deoxy-Hb have different absorption rates; therefore, their concentrations can be computed by measuring the photons left. A fair number of photons travel through a banana-shaped path to the skin and can be detected using a photon detector device at the skull (Bunce et al., 2006). A big advantage of fNIRS compared with other neuroimaging modalities is its high experimental flexibility (Quaresima & Ferrari, 2019). fNIRS generates little noise, so it doesn't interfere with certain sensitive protocols—patients don't have to lie down or be confined in a small space—its results are not affected by patients moving (Bunce et al., 2006), and it allows for continuous measurements for a longer period of time (Quaresima & Ferrari, 2019). With fewer constraints, it can be used outdoors with mobile or wireless devices (Quaresima & Ferrari, 2019), making it possible to approximate real-world settings. This advantage makes the data collection for this study on brain activation during gaming possible, as it requires the subjects to be monitored while playing games. However, it also has some disadvantages. First, current fNIRS systems have a much lower spatial resolution than fMRI (Bunce et al., 2006). Second, fNIRS systems are generally restricted to the outer 2–4 mm of the cortex and don't have the ability to image the entire brain (Bunce et al., 2006). Third, fNIRS doesn't provide anatomical information (Quaresima & Ferrari, 2019).

10.2 Machine Learning and Cognitive Neuroimaging

Cognitive neuroimaging probes the nervous system underlying human cognition. The brain images are complex and noisy data. Many data sets, populations, and scanners integrate together to form an image of brain activity. Using these rich data sets and building complex models are interesting parts of machine learning algorithms. Some questions are as follows: In what specific way can they help us in understanding the brain? What are the potential future challenges and directions? As in the mid-1990s, the revolution in statistical parametric mapping and voxel-based analysis methods (Friston 1994) enabled neuroscientists to get detailed spatial maps of brain structures and functions. The early 2000s bridged the use of machine learning approaches in neuroimaging studies, which enabled the development of single-cell analysis and provided good generalization using SVM and kernel mapping to get learned models to new data. Random forest methods were another cornerstone of this field, mainly due to their high signal to noise ratio and generalization properties (Davatzikos, 2019).

In neuroimaging, it is relatively easier to accumulate resting-state acquisition compared with a controlled cognitive state of the subject, similar to the accumulation of unlabeled data in machine learning. That is why unsupervised learning on resting-state scans holds the credit to extract intrinsic brain structures (Varoquaux and Thirion 2014). Resting-state signals demonstrate ongoing brain activity which shares common substrates with controlled cognitive functions and evoked responses (Sadaghiani et al., 2010). Finally, deep learning architectures build highly nonlinear boundaries and benefit the depth and breadth in model building, as well as providing some good examples of machine learning in neuroimaging (Kamnitsas et al., 2018).

10.2.1 Challenges

As the applications of machine learning methods are rising, so are the new challenges. Some of the aspects of machine learning are needed to be kept in mind in order to reliably apply them in neuroscience (Davatzikos, 2019). In the era of big data, deep learning models fit the data outstandingly well. However, generalization seems to still be an issue to ponder on. It is called "overfitting." Proper split-sample, cross-validation, and replication to new samples would be helpful to evaluate the accuracy of our model. One of the major studies of classical machine learning applications in clinical neuroscience is to classify patients vs. control/healthy participants. Although this is a great starting point, a more significant value would come from detecting subtle changes in the early stages before the disease is clinically detectable. This is a much tougher problem. The other challenge would be the heterogeneity of the patterns and sources. Data acquired from different sites and channels increase the problem of overfitting and generalization. This problem can be treated by appropriate statistical harmonization methods which are consequently in a growing field (Fortin et al., 2018).

10.3 Identifying Functional Biomarkers in Traumatic Brain Injury Patients Using fNIRS and Machine Learning

There are a few studies that have applied fNIRS for evaluating the dynamic of blood volume and cerebral oxygenation in patients after traumatic brain injuries (TBI) (Bhambhani et al., 2006, Hibino et al., 2013, Merzagora et al., 2014 & Merzagora et al., 2011). In Karamzadeh et al. (2016), they examined the potential prefrontal hemodynamic biomarkers identifying participants with TBI, applying multivariate machine learning methods. They also introduced a task-related hemodynamic response detection with an exhaustive quest for optimum sets of hemodynamic features. Data from a group of 31 healthy controls and 30 chronic TBI participants was recorded while the participants were performing the complexity task. In order to characterize the difference between brain activity of control and TBI subjects, 11 features were extracted from subjects' hemodynamic responses of their brains. A machine learning classification algorithm was implemented to rank all the possible features combinations, based on their classification accuracies. A spatiotemporal classification was also performed to identify regions within the prefrontal cortex (PFC) that plays a role in classification between TBI and healthy subjects. As expected, brain activity of typical participants showed significantly higher activation in Brodmann areas (BA) when comparing brain activity with subjects with TBI. Overall, the results indicated that identified hemodynamic features from hemodynamic activity of the PFC are suitable biomarkers in recognizing subjects with TBI from control (see Figure 10.2).

10.4 Finding the Correlation between Addiction Behavior in Gaming and Brain Activation Using fNIRS

Video games' association with neuropsychiatric and psychological disorders is one of the important and problematic characteristics of modern society and culture. Since establishing the first computer game, "Tennis for Two," which most people consider as the real first game, by William Higginbotham in 1958 (Overmars, 2012), the gamer audience has risen significantly. In accordance with the Entertainment Software Association (ESA), 65% of Americans adults (over 164 million) play video games and the main reasons for this have been said to be mental stimulation, relaxation, and stress relief (ESA, 2019). At the same time, the American Medical Association (AMA) added "video game addiction" to the Diagnostic and Statistical Manual of Mental Disorders in 2007 and formally included it in the new revision (DSM-5) in 2013 (APA, 2018). Following the AMA, the World Health Organization (WHO) recognized gaming addiction as a mental disorder, and gaming addiction has been added to the 11th edition of the International Classification of Disorders (ICD-11) in May 2018 (WHO, 2018).

Several studies were provided to estimate the number of populations that could be qualified as a game addicted (Ferguson, Coulson, & Barnett, 2011; Przybylski, Weinstein, & Murayama, 2017). The researchers determined that 0.3–1.0% of the general population was the range from passionate engagement to pathology. The modern tools and approaches of analysis allow us to identify and predict the possibility of brain disorders and provide recommendations to healthcare practitioners

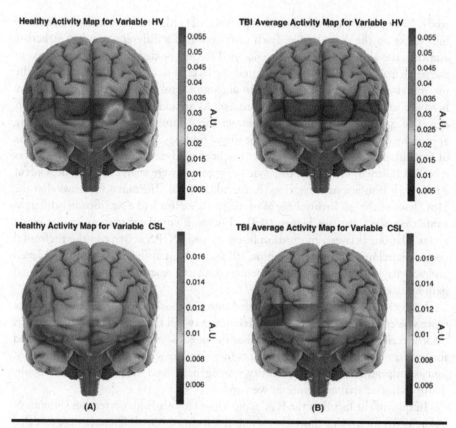

Figure 10.2 **The average activity maps for the left slope of the activity curve (CSL) and variance of the HbO signal (HV) features for the healthy (A) and TBI (B) subjects are illustrated.**

and scientists. This research study concentrates on data acquired by fNIRS and the Iowa gambling task (IGT) (Aram et al., 2019) to study how prefrontal cortex brain activation and gaming addiction are interrelated, i.e., the goal of this research is to show the interrelation of activity in the human prefrontal cortex with individual ability to make decisions and how hemodynamic changes react to gaming tasks. Thirty participants were involved in the experiment. They performed the IGT test while connected to the fNIRS instrument for measuring activity in their brains. The task for detecting patients with damage to the ventromedial sector of prefrontal cortices was developed by Bechara et al. (1994). This method simulated the real-life decision-making process and allowed identifying the elusive deviation of patients with different disorders in the laboratory environment. In recent studies, the IGT was used for investigations into whether brain activity increased during a video game (Dong et al., 2017), examining internet addiction and internet gaming disorder (Lin et al., 2019), and others. The same approach was executed in this study. Each participant was offered the choice of cards one by one from one of the four decks on the digital table. Each card deck had a different gain-loss structure and thus the ability to lose or win money. During the decision-making process in the participant's brain, fNIRS measured the level of oxyhemoglobin (HbO) of the prefrontal cortex and eventually brain activation and characteristics of addictive behavior in the video game playing process. As an additional task, the same strategy as in Section 10.3 was used to extract the features using a machine learning approach and the results confirmed the initial findings. Acquired data in the results of experiments with IGT and fNIRS has been analyzed using repeated measures ANOVA (Girden, 1992), and post-hoc comparisons were analyzed using dependent *t*-tests with Bonferroni correction (Bonferroni, 1936). The outcome shows that the HbO level of the left hemisphere of participants' brains had a significantly different value than the right (see Figure 10.3). This result correlates with an earlier study about relations between motivation intensity and fNIRS activity in the prefrontal cortex (Fairclough, Burns, & Kreplin, 2018), and depicts the relation of HbO levels and activity in the brain during a memory task as a reaction on probable financial gain or loss.

In the IGT test, the task was divided into five blocks of 20 trails each, and the score was calculated based on the difference between the number of advantageous deck selections with the number of disadvantageous selections. Data was screened for errors, missing data (none), outliers (none found with Mahalanobis distance), and assumptions. Normality, linearity, homogeneity, and Mauchly's test (Mauchly, 1940) indicated that assumptions were met.

In spite of the fact that the IGT score using Huynh-Feldt correction (Huynh & Feldt, 1976) for p-value showed different results, no group differences were revealed by post-hoc comparisons analyzed using dependent pairwise *t*-tests with Bonferroni correction. Based on achieved results, the conclusion could be made that the elements of a deep learning approach used in this study allow us to judge their effectiveness in identifying the correlation between addiction behavior in gaming and brain activity. The results of these experiments do not contradict the previously conducted experiments (Fairclough, Burns, & Kreplin, 2018; Lin et al., 2019) in the field of psychology and can be used as a basis for further research.

10.5 Current Research on Machine Learning Applications in Neuroimaging

In this section, we will review some of the recent studies on machine learning applications in neuroimaging. Rajus et al. (2019) has proposed the application of machine learning and fNIRS for identifying the potential biomarkers of pain in humans (Rajus et al., 2019). Machine learning is helping to create a mapping of features as the signatures of different types of pain in clinical and experimental data.

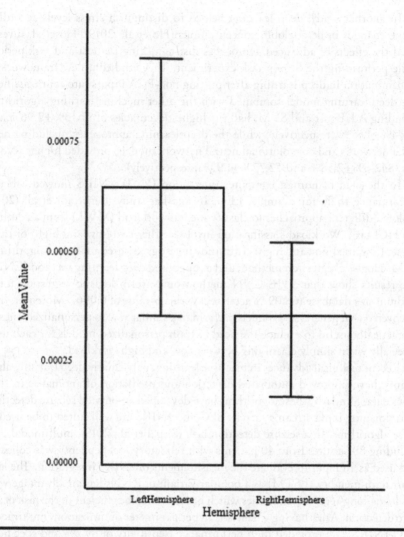

Figure 10.3 **Mean oxygenated hemoglobin with 95% confidence intervals for left and right hemispheres of the prefrontal cortex of the brain.**

Clinical measurements of pain collected from 18 subjects, based on the temperature and intensity levels of quantitative sensory testing (QST) protocol was shown. A total of 69 features were extracted from time, frequency, and wavelet domain. Three learning algorithms including SVM, linear discriminant analysis (LDA), and K-nearest neighbor (K-NN) were used to evaluate the significance of each feature independently. Based on the results, most of the features are not linearly separable and a Gaussian kernel provided the highest accuracy (94.17%) by using only 25 features to identify the four types of pain in the database.

In another study, deep learning helped to distinguish stress levels according to the changes in hemoglobin concentrations (Ho et al., 2019). Ho et al. investigated the effects of advanced approaches distinguishing the rest and task periods while performing the Stroop task experiment. They studied a new framework of discrimination in deep learning after putting non-PCA inputs into four classifiers. The deep learning model combined with the other machine learning algorithms, including AdaBoost and SVM, had the highest accuracies of 71.13%±2.96% and 64.74%±1.57%, respectively, while the deep learning approaches, including deep belief networks and convolutional neural network models, provided higher accuracies (84.26%±2.58% and 72.77%±1.92%, respectively).

In the field of human computer interaction (HCI), fNIRS showed a better performance than, for example, EEG. In another study, Benerradi et al. (2019) explored different approaches to classify mental workload (MWL) from a continuous HCI task. Workload classification involves either two (low and high) or three classes (low, medium, and high). This study investigates three analytical algorithms: SVM, a logistic regression method, and a supervised deep learning method (CNN). The results show that THE CNN method outperform logistic regression for A medium size database (68.09 % accuracy) with a p-value of 0.0967. Moreover, they discovered that generalized models perform in a similar way to personalized ones. It is practically useful to exclude the need to train personalized models for each user, especially when simply classifying between low and high workload.

Recent technical advances in machine learning, particularly deep learning algorithms, have improved automated detection and prediction of anomalies in time series data. Similarly, these algorithms have developed automated seizure detection; neuroimaging input streams such as EEG and fNIRS are well suited to be used in these algorithms. In a seizure detection task (Sirpal et al., 2019), multimodal data including 89 seizures from 40 patients with refractory focal epilepsy was collected and used as an input to evaluate the measurements of fNIRS integration. The long short-term memory (LSTM) as a popular variant of RNNs has an advantage with modeling long-term dependencies which has proven to be efficient in the task of seizure detection. After having a heuristic hyper parameter optimization, multimodal EEG-fNIRS data provided high performance (sensitivity of 89.7% and specificity of 95.5%) with a low generalization error of 11.8% and false detection rates (4.5% for EEG and multimodal data).

10.6 Summary

In recent years, AI, machine learning, and deep learning have become increasingly popular as methodologies not only for analyzing research results in cognitive neuroscience and brain research but also for confirming diagnoses and supporting the treatment of diseases. In turn, these methods, as based on mathematical algorithms and problems, need reliable tools and approaches for collecting and structuring the information obtained as a result of experiments. Some of these tools are fNIRS and the IGT, widely used in recent research (Fairclough, Burns, & Kreplin, 2018; Benerradi et al., 2019; Lin et al., 2019) and as a powerful tool for the current study. In this chapter, reviews of two applications using modern machine learning approaches to the analysis of data obtained with fNIRS were provided. The first was to identify functional biomarkers in the human prefrontal cortex for individuals with TBI. As discussed, during the analysis of several studies, it has been found that machine learning algorithms can be applied and successfully contribute to the scoring and analysis of possible combinations performed as a result of research. The second review looked for a correlation between addictive behavior in games and brain activation. Along with the already used fNIRS, IGT was used as a simulation of the video game process, ordinarily used to detect activity in the brain during the decision-making process (Aram et al., 2019). As in the previous application, machine learning analytical methods, such as ANOVA (Girden, 1992) in combination with Bonferroni correction (Bonferroni, 1936), Mauchly's test (Mauchly, 1940), and others, were applied to analyze and calculate deviations and corrections in the data obtained in the results of the experiment. These methods also demonstrated their effectiveness. Thus, the task set in this study, showing the effectiveness of elements of machine learning in cognitive neuroimaging, can be called fulfilled and demonstrates the effectiveness of solving the problems facing modern scientists, experimenters, and researchers.

References

Alexander, G.F., Chen, K., Pietrini, P., Rapoport, S.I., & Reiman, E.M. (2002). Longitudinal PET evaluation of cerebral metabolic decline in dementia: a potential outcome measure in Alzheimer's disease treatment studies. *The American Journal of Psychiatry, 159*(5), 738–745.

American Medical Association (2007). *AMA takes action on video games.* Retrieved October 15, 2018, https://www.ama-assn.org/sites/default/files/media-browser/public/about-ama/councils/Council%20Reports/council-on-science-public-health/a07-csaph-effects-video-games-internet.pdf.

American Psychiatric Association (2013). *Diagnostic and Statistical Manual of Mental Disorders. DSM-5® (5th Ed.).* American Psychiatric Publishing.

American Psychiatric Association (2018). *Internet Gaming.* Retrieved from https://www.psychiatry.org/patients-families/internet-gaming.

Aram, S., Levy, L., Patel, J.B., Anderson, A.A., Zaragoza, R., Dashtestani, H., … Tracy, J.K. (2019). The Iowa Gambling Task: a review of the historical evolution, scientific basis, and use in functional neuroimaging. SAGE Open, I–I2. Retrieved from https://journals.sagepub.com/doi/full/10.1177/2158244019856911

Bechara, A., Damasio, A., Damasio, H., & Anderson, S. (1994). Insensitivity to future consequences following damage to the human prefrontal cortex. *Cognition, 50,* 7–15.

Benerradi, J., Maior, H.A., Marinescu, A., Clos, J., & Wilson, M.L. (2019). *Exploring Machine Learning Approaches for Classifying Mental Workload Using fNIRS Data From HCI Tasks.* In Proceedings of the Halfway to the Future Symposium, ACM.

Bhambhani, Y., Maikala, R., Farag, M., & Rowland, G. (2006). Reliability of near-infrared spectroscopy measures of cerebral oxygenation and blood volume during handgrip exercise in nondisabled and traumatic brain-injured subjects. *Journal of Rehabilitation Research and Development, 43*, 845.

Bonferroni, C.E. (1936). Teoria Statistica Delle Classi e Calcolo Delle Probabilità. *Libreria internazionale Seeber, 8*, 1–62.

Bunce, S., Izzetoglu, K., Izzetoglu, M., Onaral, K., Banu O., & Kambiz P. (2006). Functional near-infrared spectroscopy. *IEEE Engineering in Medicine and Biology Magazine, 25*(4), 54–62.

Chen, H., Zhang, Y., Zhang, W., Liao, P., Li, K., Zhou, J., & Wang, G. (2017). Low-dose CT via a convolutional neural network. *Biomedical Optics Express, 8*, 679–694.

Chow, D. (2018). Machine Learning in neuroimaging. *American Journal of Neuroradiology.* Retrieved from http://ajnrdigest.org/machine-learning-neuroimaging/.

Convolutional Neural Networks (CNNs / ConvNets). *Convolutional Neural Networks for Visual Recognition.* Retrieved from http://cs231n.github.io/convolutional-networks/.

Cortes, C. & Vapnik, V. (1995). Support-vector networks. *Machine Learning, 20*, 273–297.

Davatzikos, C. (2019). Machine Learning in neuroimaging: progress and challenges. *NeuroImage, 197*, 652.

De Medeiros Kanda, P.A., Anghinah, R., Smidth, M.T, & Silva, J.M. (2009). The clinical use of quantitative EEG in cognitive disorders. *Dementia Neuropsychologia, 3*(3), 195–203.

De Zubicaray, G.I. (2006). Cognitive neuroimaging: cognitive science out of the armchair. *Brain and Cognition, 60*, 272–281.

Dolan, L.J. (2008). Neuroimaging of cognition: past, present, and future. *Neuron, 60*(3), 496–502.

Dong, G., Wang, L., Du, X., & Potenza, M.N. (2017). Gaming increases the craving for gaming-related stimuli in individuals with internet gaming disorder. *Biological Psychiatry: Cognitive Neuroscience and Neuroimaging, 2*(5), 404–412.

Entertainment Software Association (2019). *Essential Facts About the Computer and Video Game Industry.* Retrieved from https://www.theesa.com/esa-research/2019-essential -facts-about-the-computer-and-video-game-industry/.

Fairclough, S.H., Burns, C., & Kreplin, U. (2018). fNIRS activity in the prefrontal cortex and motivational intensity: impact of working memory load, financial reward, and correlation-based signal improvement. *Neurophotonics, 5*(3), 035001-1-10.

Ferguson, C.J., Coulson, M., & Barnett, J. (2011). A meta-analysis of pathological gaming prevalence and comorbidity with mental health, academic and social problems. *Journal of Psychiatric Research, 45*,1573–1578.

Fortin, J.P., Cullen, N., Sheline, Y.I., Taylor, W.D., Aselcioglu, I., Cook, P.A., ... & McInnis, M. (2018). Harmonization of cortical thickness measurements across scanners and sites. *Neuroimage, 167*, 104–120.

Friston, K.J. (1994). Functional and effective connectivity in neuroimaging: a synthesis. *Human Brain Mapping, 2*(1–2), 56–78.

Girden, E.R. (1992). *ANOVA: Repeated Measures. Quantitative Applications in the Social Sciences.* Newbury Park, CA: Sage Publications.

Griffis, J.C., Allendorfer, J.B., & Szaflarski, J.P. (2016). Voxel-based Gaussian naïve Bayes classification of ischemic stroke lesions in individual T_1-weighted MRI scans. *Journal of Neuroscience Methods, 257*, 97–108.

Haller, S., Badoud, S., Nguyen, D., Garibotto, V., Lovblad, K.O., & Burkhard, P.R. (2012). Individual detection of patients with Parkinson disease using support vector machine analysis of diffusion tensor imaging data: initial results. *American Journal of Neuroradiology, 33*(11), 2123–2128.

Hibino, S., Mase, M., Shirataki, T., Nagano, Y., Fukagawa, K., Abe, A., … Ogawa, T. (2013). Oxyhemoglobin changes during cognitive rehabilitation after traumatic brain injury using near infrared spectroscopy. *Neurologia Medico-chirurgica*, 53, 299–303.

Ho, T.K.K., Gwak, J., Park, C.M., & Song, J.I. (2019). Discrimination of mental workload levels from multi-channel fNIRS using Deep Learning-based approaches. *IEEE Access*, 7, 24392–24403.

Huynh, H. & Feldt, L.S. (1976). Estimation of the box correction for degrees of freedom from sample data in randomized block and split-plot designs. *Journal of Educational Statistics*, 1(1), 69–82.

Jiang, F., Jiang, Y., Zhi, H., Dong, Y, Li, H., Ma, S., … Wang, Y. (2017). Artificial intelligence in healthcare: past, present, and future. *Stroke and Vascular Neurology*, 2(4), 230–243.

Kamal, H., Lopez, V. & Sheth, S.A. (2018). Machine learning in acute ischemic stroke neuroimaging. *Frontiers in Neurology*, 9, 945.

Kamnitsas, K., Castro, D.C,, Folgoc, L.L., Walker, I., Tanno, R., Rueckert, D., … & Nori, A. (2018). Semi-supervised learning via compact latent space clustering. *arXiv preprint arXiv:1806.02679*.

Kang, E., Min, J., & Ye, J.C. (2017). A deep convolutional neural network using directional wavelets for low-dose X-ray CT reconstruction. *Medical Physics*, 44(10), 360–375.

Karamzadeh, N., Amyot, F., Kenney, K., Anderson, A., Chowdhry, F., Dashtestani, H., … & Diaz-Arrastia, R. (2016). A Machine Learning approach to identify functional biomarkers in the human prefrontal cortex for individuals with traumatic brain injury using functional near-infrared spectroscopy. *Brain and Behavior*, 6(11), 1–14.

Li, R., Rui, G., Chen, W., Li, S., Schulz, P.E., & Zhang, Y. (2018). Early detection of Alzheimer's disease using non-invasive near-infrared spectroscopy. *Frontiers in Aging Neuroscience*, 10, 366.

Li, R., Zhang, W, Suk, H., Wang, L., Li, J., Shen, D., & Ji, S. (2014). Deep Learning-Based imaging data completion for improved brain disease diagnosis. *Medical Image Computing and Computer-Assisted Intervention*, 17(Pt 3), 305–312.

Lin, C.H., Wang, C.C., Jia-Huang Sun, J.H., Ko, C.H., & Chiu, Y.C. (2019). Is the clinical version of the Iowa Gambling Task relevant for assessing choice behavior in cases of Internet addiction? *Frontiers in Psychiatry*, 10, 232.

Mauchly, J.W. (1940). Significance test for sphericity of a normal n-variate distribution. *The Annals of Mathematical Statistics*. 11(2), 204–209.

Mazurowski, M.A., Buda, M., Saha, A., & Bashir, M.R. (2018). Deep Learning in radiology: an overview of the concepts and a survey of the state of the art. *Journal of Magnetic Resonance Imaging*, 49(4), 1–27.

McCarthy, J. (2017). *What is Artificial Intelligence?* Retrieved from http://jmc.stanford.edu/articles/whatisai/whatisai.pdf.

Merzagora, A.C.R., Izzetoglu, M., Onaral, B., & Schultheis, M.T. (2014). Verbal working memory impairments following traumatic brain injury: an fNIRS investigation. *Brain Imaging and Behavior*, 8, 446–459.

Merzagora, A.C., Schultheis, M.T., Onaral, B., & Izzetoglu, M. (2011). Functional near-infrared spectroscopy-based assessment of attention impairments after traumatic brain injury. *Journal of Innovative Optical Health Sciences*, 4, 251–260.

Mosso, A. (1881). *Concerning the Circulation of the Blood in the Human Brain*. Leipzig, Germany: Verlag von Viet & Company.

Mosso, A. (1882). *Applicazione della bilancia allo studio della circolazione del sangue nell'uomo*. Atti della R. Accademia delle scienze di Torino, XVII, 534–535.

Nie, D., Cao, X., Gao, Y., Wang, L., & Shen, D. (2016). Estimating CT image from MRI data using 3D fully convolutional networks. *Deep Learning and Data Labeling for Medical Applications, 2016,* 170–178.

O'Brien, J.T. (2007). Role of imaging techniques in the diagnosis of dementia. *The British Journal of Radiology 80*(2) Spec No 2, 71–77.

Odinak, M.M., Emelin, A.Y., Lobzin, V.Y., Vorobyev, S.V., & Kiselev, V.N. (2012). Current capacities for neuroimaging in the differential diagnosis of cognitive impairments. *Neurology, Neuropsychiatry, Psychosomatics 4*(2S), 51–55.

O'Shea, M. (2013). The brain: milestones of neuroscience. *The New Scientist, 218*(2911), ii–iii.

Overmars, O. (2012). *A Brief History of Computer Games.* Retrieved from https://www.stichtingspel.org/sites/default/files/history_of_games.pdf.

Przybylski, A.K, Weinstein, N., & Murayama, K. (2017). Internet gaming disorder: investigating the clinical relevance of a new phenomenon. *The American Journal of Psychiatry, 174,* 230–236.

Quaresima, V. & Ferrari, M. (2019). A Mini-Review on functional near-infrared spectroscopy (fNIRS): where do we stand, and where should we go? *Photonics, 6*(3), 87.

Rehme, A.K., Volz, L.J., Feis, D.L., Bomilcar-Focke, I., Liebig, T., Eickhoff, S.B., Fink, G.R., Grefkes, C. (2015). Identifying neuroimaging markers of Motor Disability in acute stroke by Machine Learning Techniques. *Cerebral Cortex, 25,* 3046–3056.

Rojas, R.F., Huang, X., & Ou, K.L. (2019). A Machine Learning approach for the identification of a biomarker of human pain using fNIRS. *Scientific Reports, 9*(1), 5645.

Sadaghiani S, Hesselmann G, Friston KJ, Kleinschmidt A. (2010). The relation of ongoing brain activity evoked neural responses and cognition. *Frontiers in the Systems Neuroscience, 4,* 20.

Sandrone, S., Bacigaluppi, M., Galloni, M.R., Cappa, S.F., Moro, A., Catani, M. … Martino, G. (2013). Weighing brain activity with the balance: Angelo Mosso's original manuscripts come to light. *Brain, 259*(11), 1–13.

Schlemper, J., Caballero, J., Hajnal, J.V., Price, A., & Rueckert, D. (2017). A deep cascade of convolutional neural networks for dynamic MR image reconstruction. *IEEE Transactions on Medical Imaging, 37*(2), 491–503.

Sirpal, P., Kassab, A., Pouliot, P., Nguyen, D.K., & Lesage, F. (2019). fNIRS improves seizure detection in multimodal EEG-fNIRS recordings. *Journal of Biomedical Optics, 24*(5), 1–9.

The World Health Organization (2018). *Gaming Disorder.* Retrieved from https://www.who.int/features/qa/gaming-disorder/en/.

Uhlhaas, P.J., Liddle, P., Linden, D.E.J., Nobre, A.C., Singh, K.D., & Grossa J. (2017). Magnetoencephalography as a tool in psychiatric research: current status and perspective. *Biological Psychiatry: Cognitive Neuroscience and Neuroimaging, 2*(3), 235–244.

Van Straaten, E.C., Scheltens, P., & Barkhof, F. (2004). MRI and CT in the diagnosis of vascular dementia. *Journal of the Neurological Sciences, 226*(1/2), 9–12.

Varoquaux, G., & Thirion, B. (2014). How Machine Learning is shaping cognitive neuroimaging. *GigaScience, 3*(1), 28.

Zhu, G., Jiang, B., Tong, L., Xie, Y., Zaharchuk, G. & Wintermark, M. (2019). Applications of Deep Learning to neuro-imaging techniques. *Frontiers in Neurology, 10,* 869.

Chapter 11

People, Competencies, and Capabilities Are Core Elements in Digital Transformation: A Case Study of a Digital Transformation Project at ABB

Ismo Laukkanen

Contents

11.1 Introduction 184
     11.1.1 Objectives and Research Approach 186
     11.1.2 Challenges Related to the Use of Digitalization and AI 187
11.2 Theoretical Framework 187
     11.2.1 From Data Collection into Knowledge Management and
             Learning Agility..187
     11.2.2 Knowledge Processes in Organizations 189
     11.2.3 Framework for Competency, Capability, and Organizational
             Development...190

11.2.4 Management of Transient Advantages Is a Core Capability in
Digital Solution Launch and Ramp-Up 190
11.3 Digital Transformation Needs an Integrated Model for Knowledge
Management and Transformational Leadership.......................................191
11.4 Case Study of the ABB Takeoff Program: Innovation, Talent, and
Competence Development for Industry 4.0..194
11.4.1 Background for the Digital Transformation at ABB...................194
11.4.2 The Value Framework for IIoT and Digital Solutions.................194
11.4.3 Takeoff for Intelligent Industry: Innovation, Talent, and
Competence Development for Industry 4.0 194
11.4.4 Case 1: ABB Smartsensor: An Intelligent Concept for
Monitoring...199
11.4.5 Case 2: Digital Powertrain: Optimization of Industrial
System Operations 202
11.4.6 Case 3: Autonomous Ships: Remote Diagnostics and
Collaborative Operations for Ships..203
11.5 Conclusions and Future Recommendations..205
11.5.1 Conclusions..205
11.5.2 Future Recommendations 205
11.5.3 Critical Roles of People, Competency, and Capability
Development...207
References 207

11.1 Introduction

Digitalization or the widespread adoption of digital technologies, industrial Internet of Things (IIoT), artificial intelligence (AI), and advanced analytics is driving digital transformation in various industrial sectors. The major drivers for this development have been energy and industrial revolutions, as illustrated in Figure 11.1. Industrial revolution is a major driver for digitalization, IoT, and AI. The transformation will disrupt several industrial sectors including, for example, energy production, industrial manufacturing, transportation, and infrastructure.

As one real-life example, electric utilities are facing both opportunities and challenges in the emerging energy revolution. Some key questions are how to boost productivity out of aging and regulated assets and how to manage distributed renewable energy resources, along with the future massive integration of electric plug-in vehicles and the complications and changes in the regulatory landscape. At the same time, the decline in demand and revenue from the regulated asset base has them thinking about digitalization, monetization of data, and alternate sources of revenue (ABB, 2018a).

Based on our analysis related to the use of digital technologies in industry, there is a remarkable potential in the use of digital, industrial IoT, analytics, and AI

Why: Energy and Industrial Revolutions
World as we know it is being disrupted – at unprecendented rate of change

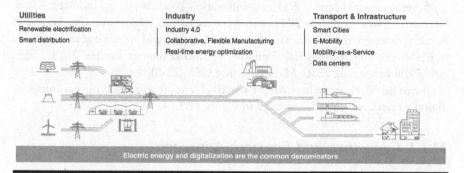

Figure 11.1   Industrial revolution is a major driver for digitalization, IoT, and AI (ABB, 2019a).

technologies in different industries as an S-curve, which is illustrated in Figure 11.2 (Jouret, 2017).

Digital transformation will disrupt existing business models, create efficiencies, and enhance customer experiences in different industrial sectors. The digital transformation of industrial sectors like energy management and automation lies at the core of this journey, enabling a paradigm shift for the industry (World Economic Forum, 2018).

Both competitiveness and productivity of industrial companies can be increased with AI, IoT, and digitalization technologies. Based on the business analysis of the World Economic Forum and Accenture (2019) and data from 16,000 companies, there is a strong positive return on investment, although most of the gains

Industrial markets to adopt digital technologies
Computing + connectivity + cloud + analytics set to unlock value

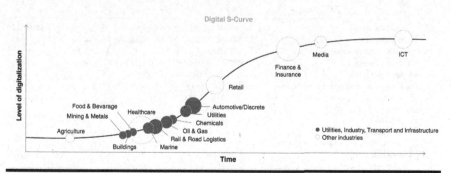

Figure 11.2   S-curve of digital technologies in different industrial sectors (ABB, 2018; 2017).

are clustered among industry leaders. These early adopters saw a 70% productivity increase, compared with just 30% for industry followers.

Several national level R&D and innovation programs (e.g., Industry 4.0 in Germany, Made in China 2025, and Manufacturing USA) have a strong focus in the development in IIoT, AI, advanced analytics, and intelligent technologies to enable the fourth industrial revolution (World Economic Forum, 2018; CSIS, 2019; Wübbeke et al., 2016; Manufacturing USA, 2019).

Based on McKinsey, there will be remarkable value migration opportunities in digital services, which are illustrated in Figure 11.3.

11.1.1 Objectives and Research Approach

The objectives of the research are:

1. To develop a value-based framework for industrial digital solutions which can be used in the ramp-up of digital, IoT, and AI solutions in organizational digitalization programs.
2. To find out the impacts of a digital solutions framework for people, competence, and capability development needs in organizations.
3. To find out what the major customer benefits are of digitalization in industrial solutions.

The research and development efforts reported here wish to serve both as useful theoretical insights and as practical solutions to the described overall challenge and to the problems of particular cases. The report is based on the results from the project "TAKEOFF innovation, talent and competence development for industry 4.0."

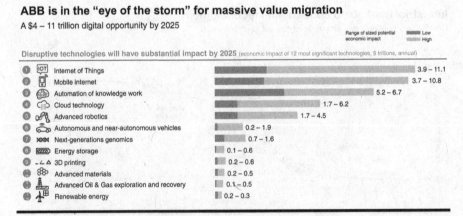

Figure 11.3 Business opportunities related to digitalization (ABB, 2018).

This research has been partly funded by EIT Digital and done in collaboration with Aalto University, Aalto Executive Education, and some partner companies of ABB.

11.1.2 Challenges Related to the Use of Digitalization and AI

Despite all the potential benefits of digitalization, many industrial companies have been facing challenges in how to utilize all opportunities and benefits of digitalization, IoT, analytics, and AI. According to Furr and Shipolov (2019), there are myths and challenges in the digital transformation, which are summarized in Table 11.1.

Also based on the findings of Fountaine, McCarthy, and Saleh (2019), technology is not the biggest challenge for building AI-powered organizations—it is culture, people, and competencies. Based on the McKinsey research of several thousands of companies, AI and advanced analytics support core practices are in widespread use in only 8% of the companies, while in most of the companies, ad-hoc pilots or applying AI and analytics in single process pilots are the norm. Only 23% of companies have budgeted resources for non-technical development, for example, training and adoption of new ways of working. The reason for this is because of cultural and organizational barriers but also myths and unrealistic expectations of AI as a plug and play technology with immediate returns.

Many organizations have failed to realize that digital transformation and AI cannot be done solely through innovation and technology. Transformation also requires investment in people and culture (Furr and Shipolov, 2019). People need upskilling in order to apply new skills and ways of working, as well as using the latest technology in their daily work. Regardless of how good the new technology is, investment will be partly wasted if the people do not accept the change (Fountaine et al. 2019). Unlearning of old habits and upskilling of competencies are needed to realize the benefits of digital, IoT, and AI tools.

11.2 Theoretical Framework

11.2.1 From Data Collection into Knowledge Management and Learning Agility

The role of knowledge and knowledge work as a competitive advantage has received considerable attention in management theories (e.g., Drucker, 1994; Liebowitz, 1999, 2000, 2012), Davenport, 2005). The common hierarchy of knowledge, as a part of organizational information and knowledge management, can be defined as follows: data, information, knowledge, expertise/intelligence, and wisdom as illustrated in Figure 11.4. The key challenge in advanced analytics and AI solutions is how to identify the critical data variables to be collected, how to get enough rich

Table 11.1 Some Myths and Realities Related to Digital and AI Transformation

Myths in digital	Reality
Technology innovation is the major focus in AI, advanced analytics, and digital solutions	Digitalization is about customer value, culture, and organizational development for a new way of working
Digital requires radical disruption on the value proposition and business model	The best results can come from adaptation on how to better serve customer needs
Digital will replace physical products	Physical product and digital solution will be integrated solutions
Digital involves buying startups	Digital also involves protecting startups
Digital involves overhauling legacy systems	Digital is more about incremental bridging
AI and advanced analytics are plug and play technologies with immediate returns	AI requires alignment of culture, structure, and ways of working for wide adoption
AI and advanced analytics can be developed by teams of data scientists, AI, and ICT consultants	AI and digital requires collaborative cross-functional teams with strong business, ICT, and analytics expertise
Digitalization is a bottom-up exercise based on pilots in single processes	Digitalization requires organizational development at all levels from top leaders into operations and support roles
Digital transformation is technical plug and play change without any impacts to organization or culture	Widespread adaptation of digital, AI, and analytics solutions requires agile, experimental, and adaptable culture
Budgeting for technology development is enough and people, integration, and adoption is not needed	Budgeting for training, on-the-job coaching, and change management is critical

Adapted from Furr and Shipolov [2019] and Fountaine, McCarthy, and Saleh [2019].

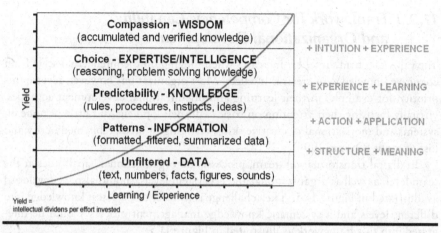

Figure 11.4   Common hierarchy of knowledge. (Adapted from Laukkanen, 2008.)

and reliable data for advanced analytics algorithms, and how to refine collected data into useful knowledge and intelligence.

The creation and diffusion of knowledge have also become increasingly important factors in competitiveness, especially when knowledge as a high valuable commodity is embedded in products (especially high technology) and knowledge services (knowledge intensive and digital services) (Hertog, 2000; Dalkir, 2017). At the same time, the competitive advantage and value of knowledge is becoming shorter, emphasizing the need for combining knowledge management and transformational leadership to enable the transient competitive advantage which will be introduced in Section 11.3.

11.2.2 *Knowledge Processes in Organizations*

The major knowledge processes can generally be represented as four subprocesses: knowledge scanning/mapping; knowledge generation; knowledge codification; and knowledge transfer/realization (Liebowitz, 1999; Dalkir, 2017). The knowledge scanning and mapping process includes, for example, business and technology foresight, where potential new areas are systematically scanned. The knowledge generation process includes the processes of creation, capturing/acquisition, and development of knowledge.

The knowledge codification process covers the conversion of knowledge into an accessible format and the storing of knowledge. The knowledge transfer process includes the sharing of knowledge from the point of generation or codification to the point of using and applying it in an organization (Davenport, 2005).

Nonaka (1995) defined the goal for knowledge transfer in organizations as "tapping of tacit, highly subjective insights or intentions of an individual employee and making these insights available for the whole company."

11.2.3 Framework for Competency, Capability, and Organizational Development

The value of a firm's intellect increases when moving up the intellectual scale from cognitive knowledge to creative intellect. Most organizations however, reverse this priority, for example, in their learning and organizational development activities, virtually focusing their attention on basic skills development and little or none on systems and motivational or creative skills, resulting in predictable mediocrity and loss of profit (Quinn, 1996).

In digital transformation, team, process, and organizational capabilities at the team level, as well as organizational and ecosystem levels, should also be developed as illustrated in Figure 11.5. A key challenge is transfer of the latest knowledge into different levels and a systematic knowledge management process should be integrated into this framework as illustrated in Figure 11.5.

11.2.4 Management of Transient Advantages Is a Core Capability in Digital Solution Launch and Ramp-Up

Almost all traditional strategy frameworks and tools in use today are based on a single dominant idea: the purpose of corporate strategy today is to achieve a sustainable competitive advantage. This idea is strategy's most fundamental concept but it's no longer relevant for more and more companies, especially in the digital solution business. Sustainable competitive advantage is eroding due to "volatile" and "uncertain" environments. Because of this volatility, strategy must increasingly be based on transient competitive advantage, exploiting short-term opportunities with speed and agility (McGrawth, 2013).

Transient advantage is a business strategy that accepts competitive advantages as being less industry bound and more customer centric based on finding ways of

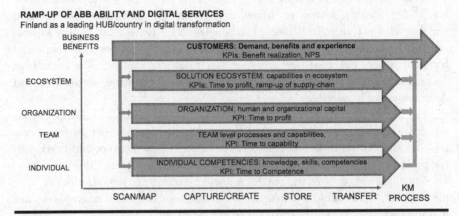

Figure 11.5 Integrated framework competency and capability development.

leveraging short and temporary advantages, which are illustrated in Figure 11.6. According to McGrawth (2013), the wave of transient advantage consists of five phases:

1. Launch Phase: An organization identifies a business opportunity and mobilizes resources to capitalize on it. Organizations need people with ideas, who are comfortable with experimentation and iteration. Analysis and strategic planning of resources, competencies, and capabilities are also critical.
2. Ramp-Up: The business idea is brought to scale. Organizations need people who can assemble the right resources at the right time with the right quality and deliver on the promise of the idea. Organizational learning, development of competencies, and dynamic capabilities confirm the quick ramp-up of the business.
3. Exploitation: The organization captures profits and market share and forces its competitors to react. At this point, a company needs people who are good at analytical decision-making and efficient in process execution.
4. Reconfiguration: Organizations have to reconfigure what it is doing to keep the temporary advantage fresh. Reconfigurations require transformational leadership and people who are not afraid to radically rethink business models or resources.
5. Disengage: Disengagement requires people who can see early evidence of decline and are willing to make hard decisions fast.

In transient advantage, company CEOs are managing and orchestrating "how these waves are managed."

11.3 Digital Transformation Needs an Integrated Model for Knowledge Management and Transformational Leadership

An integrated framework combining knowledge management and learning and transformational leadership is presented in Figure 11.7 as proposed by Nissinen and Laukkanen (2018). The ontological dimensions in the framework are individual, team/process, organizational, and inter-organizational levels where both knowledge management and transformational leadership processes take place normally. Four learning loops are the integrating mechanisms of knowledge management and transformational leadership in these levels. From a strategy perspective, the key challenge is to effectively integrate and synchronize all these four learning loops for knowledge transfer, organizational development, and change. At the *individual level*, the focus is on knowledge, skills, and competencies which can be developed with personal feedback tools, competence profiles/maps, competence assessments, and HRD tools

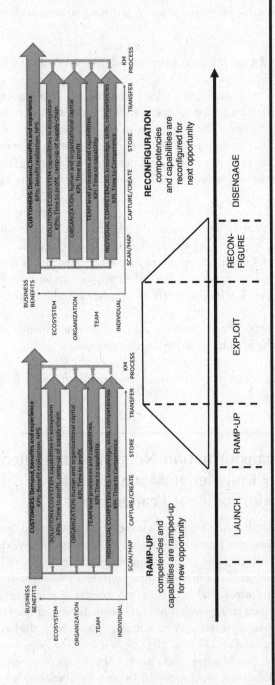

Figure 11.6 **Ramp-up and reconfiguration of competencies and capabilities in management of transient advantage. (Adapted from McGrawth, 2013.)**

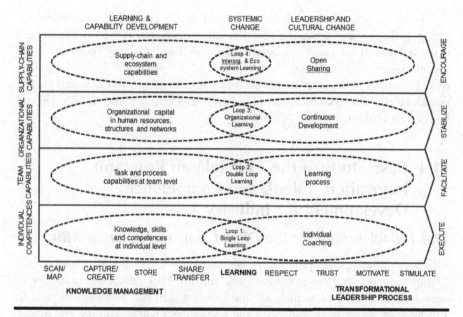

Figure 11.7 Conceptual framework for knowledge management and transformational, deep leadership. (Adapted from Nissinen and Laukkanen, 2018.)

(e.g., 70:20:10 model). Transformational leadership aims for the full commitment of the cornerstones of leadership seen like shared practical values. The focus on learning is to confirm single loop learning which can be a challenge in complex and dynamic work environments having a focus on troubleshooting and firefighting. The presence of the idea and practices of deep learning is vital. At the *team level*, the focus is on the development of cross-functional team and process capabilities which are often dynamic capabilities (Teece et al., 1997). The learning process is based on double loop learning where the best practices of processes are systematically identified and improved. Transformational leadership is based on a team level learning process. Understanding and using the unique personalities, personal skills, and knowledge are the source of creative and motivating team processes.

At the *organizational level*, the focus of development is on organizational capital including human resources, organizational structures, and networks. The learning process is organizational learning where strategic capabilities are identified and developed based on strategic targets. Transformational leadership focuses on continuous improvement of the leadership system and the development of the culture.

At the *inter-organizational level*, the development of capabilities focuses on business ecosystems or supplier network capabilities which often are complementing capabilities. The learning process is inter-organizational, combining benchmarking and learning from the best partners. Deep leadership focuses on creating open interaction and accelerating open or semi-open innovation in a supplier network type of organizational structure.

Systematic organizational development and change are the key areas when analyzing, planning, and executing transformation programs. A typical challenge is that the focus of the programs covers mainly individual competences and team, organizational, and inter-organizational aspects are neglected. Beyond this, the synchronization of these levels and the respective learning loops is mostly forgotten. Detailed theoretical background of this model can be found in Nissinen and Laukkanen (2018).

11.4 Case Study of the ABB Takeoff Program: Innovation, Talent, and Competence Development for Industry 4.0

11.4.1 Background for the Digital Transformation at ABB

ABB is one of the global leaders in power, automation, and digital technologies—having business operations in around 100 countries. ABB is dedicated to helping its clients use electrical power efficiently and lowering their environmental impact. As a technology leader, both leadership and knowledge management are key success factors for ABB, in order to drive innovation, to attract and retain talent, and to act responsibly (ABB, 2019a).

The latest update in corporate strategy involves a strong emphasis in digitalization with the corporate vision "Technology Leader in Digital Industries."

ABB has been a strong player in robotics, automation, and control system technologies for decades, but in 2017, a common cloud-based platform called ABB Ability for digital customer solutions was introduced. Digital services within ABB are integrated into the ABB Ability platform, and in 2019, there were more than 210 solutions for different industries (ABB, 2019b). This customer value and solution-based approach is illustrated in Figure 11.8.

11.4.2 The Value Framework for IIoT and Digital Solutions

The industrial solution framework is a complex mesh of different IIoT technologies, from simple sensors developed for monitoring to machine learning applications that turn sensor data into predictive maintenance actions. Customer solutions can be classified in five different hierarchy levels as illustrated in Figure 11.9 and Table 11.2.

11.4.3 Takeoff for Intelligent Industry: Innovation, Talent, and Competence Development for Industry 4.0

This case study focuses on the ramp-up of innovation, talent, and competency development at a country level program in Finland 2018–2020. The primary goal for the program was a systematic ramp-up of digital business in Finland. The secondary

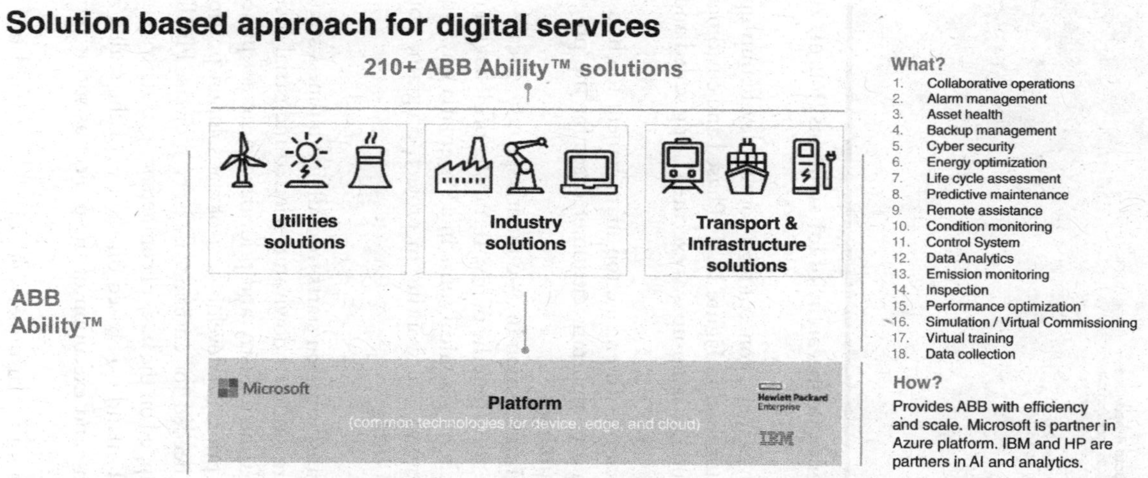

Solution based approach for digital services

ABB Ability™

210+ ABB Ability™ solutions

| Utilities solutions | Industry solutions | Transport & Infrastructure solutions |

Platform
(common technologies for device, edge, and cloud)

Microsoft

Hewlett Packard Enterprise

IBM

What?
1. Collaborative operations
2. Alarm management
3. Asset health
4. Backup management
5. Cyber security
6. Energy optimization
7. Life cycle assessment
8. Predictive maintenance
9. Remote assistance
10. Condition monitoring
11. Control System
12. Data Analytics
13. Emission monitoring
14. Inspection
15. Performance optimization
16. Simulation / Virtual Commissioning
17. Virtual training
18. Data collection

How?
Provides ABB with efficiency and scale. Microsoft is partner in Azure platform. IBM and HP are partners in AI and analytics.

Figure 11.8 ABB Ability service ecosystem and customer value elements.

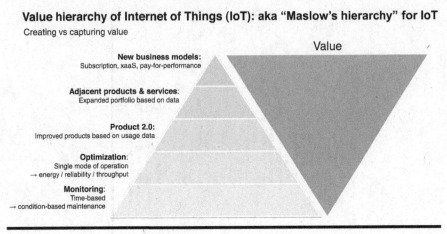

Figure 11.9   Customer value hierarchy of IoT solutions (Jouret, 2017).

goal was to develop a systematic concept for a country level ramp-up of digital business. The concept is illustrated in Figure 11.10. Phased and customer focused ramp-up of digital services and the ramp-up was executed using scaled and agile methods:

1. Management kick-off. To engage top management to choose customer verticals and the most important customer cases for the program, as well as confirming resourcing.
2. Piloting with agile execution in 3–6 month sprints; 3) scale-up to the global scale based on results from the pilots; 4) transfer of global know-how and best practices between geographical units in a systematic way; and 5) to create a concept for a new way of working in project, program, portfolio, and risk management.

Execution of digital transformation starts from digital business strategy and targets. The strategic targets are cascaded down into selected industrial focus segments, for example, intelligent marine industry and prioritized customer projects. These verticals and projects will prioritize development of the solution portfolio, capabilities, and operating model needed for customer delivery projects. Finally, competencies and capabilities are mapped on the basis of competence gap analysis in different levels.

The execution in Finland was based on the use of the scaled and agile model (SAFe) in the planning and execution of the project as sprint type increments as illustrated in Figure 11.11.

The framework based on customer solutions is illustrated in Figure 11.12 and examples of competence and capability mapping for these customer solutions in different levels are illustrated in Figure 11.13. Critical elements in the development of digital business capability are competencies, skills, and capabilities. In Figure 11.13, competencies and capabilities needed in the delivery of industrial IoT solutions are illustrated for different hierarchy levels.

Table 11.2 Value Hierarchy of IoT and Examples of Customer Solutions

Level in hierarchy	Customer value
Monitoring Solution: Smartsensor	At the first level of hierarchy, organizations start with monitoring, which is also the base for the pyramid. According to research, 60–70% of all use cases are based on monitoring providing sensors on machinery to keep track of performance, maintenance schedules, and monitoring.
Optimization Solution: Digital Powertrain	The second level in the pyramid is optimization, where an organization can have IoT devices start automating changes to equipment and other business inputs based on the conditions they read. As a result, users can go beyond monitoring and with optimization things run faster, consume less energy, and are more reliable in extreme operation situations.
Product 2.0 Solution: Digital Powertrain	The next level is called Product 2.0 and it is a by-product of continuous monitoring giving manufacturers insight into the features that their industrial customers use most. For R&D and software development, this data gives very important insight and helps to decide how to make products better based on usage data.
Adjacent products and portfolio Solution: Circuit breaker	Technology convergence in smartphones with additional new features year by year and manufacturers of IoT and industrial services are going to establish more converged industrial devices that will add unheard-of features to industrial equipment. As an example, a circuit breaker measures power quality and can shed unnecessary loads if the customer wants to do demand response. Those features can be offered as apps that can be downloaded onto the computer in the circuit breaker.
Business Model innovation Solution: Autonomous ship	The final tip of the hierarchy is business model innovations for B2B industrial companies. With the power of IoT, customers have the choice to choose how they buy their industrial systems. With predictive maintenance down to a science, manufacturers of this equipment may offer subscription models where the customer pays a flat monthly fee or even on a usage basis because with so much telemetry, the manufacturer of a widget maker can know exactly how many widgets are made at any given time and under what conditions.

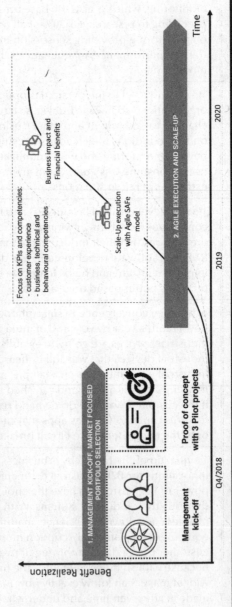

Figure 11.10 Phased and customer focused ramp-up of digital services.

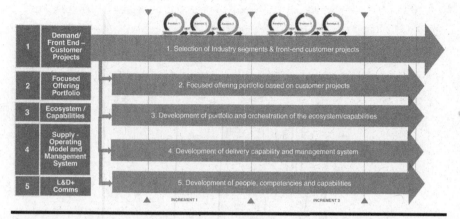

Figure 11.11 Scaled and agile model for ramp-up of digital solutions.

Already the development of monitoring level solution requires extensive technical competencies. The higher levels require more and more leadership competencies, for example, transformational and change leadership plus other business capabilities like business model development. As discussed in Section 11.3, systematic planning of competencies and capabilities is needed at individual, team, organizational, and ecosystem levels, which are illustrated in Figure 11.13.

11.4.4 Case 1: ABB Smartsensor: An Intelligent Concept for Monitoring

ABB wants to help customers utilize the power of IIoT to translate machinery asset data into actionable insights. ABB's Motors and Generators business developed an IIoT device called the "Smart Sensor," which can be used to retrofit almost any low-voltage electric motor to help monitor its condition. The device's sensors measure vibration, temperature, electro-magnetic field strength, and other parameters to help reduce downtime, increase the product lifecycle, and reduce energy costs (Accenture, 2019).

Solution elements:

- *Mobile app.* An IIoT gateway was used in addition to service personnel to commission the sensors and monitor the motors on the shop floor in order to react quickly in emergencies.
- *Customer portal.* The portal collects asset data to help ABB customers manage plants, teams, relationships between teams, assets, and organizations. APIs integrate customers and their service providers into the Smart Sensor portal and cloud ecosystem.
- *ABB Ability digital Powertrain platform.* The platform helps customers monitor large parts of their shop floor and group assets using different sensors. This allows customers to monitor the whole turbine, not just one small piece of it.

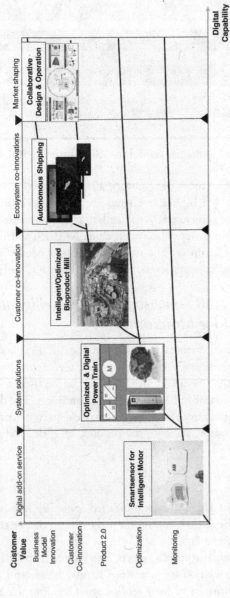

Figure 11.12 IoT solution framework and examples of customer solutions in ramp-up.

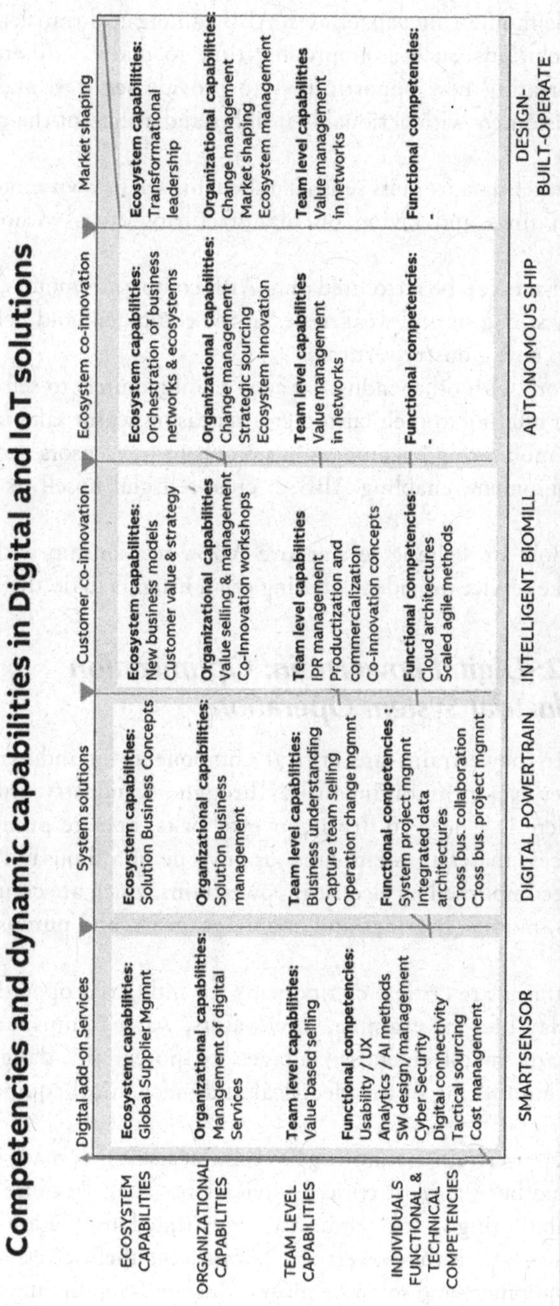

Competencies and dynamic capabilities in Digital and IoT solutions

	Digital add-on Services	System solutions	Customer co-innovation	Ecosystem co-innovation	Market shaping
ECOSYSTEM CAPABILITIES	Ecosystem capabilities: Global Supplier Mgmnt	Ecosystem capabilities: Solution Business Concepts	Ecosystem capabilities: New business models Customer value & strategy	Ecosystem capabilities: Orchestration of business networks & ecosystems	Ecosystem capabilities: Transformational leadership
ORGANIZATIONAL CAPABILITIES	Organizational capabilities: Management of digital Services	Organizational capabilities: Solution Business management	Organizational capabilities: Value selling & management Co-Innovation workshops	Organizational capabilities: Change management Strategic sourcing Ecosystem innovation	Organizational capabilities: Change management Market shaping Ecosystem management
TEAM LEVEL CAPABILITIES	Team level capabilities: Value based selling	Team level capabilities: Business understanding Capture team selling Operation change mgmnt	Team level capabilities: IPR management Productization and commercialization Co-innovation concepts	Team level capabilities: Value management in networks	Team level capabilities: Value management in networks
INDIVIDUALS FUNCTIONAL & TECHNICAL COMPETENCIES	Functional competencies: Usability / UX Analytics / AI methods SW design/management Cyber Security Digital connectivity Tactical sourcing Cost management	Functional competencies : System project mgmnt Integrated data architectures Cross bus. collaboration Cross bus. project mgmnt	Functional competencies: Cloud architectures Scaled agile methods	Functional competencies:	Functional competencies:
	SMARTSENSOR	DIGITAL POWERTRAIN	INTELLIGENT BIOMILL	AUTONOMOUS SHIP	DESIGN-BUILT-OPERATE

Figure 11.13   Competencies and capabilities needed in the delivery of IoT solutions.

Summary: Smartsensor monitoring solution (Accenture, 2019):

- With mobile monitoring capabilities, ABB can create a transient advantage in digital solutions, such as improving time to market, differentiating its products, creating new opportunities to provide services, and generating value for customers with actionable insights and a state-of-the-art customer experience
- ABB can gather data from its sensors to benchmark its own motors, improving product lines and saving on manufacturing costs without reducing quality.
- Since the sensors can be retrofitted onto ABB competitor motors, the insights can identify strengths and weaknesses in the equipment and help ABB gain insights into new industry verticals.
- ABB can work with other industrial asset manufacturers to sell its sensor as part of their offering to their customers, increasing sensor sales indirectly.
- Powertrain monitoring encourages customers to use sensors across different types of equipment, enabling ABB to cross-sell and upsell its sensors and services.
- The new tools are helping to improve ABB's relationship with ecosystem members like service providers, offering them insights to do their jobs better.

11.4.5 Case 2: Digital Powertrain: Optimization of Industrial System Operations

Electrically driven powertrains are critical components in industry, and it is essential that they can run continuously. Throughout industry, infrastructure, and buildings there is a need to drive conveyor belts, operate pumps and mixers, move or process material, rotate fans, or any one of a thousand other tasks. These tasks are accomplished by electrical powertrains which are connections of a number of drives, motors, bearings and couplings, gears, and pumps in different configurations.

These powertrains are critical components for industrial operations, as well as for our everyday life, for example, in elevators, water pumps, and conveyor belts. To avoid any inconveniences, outages, or potentially dangerous situations, condition monitoring of the electrical and mechanical equipment is very important.

Traditionally, powertrain monitoring has come at a cost that made it prohibitive to use for anything but the most critical applications. That's because putting in a comprehensive monitoring system requires a sophisticated installation that is sometimes more expensive than the powertrain components themselves! Furthermore, the monitoring equipment and software must be installed and maintained by external specialists.

The availability of a digital powertrain—low-cost and IoT-based: wireless sensors and a data transmission solution that allows for permanent monitoring at a fraction of the cost of traditional condition monitoring systems.

Summary of a digital powertrain solution:

- ABB Ability Condition Monitoring for powertrains is a cloud service that makes this data permanently available online at minimal installation and maintenance costs.
- Fast commissioning and installation are other benefits, as motors, bearings, and pumps do not need to be cabled separately. This is very important, because if you do get problems during commissioning or operation, the cabling is often the culprit.
- Other customer benefits are ease of use and integration, manufacturer independence, scalability, and flexibility.

11.4.6 Case 3: Autonomous Ships: Remote Diagnostics and Collaborative Operations for Ships

ABB is a supplier of the Azipod propulsion system for ships. An autonomous ship pilot was carried out in Finland in 2019 (ABB, 2019e) where ABB Ability™ Marine Pilot Vision as a virtual model of the ship was superimposed on real surroundings measured using various sensor technologies, making it possible to monitor the vessel and its surroundings from a birds-eye view while switching to other views instantaneously. The solution predicts vessel motions with respect to the actual surroundings and gives the user visibility of previously hidden obstacles or collision risks. The operating architecture of the system is illustrated in Figures 11.14 and 11.15.

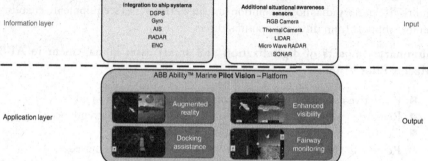

Figure 11.14 ABB Ability Marine Pilot vision system for ships (Moratella, 2019).

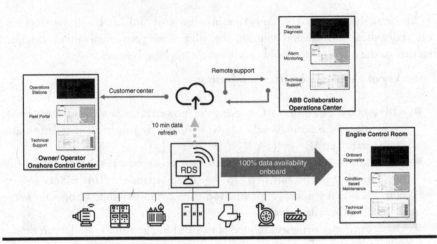

Figure 11.15 Smart asset management and collaborative operations center model in Marine applications (Moratella, 2019).

Summary of ABB Marine Pilot Vision system benefits (ABB, 2019f):

- It improves the safety of the passengers and the crew by improved situational awareness, real time docking assistance, and incident and damage prevention for infrastructure and other ships.
- There are also significant time savings in docking operations, which will also result in significant annual fuel savings.

In addition to ABB Marine Pilot vision, there is an ABB diagnostic tool providing troubleshooting and condition monitoring for electrical and mechanical systems installed onboard the vessel with possibilities for remote assistance from the ABB Collaborative Operations Center. To address the individual needs of each vessel, the RDS is completely modular. This allows for the expansion of the diagnostic capability from monitoring a few critical components or subsystems, to a fully multi-disciplinary diagnostic solution for an entire vessel's equipment, enabling remote support from different manufacturers.

Summary: Impacts of digitalization and smart asset management in ABB Marine Pilot Vision:

- Predictive maintenance: remarkable ten times reduction in costs
- Remote monitoring: 70% reduction in service engineer attendance
- Condition based maintenance: 50% cost reduction
- Remote diagnostics: 90% of cases could be remotely diagnosed
- Summary of customer benefits:
  - Availability: always onboard, direct contact, remote access
  - Safety: critical alarms, condition monitoring, risk mitigation
  - Savings: Asset management, less downtime, minimal failures

11.5 Conclusions and Future Recommendations

11.5.1 Conclusions

Many organizations have failed to realize that digital transformation and AI are not only investments into the innovation and technology, but successful transformation requires investments into people, culture, competencies, and capabilities. In order to apply new skills and new ways of working and use the latest technology in their daily work, people need upskilling. Also, a stronger focus on better communication, demystification, and expectation management related to people and their feelings, for example, fears, change resistance, or unlearning to IoT, robotization, digitalization, and AI are needed. Regardless of how good the new technology is, investment will be partly wasted if the people do not accept change and if transformational leadership is not managed.

Based on the industrial case studies, frameworks and concepts for ramping-up IIoT solutions were' proposed and used in the ABB digitalization program. Industrial digital applications based on digital, AI, and IoT technologies provided remarkable savings and benefits for customers.

11.5.2 Future Recommendations

ABB Marine solutions is one of the leading businesses in the utilization of technologies and other industrial sectors will follow the steps toward autonomous operations which are illustrated in Figure 11.16. An industrial case pilot for autonomous ships has already been piloted (ABB, 2019c) and a concept for collaborative operations has been launched.

The journey and lessons learned from autonomous shops show that the time needed for digital transformation from product business into solution and service can take several years as illustrated in Figure 11.17. Integration of different digital,

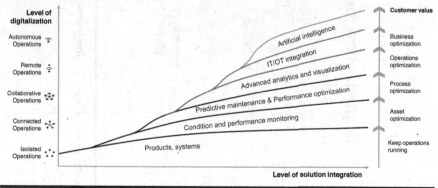

Figure 11.16   Steps toward autonomous operations.

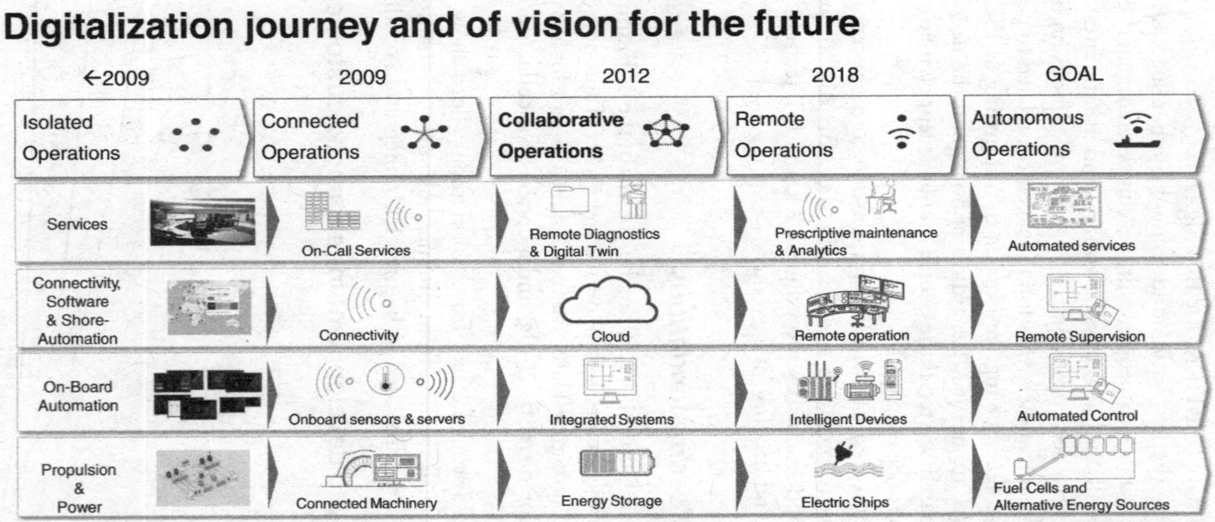

Figure 11.17   Digitalization journey toward autonomous ships.

mobile, AI, and advanced analytics technologies will speed up this development, and ABB Finland had the first industrial case pilot of using a 5G network, AI, and the ABB Ability platform in industrial operations. The use of scaled and agile methods in this transformation will accelerate the change.

11.5.3 Critical Roles of People, Competency, and Capability Development

As a future recommendation, a bigger emphasis should be placed on knowledge transfer and competence development at individual, team, and organizational levels. Further research in the integration of KM and transformational leadership is also needed. A core capability for organizations will be how to manage simultaneous transient advantages leading into dynamic optimization of knowledge transfer, and continuous upskilling and reskilling of competencies.

The role of HR, talent, and learning and development (L&D) will change from training programs into strategic business and organizational development. In the future, holistic and updated frameworks for knowledge management in transient business organizations will also be needed where people change management and the management of feelings and fears, and personal level psychological reasons for change resistance, are better managed.

References

ABB, 2018a, Digital road to the energy revolution, Rob Massoudi, https://www.abb-conversations.com/2018/06/digital-road-to-the-energy-revolution/ (Retrieved 10.12.2019).

ABB, 2019a, ABB group web page, http://www.abb.com (Retrieved 10.12.2019).

ABB, 2019b, ABB Ability web page, https://ability.abb.com (Retrieved 10.12.2019).

ABB, 2019c, ABB enables groundbreaking trial of remotely operated passenger ferry, https://new.abb.com/news/detail/11632/abb-enables-groundbreaking-trial-of-remotely-operated-passenger-ferry (Retrieved 10.12.2019).

ABB 2019d, ABB Customer case: Metsä Group, Äänekoski bioproduct mill https://new.abb.com/motors-generators/iec-low-voltage-motors/references/metsa-group (Retrieved 10.12.2019).

ABB, 2019e, ABB Reference case: World's first industrial application utilizing 5G and AI adopted at ABB drives factory in Helsinki, https://new.abb.com/news/detail/25464/worlds-first-industrial-application-utilizing-5g-and-ai-adopted-at-abb-drives-factory-in-helsinki (Retrieved 10.12.2019).

ABB, 2019f, ABB Ability Marine Pilot Vision, https://new.abb.com/marine/systems-and-solutions/digital/abb-ability-marine-pilot/abb-ability-marine-pilot-vision (Retrieved 10.12.2019).

ABB, 2019g, ABB Ability Marine Pilot Vision, https://new.abb.com/marine/systems-and-solutions/digital/abb-ability-marine-pilot/abb-ability-marine-pilot-vision (Retrieved 10.12.2019).

ABB Review, 2019, Unleashing the electrical powertrain through digital monitoring, *ABB Review* 4, 52–55.

Accenture, 2019, Client case study – ABB Making machinery speak volume, https://www.accenture.com/us-en/success-making-machinery-speak-volumes (Retrieved 10.12.2019).

Bontis, N., Crossan, M.M., and Hulland, J., 2002, Managing and organizational learning system by aligning stocks and flows, *Journal of Management Studies* 39(4), 437–469.

CSIS, 2015, Made in China 2025, Center for strategic and international studies, https://www.csis.org/analysis/made-china-2025 (Retrieved 10.12.2019).,

Dalkir, K., 2017, *Knowledge Management in Theory and Practice*, MIT Press., Cambridge, MA.

Davenport, T., 2005, *Thinking for a Living, How to Get Better Performance and Results from Knowledge Workers*. Boston, MA: Harvard Business School Press.

Dixon, N.M., 2000, *Common Knowledge – How Companies Thrive by Sharing What They Know*, Boston: Harvard Business School Press,188 p.

Drucker, P., 1994, Post-Capitalist Society, New York: Collins, 240 p.

Fountaine, T., McCarthy, B., and Saleh, T., 2019, Building the AI-poweredorganization, *Harvard Bussines Review* 97(July–August), 63–73.

Furr, N., and Shipilov, A., 2019, Digital doesn't have to be disruptive, *Harvard Bussines Review* 97(July–August), 94–103, https://hbr.org/2019/ 07/digital-doesnt-have-to-be-disruptive.

Hertog, P., 2000, Knowledge intensive business services as co-producers of innovation, *International Journal of Innovation Management* 4(04), 491–528.

Laukkanen, I., 2008, Knowledge transfer and competence development in complex paper production environments, D.Sc. Thesis, TKK Dissertations 103, Helsinki University of Technology, Espoo.

Li- L., 2018, China's manufacturing locus in 2025: With a comparison of "Made-in-China 2025" and "Industry 4.0," *Technological Forecasting and Social Change*, 135, 66–74.

Liebowitz, J. (ed.) 1999, *Knowledge Management Handbook*, Boca Raton, FL: CRC Press.

Liebowitz, J. (ed.) 2012, Knowledge Management Handbook: *Collaboration and Social Networking*, 2nd edition, CRC Press, Boca Raton, FL.

Liebowitz, J., 2000, *Building Organizational Intelligence – A Knowledge Management Primer*, Taylor & Francis., Boca Raton, FL.

Manufacturing USA programme, https://www.manufacturingusa.com/ (Retrieved 10.12.2019).

McGrath, R.G. 2013, *The End of Competitive Advantage: How to Keep Your Strategy Moving as Fast as Your Business*, Boston, MA: Harvard Business Review Press.

Moratella, L., 2019, Electric. Digital. Connected., The future platform for the shipping industry, Mari-*Tech conference*, Ottawa, Canada.

Nissinen, V., and Laukkanen, I., 2018, Deep leadership and knowledge management: Conceptual framework and a case study, *In KMO 2018 - International Conference on Knowledge Management in organizations*, Springer, p. 48–59.

Nonaka, I., and Takeuchi, H., 1995, *The Knowledge-Creating Company: How Japanese Companies Create the Dynamics of Innovation*, New York: Oxford University Press, 304 p.

O'Halloran, D, and Kvochko E., 2015, Industrial internet of things: Unleashing the potential of connected products and services, World Economic Forum, Switzerland: Davos-Klosters.

Quinn, J.B., Anderson, P., and Finkelstein, S., 1996, Managing professional intellect: Making the most of the best, *Harvard Business Review* 74(2), 71–80.

Teece, D.J., Pisano, G., and Shuen, A., 1997, Dynamic capabilities and strategic management, *Strategic Management Journal* 18(7), 509–533.

World Economic Forum 2018, in collaboration with Accenture, "Maximizing the Return on Digital Investments," May 2018, http://www3.weforum.org/docs/DTI_Maximizing_Return_Digital_WP.pdf (Retrieved 10.12.2019).

World Economic Forum 2019, "HR4.0: Shaping people strategies in the fourth industrial revolution," December 2018, http://www3.weforum.org/docs/WEF_NES_Whitepaper_HR4.0.pdf (Retrieved 10.12.2019).

Wübbeke, J., Meissner, M., Zenglein, M., Ives, J., and Conrad, B., MADE IN CHINA 2025 The making of a high-tech superpower and consequences for industrial countries, *Merics Papers on China*, https://www.merics.org/sites/default/files/201807/MPOC_No.2_MadeinChina2025_web.pdf (Retrieved 10.12.2019).

Chapter 12

AI-Informed Analytics Cycle: Reinforcing Concepts

Rosina O. Weber and Maureen P. Kinkela

Contents

12.1 Decision-Making...212
    12.1.1 Data, Knowledge, and Information 214
    12.1.2 Decision-Making and Problem-Solving 215
12.2 Artificial Intelligence 216
    12.2.1 The Three Waves of AI...216
12.3 Analytics..218
    12.3.1 Analytics Cycle 223
12.4 The Role of AI in Analytics 224
12.5 Applications in Scholarly Data..229
    12.5.1 Query Refinement...230
    12.5.2 Complex Task and AI Method..231
12.6 Concluding Remarks..232
References 233

12.1 Decision-Making

Decisions are the essence of dynamics of all entities. Organizations, people, animals, and agents all progress into new states through decisions. When you get up from bed, it is because you made a decision to do so. A soccer player makes a choice to run a certain direction because of a decision. Organizations rise and fall based on daily decisions that go from simple to immensely complex. Decisions are triggered by goals. Decisions lead agents to move closer to goals because they change states of facts. Productive humans get up to live a fulfilled life, so they make decisions to get up and go to work. Soccer players want to score, so they decide to seek the ball and predict where it will be next to reach it.

We adopt the simplified model of decision-making proposed by Simon (1957) that describes decisions through three steps, namely, *intelligence*, *design*, and *choice*. These three steps are executed in a cycle. The *intelligence* step is when the decision-maker obtains information about the decision to be made. For example, weather and traffic conditions are information points obtained during the intelligence step for a decision on how to get to work. Information gathered in the intelligence step describes attributes of entities associated to the decision context such as the train is late.

In the *design* step, the decision-maker enumerates alternative decisions such as driving, getting a scooter, and taking the train. Finally, the decision-maker selects one decision such as getting a scooter—this is the *choice* step.

Figure 12.1 shows these three steps in a cycle. We particularly chose to depict the decision-making process in a gear cycle because the decision-maker may go back and forth through these steps in no particular order; we want to emphasize that changes in any step may impact all other steps.

The implications of the decision-making process for analytics and AI require further exploration of the process. Figure 12.2 depicts a semantic network of concepts related to the decision-making model originally proposed by Simon (1957) and later complemented by Huber (1980) who included *implementation* and *monitoring*. Contextualizing decision-making within problem-solving provides motivation to decisions. Even if not all motivations are problematic, referring to the context as a problem emphasizes how decisions are part of a process that requires an action. The action is taken when the decision is made and implementing the decision means that the information points of the decision may change. After one or more decisions are made, you may be on your way to work and the soccer player may be at a different position. These changes in the values of state variables and attributes of entities represent new information, which characterizes a new context to trigger new decisions depending on an agent's goals.

In Figure 12.2, we extend the decision-making and problem-solving process to give prominence to the concepts that decision-makers take into account when making decisions. On the right-side of the network, we show concepts that are directly considered in each of the steps. This semantic network of concepts should facilitate

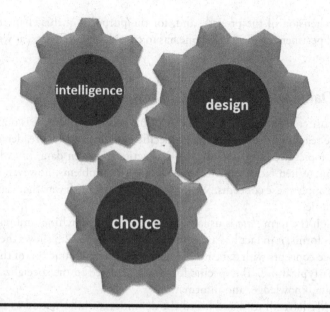

Figure 12.1 Proposed gear cycle view of the decision-making process proposed by Simon (1957).

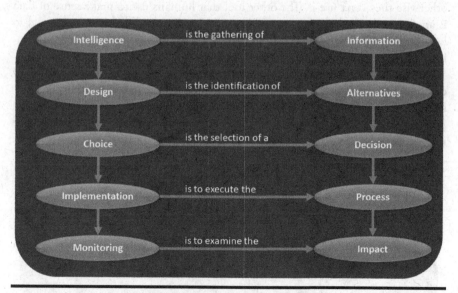

Figure 12.2 Decision-making and its contextual elements.

the comprehension of the process, and, for the purposes of this chapter, helps us identify all pertinent elements that one has to consider for analytics, as will become clear later on.

12.1.1 Data, Knowledge, and Information

As we discuss concepts involved in the decision-making process, it is opportune to remind the reader of the definitions of specific data forms. Most readers of analytics-related topics are familiar with the distinction between data, knowledge, and information. When faced with real-world analytics problems, however, many still struggle to apply these concepts. We hope to present this in a way that clarifies their use in analytics.

Although the term *data* is usually adopted as an overarching umbrella term to describe all forms, it in fact has a specific meaning. Figure 12.3 shows the organization of these concepts with data at the top as the general abstraction of these forms, which is its typical use. The specific forms are depicted in the specialization level, namely, data, knowledge, and information.

Data. We have all read and heard the definition of information as contextualized data. We prefer not to define a term using yet another undefined term. For the purposes of AI and analytics, data is the form that humans can't use. Data is what is stored in databases. Humans require database management systems to process data into information they can absorb. Think of an image of a database table scrolling down a screen. That is data, and humans require tools to make sense of data, otherwise they can't use it. The other tool that humans use to make sense of data is analytics. Particularly the step where machine learning algorithms are used to learn knowledge from data. Machine learning is a subfield of AI focused on data-intensive algorithms that learn knowledge from data.

In summary, there are two methods that convert data for humans to use: 1) databases convert data into information, and humans use information in the intelligence step of the decision-making process to characterize contexts so they can progress toward their goals. 2) Machine learning algorithms convert data into knowledge, which is discussed next.

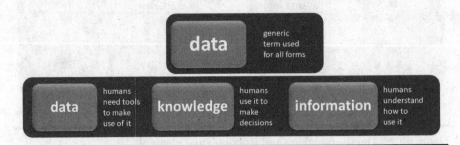

Figure 12.3 Diagram of data forms commonly referred to as data.

Knowledge. The most challenging of the data forms is undoubtedly knowledge. Alavi and Leidner (2001) present six different perspectives of knowledge. Of course, a complex and ubiquitous form that bears relevance in so many different fields such as cognitive science, psychology, philosophy, neuroscience, knowledge management, knowledge engineering, and probably many others, will have various perspectives to it. For the purposes of AI and analytics, knowledge is a belief used to make decisions, it is what equips humans and agents to implement the choice step and select one out of all alternatives identified in the design step of the decision-making process; knowledge is contextual and informed by the process it is meant to benefit. Humans have knowledge to predict that driving may be slow on a day with bad weather when even trains are delayed. They use that knowledge to select the alternative to work from home. The soccer player has knowledge to predict the behavior of an opponent and chooses a direction to run to be well positioned to reach the ball and attempt to score. Although subjective and difficult to represent, the result of knowledge is to enable agents to make decisions through hypothetical simulation of tasks and examination of their potential impact on the variables pertinent to their goals.

This view of knowledge proposed herein has been developed through studies and discussions proposed by various authors (e.g., Alavi and Leidner, 2001; Weber, 2018; Huber, 1980). This view explains why we provided all those elements that are considered in the decision-making process (see Figure 12.2). The impact of a decision in its environment determines whether an alternative decision can be selected. The concept used to make the selection is *knowledge*.

Information. As mentioned earlier, information describes the state of the world; it is found as the output of databases. Consider how database records are structured in fields and each record is populated with values for those fields. The values assigned to each field are information. They describe states and provide attributes for entities. They define problems by describing the state of their relevant entities. The goal of a decision is to change information. For example, a human is hungry and makes the decision to eat and then the human is no longer hungry. Being hungry and then not hungry are attributes of the entity human. In a database record to describe a human, hunger would be a field, and values yes or no would populate the record. A device is malfunctioning and then a decision is made to fix it and then it is no longer malfunctioning. The player is in a location and makes a decision to move to a different location and in the new location the player can score.

Information is not converted into knowledge in any computational tool. Humans, however, can absorb information and learn from it. This relationship between information and knowledge occurs within the human mind.

12.1.2 Decision-Making and Problem-Solving

As mentioned above, the decision-making model (Simon, 1957) was completed by Huber (1980) who added the steps *implementation* and *monitoring*, wrapping all the decision-making steps and these two last steps within problem-solving. Huber defined decision-making as "the process through which a course of action is chosen" (Huber, 1980, p. 9). The definition of knowledge given by Alavi and Leidner (2001) is a "justified belief that increases an entity's capacity for effective action" (2001, p. 109). Note that both consider the idea that a decision implies an action. As we did in Figure 12.2, we label this action a process. This process is the one that has to be effective and this is what decision-makers need to envision to decide on which alternative decision to adopt.

A process has a goal, a purpose, and an end. The concept of *processes* is typical in business organizations and ubiquitous in mundane life. Taking a shower or preparing a meal are processes. Processes are subsets of projects, i.e., a project entails multiple processes. For example, organizing a party is a project that entails a series of processes such as inviting guests, deciding what to serve, planning the venue and its layout, and so on. These processes require the execution of different complex tasks such as planning, design, configuration, classification, and so on. These complex tasks serve as frameworks to execute these processes. They provide context for the decisions that lead to their execution. These complex tasks are also the core of the relationship between analytics and artificial intelligence (AI) that we discuss next.

12.2 Artificial Intelligence

AI is a field of study dedicated to the advancement of intelligent agents, which are those entities that exhibit rational behavior when making decisions through complex tasks such as planning, classification, recommendation, interpretation, prescription, and so on. It is very important not to confuse the name of this field of study with the adjective and noun it contains because "artificial intelligences" are not really the focus of this computing-related field. The name of the field was coined at a workshop in 1956 (Moor, 2006). The vision for the field was never to create any "artificial intelligences," but simply to replicate the execution of tasks. Many of the complex tasks they proposed to replicate computationally are typically performed by humans. This vision of AI would later be perceived as its first wave (DARPA, 2019).

12.2.1 The Three Waves of AI

The First Wave of AI starts with the 1956 workshop (Moor, 2006), where the name is coined and the vision for the field is conceptualized. All AI methods in use today are conceived in the first wave. These methods are used in multiple industries in narrow application domains and execute multiple complex tasks. During the first wave, society in general is not aware of these methods even if they are widely used in well-known applications such as detecting fraudulent credit card transactions, filtering spam emails, and enabling robotic vacuum cleaners to function autonomously.

The first wave AI methods can roughly be categorized as data-oriented, knowledge-oriented, natural language, and evolutionary, as shown in Figure 12.4. Data-oriented methods typically learn from data and characterize the subfield of AI called machine learning. Machine learning methods (Russell and Norvig, 2014) include neural networks, decision trees, naive Bayes and support vector machines, and so on. These methods require large data sets to work well. Knowledge-based methods include rule-based reasoning, constraint satisfaction, and ontologies. Case-based reasoning combines both knowledge-based and machine learning aspects. Knowledge-based methods require some type of knowledge engineering and maintenance. Natural language processing combines techniques to treat sentences and grammar (ibid.), whereas natural language understanding theorizes the existence of a language model that can be used to process natural language segments (Allen, 1995). An example of an evolutionary method is genetic algorithms (Russell and Norvig, 2014), which evolve solution representations. This type of method is usually combined with others for best results. It requires a reference of quality as a fitness function to guide the evolution.

The Second Wave of AI starts with the increased volume of data produced by social media, electronic sensors, widespread use of the web, and reduced memory storage costs. In May 2019, a private statistics company revealed that they computed an average of 500 hours of video uploaded to YouTube by minute (Statista, 2019). This increased volume of data pushes the bar of data-oriented AI methods. In response to the need to deal with big data, these data-oriented methods become more robust and start achieving never-before-seen results. Machine learning methods, particularly neural networks, evolve into much more complex functional networks to deal with big data that became known as deep learning.

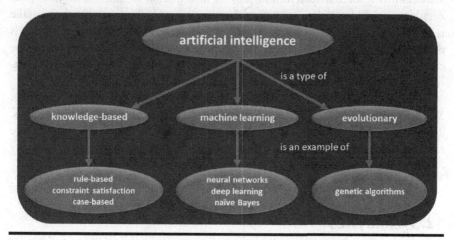

Figure 12.4 Artificial intelligence and its main subfields as established in the first wave.

Similar to the early gold-rush days, businesses start a data-rush to commercialize data and offer services based on machine learning. User data becomes the most valuable asset. Dealing with large amounts of data becomes a field of study and a profession: data science. Universities rush to create data science programs to educate professionals to process and make sense of data. Companies do not have to produce data; all they need to succeed is to own user data. Gaining user trust and becoming the central point of access to users is believed to be the main assets of tech giants (Holmen, 2018; Galloway, 2017). The second wave makes the public aware of AI. The methods from the other subfields continue to be used and evolve at the same pace as before; they remain mostly unknown by the general public. Machine learning, representing a subset of AI, starts to overtake AI in popularity and the ill-informed can confuse the two. The gains in accuracy in classification associated to images are impressive. Data-oriented approaches produce powerful language models for natural language understanding. The separation between machine learning and natural language understanding becomes fuzzy.

The problem with the second wave is that machine learning methods lose transparency when they increase their complexity and it is not possible to trace the steps taken by a machine learning method to make a decision. A crisis resulting from lack of trust, reports of machine learning bias, and prejudice takes over the news. Many companies are profitable, but they cannot be sure whether their business rules are being carried out in such automated decisions. The second wave should still last, but scientists are already working on the third wave.

The Third Wave is the response to the limitations of the second wave. The vision is of a radical paradigm change from humans not knowing how or why AI agents make decisions, to humans and AI agents working together as partners, placing complete trust and reliance in one another's decision. Third-wave agents are designed to be transparent and provide information to humans on how their decisions are made so that if a wrong decision is made, the source of the mistake is identified. Third-wave agents are able to use context and adapt their solutions depending on said context. These characteristics are necessary for humans to be comfortable partnering with AI agents. Until the third wave is fully realized, analytics will still have limitations.

The comprehension of AI empowers analytics to levels beyond its typical use. We next discuss some specifics of analytics and cycles proposed for its process. Today, as we still live in the second wave, analytics cycles utilize only second-wave methods. Later, we will describe how to move beyond this typical use and employ AI-informed analytics.

12.3 Analytics

A widely adopted (e.g., Edwards and Rodriguez, 2018) framework to classify analytics characterizes it through three technical types (Robinson et al., 2010):

- *Descriptive Analytics.* The use of data to figure out what happened in the past.
- *Predictive Analytics.* Uses data to find out what could happen in the future.
- *Prescriptive Analytics.* Uses data to prescribe the best course of action to increase the chances of realizing the best outcome.

Analytics explores several purposes of data motivated by queries in specific contexts. It is important thus to comprehend how queries, their purposes, and technical types can vary and evolve in certain business contexts. Next, we describe a series of steps where analytics can help answer questions in various business segments.

Table 12.1 shows the evolution of the complexity level of the analytics from less to more complex in the use of data for strategic planning by an organization. Generally, it is a more complex goal to determine what could happen in the future or to prescribe the best course of action, than it is to determine what happened in the past, in part because these activities often involve human intuition and because they require the combination of many pieces of descriptive analysis which can combine in more than one way. In the examples in this table, the goals associated with the various uses of the data build upon each other as the complexity of the objectives increases.

How can analytics truly benefit from Artificial Intelligence? We can discuss this for each type, in turn, using the evolutionary steps described in Table 12.1. These steps describe increasingly complex uses of an organization's sales and procurement tables for strategic planning.

In the first row, the data are used to record sales and procurement transactions. The formation of tables for database storage is an early and mandatory part of any business system development. Persistent storage is critical for any non-trivial computer activity, since transactions in memory are lost as soon as the power goes off or the program that is running closes. Companies do not allow this data to just sit in the tables, however. Once data tables are built and populated with some data, the normal next activity is to organize the data into reports about what happened in the past, which by Robinson et. al.'s definition (2010) makes this activity descriptive. These reports can be simple lists of transactions (i.e., data dumps), or more likely, the data will be sorted on some significant field or fields and possibly subtotaled. With these reports, the decision being made (or the question being asked) is simply, "How much?" "How much did we buy" or "How much did we sell?"

One of the important uses of data by the financial or controlling departments of an organization, is to compare the history acquired and described in the second row in Table 12.1, against some standard, benchmark, or plan. At that point, the company utilizes the data to create budget-versus-actual reports. These are important management documents that enable the company to see if it is on track with its strategic planning. Despite their descriptive nature, these reports can benefit from sophisticated visualization methods and AI algorithms. As we will discuss later, clustering analysis can be used. Analysis of the changes and automated similarity assessment may provide insights on the relationship between behaviors. The

Table 12.1   Examples of Analytics Considering Motivating Questions, Purpose, and Type of Analytics

Row	Purpose of data use	Technical type	Products	Motivating question
1	Data are used to record transactions.	Descriptive	Sales and procurement listings: sorted and/or subtotaled.	How much did we sell? How much did we buy?
2	Data are used to make comparisons of activity from period to period.	Descriptive	Budget-versus-actual reports; quarterly and annual reports.	How much did we sell compared with what we thought we would sell? How much did we buy compared with what we thought we would buy?
3	Comparisons are used to make predictions of future activity.	Predictive (Study #1)	Comparisons of same fields for multiple years with predictive methods.	How much did we sell (or buy) in each of the ten years? Based on this, what will happen this year?
4	Predictions are used to adjust plans.	Prescriptive	Budgets, schedules, estimates.	Since Study #1 predicts that sales will drop dramatically in the summer this year, how do we adjust revenues, costs, estimates, and production schedules?
5	Data are used to make comparisons of activity from period to period and demographic to demographic.	Descriptive (Study #2)	Listings of sales by demographic and time of year.	Do we have data that demonstrate certain demographics tending to buy these products at unusual times of the year?

(Continued)

Table 12.1 (Continued) Examples of Analytics Considering Motivating Questions, Purpose, and Type of Analytics

Row	Purpose of data use	Technical type	Products	Motivating question
6	Studies are combined in order to arrive at an advertising strategy.	Prescriptive	Advertising campaigns.	Since Study #1 predicts that sales will drop dramatically in the summer this year and Study #2 demonstrates that certain demographics buy our product at unusual times, what is our advertising strategy?
7	Studies are combined in order to predict the results of the advertising strategy.	Predictive (Study #3)	Predictive report.	What do we predict will be the results of this advertising strategy?
8	Data are used to identify demographic factors which might affect the success of our advertising campaign in various areas.	Predictive (Study #4)	Predictive report.	Study #3 demonstrates a 25% uptick in sales in areas where this type of advertising strategy is employed. What factors will determine if this will be the effect of an advertising campaign in certain demographics? Based on studies of these factors, what do we predict will be the effect of our advertising strategy in various areas?
9	Heuristics are applied to ascertain the wider effect of current events on these results.	Predictive (Study #5)	Predictive report.	Based on politics, world conditions, and the economy, do you think this prediction will come true this year?
10	New predictions used to adjust planning documents.	Prescriptive	Updated budgets, schedules, estimates.	Based on the results of Study #5, adjust budgets, schedules, and estimates to account for a predicted increase over the average of the past ten years.

ability to simulate budgets and business activity through plans can provide a more realistic measure of the impact of variations. Finally, even more important than answering the decisions, "How much did we sell compared with what we thought we would sell?" and "How much did we buy compared with what we thought we would buy?", would be to answer, "How much more or less do we have to sell or buy to meet our goals?"

The step described in the third row is predictive. It answers the decision, "What will this year or next year look like?" By examining historical data, regression models can suggest what the future may look like. For truly effective prediction, it may be beneficial to combine purely data-oriented methods based on statistics with knowledge-based methods that incorporate judgement. This activity is more complex in the sense that it usually involves combining data from multiple periods.

The logical next step in the evolution is prescriptive. Based on results from the previous step, the goal is to update plans such as budgets, schedules, and estimates. The decision is, "How do we use the prediction in the previous step to make these adjustments?" This step is more complex than the previous ones, both from a processing standpoint and from a human judgement standpoint. Here again analytics benefits from automated plans to simulate business activity.

These analytics discussed in the first four rows in Table 12.1 are a type of cycle that we often see in business: examine the past, predict the future, simulate its impact, and adjust plans to accommodate the prediction and steer the business to its goals. Another cycle can be: examine the past and make plans to accommodate the information, without real predicting being necessary. For example, when a budget-versus-actual report shows that we are spending too much, often the next step is to figure out where to cut spending. Predictive informatics may not be used in this case. We don't have to predict—we already know we are over budget, and by exactly how much. It would, however, be fundamental to find out why. This is where methods from the third wave will help.

On the fifth row, we go back to a descriptive analytics goal. A two-step cycle is what happens next in Table 12.1. This goal arises because planners looking at the prediction, which came out of the step in the third row, and arrived at another piece of descriptive information needed. The decision associated with this query was, "Are there customers in any demographics who make purchases at an unusual time of year?" This report can be produced through data warehousing, or *pivot tables*, which sets up the data to count based on an examination of more than one field simultaneously. The goal of finding this information arose from a problem-solving activity of human planners trying to figure out how to advertise during the low sales months. With the advances of the second wave, deep learning networks can combine multiple predictions and conditional functions to automate such analyses.

As a result of the step in the fifth row, the step in the sixth row is prescriptive and answers the decision, "How do we change our advertising to accommodate the demographical information arrived at in the fifth row?" Planning the advertising strategy is a complex human problem-solving activity and could likely involve examining other data elements in addition to the sales and procurement tables we have looked at thus far. It could spin off a whole new cycle of descriptive, predictive, and prescriptive analytics. The simulation of an advertising strategy requires careful contemplation of highly sensitive variables. With the speed at which information spreads with social media, automated methods are required to keep track of their impact. One area to consider for this tracking used in textual analytics is sentiment analysis (Liu, 2015).

Steps in rows 7, 8, and 9 are predictive steps which examine the new advertising plan in increasingly complex ways. The decisions are, "Will this new strategy be effective? Will the effectiveness of the new strategy be altered in various demographics? Will the effectiveness be altered based on possible future changes in the status quo?" These steps are complex because they can involve a combination of steps considering what has happened in the past as indicated by the data, predicting what it implies using both human and statistical analysis, and using human intuition to analyze the overall meaning of this combination of information items. It is always important to remember that prediction methods are only as good as the data they use. For effective predictions, high quality data has to be used that contemplates all variations of trends and directions.

The users having arrived at some decisions as a result of the previous steps, Step 10 is again prescriptive. The results can help us update plans to simulate budgets, schedules, and estimates, now with greater confidence based on the analytics we have engaged in.

12.3.1 Analytics Cycle

Process cycles represent steps to follow in order to implement methodologies. Such cycles are useful to guide practitioners and to help create mental models of such methodologies. As disciplines evolve, they earn new names and their process cycles evolve. Analytics is no exception. It evolved directly from the knowledge discovery from databases (KDD) process, which was popularized by publications such as Fayyad et al. (1996). Despite the goal of their vastly referenced article, which was to distinguish data mining from KDD, the term data mining became the catch-all term for KDD.

As the world and its technologies evolved and the amount of data involved grew exponentially, we entered a new era, the era of data science and data analytics. The business world and academia have advanced along very similar lines in their respective adoption and investigation of data technologies. The business world adopted the term business intelligence (Pearlson et al., 2019) for the general set of methods and capabilities that enable businesses to learn and advance from data. In academia, the analogous term is data science, the field of study dedicated to advancing the set of methodologies and capabilities that produce new knowledge from data.

On the other hand, the term analytics is rather reserved for the process that is driven by a question or query, similar to the motivation of KDD. Earlier, we explained that decisions are what drives business. Business analytics (Pearlson et al., 2019) is hence the analytics process driven by the need for decision-making. We refer to the process as analytics because we describe it to be used beyond the business context.

The KDD process proposed by Fayyad et al. (1996) consists of these steps: Selection, Preprocessing, Transformation, Data Mining, and Interpretation/ Evaluation. Delen (2018) adopts the Cross-Industry Standard Process for Data Mining (CRISP-DM) for data analytics, which includes Business Understanding, Data Understanding, Data Preparation, Model Building, Testing and Evaluation, and Deployment. We could keep going as there are multiple variations of analytics cycles. Based on a thorough examination of various cycles (EMC, 2015), an overview cycle consists of the steps: Discovery, Data Preparation, Model Planning, Model Building, Communicate Results, and Operationalize. EMC (2015) appropriately suggests arrows going back to the previous step of the cycle as a way to remind data analysts to move back a step and reconsider the results of the previous steps in order to promote success. Due to our educational focus, in our proposed cycle, we once again utilize the gear cycle representation to emphasize that all previous steps may be revisited if any change in direction becomes necessary. Given the presence of a motivating question or query in analytics, we rename Discovery with Query Refinement. We also adopt the final two steps from the KDD process and use Testing and Evaluation, and Deployment, as shown in Figure 12.5.

12.4 The Role of AI in Analytics

These cycles described above are good representations of how the vast majority of analytics is carried out; they are not, however, ideal representations of the true potential of analytics. To realize its true potential, we propose an analytics cycle that is informed by the comprehension of AI and considers the entire extent of AI rather than simply machine learning. Our proposed cycle is not limited to businesses but expands to the application of analytics to any data context. We call it AI-informed analytics and represent it in the cycle depicted in Figure 12.6. This version of data analytics is one that is employed by analysts who comprehend AI and its contribution to analytics, and hence can explore the full potential of their synergy.

The AI-informed analytics cycle may sound a bit redundant given that many authors describe analytics as a process that utilizes AI. As we noted earlier, various cycles for the analytics process have been proposed, and our proposed cycles in Figure 12.5 and Figure 12.6 have been developed from those cycles. Let us now examine the steps of the cycle that we propose in Figure 12.6 that differ from others because those are the steps that describe an AI-informed cycle.

Query Refinement. The query driving the process has to be refined and confirmed for efficiency. Poorly defined queries can be misleading. Experience will tell

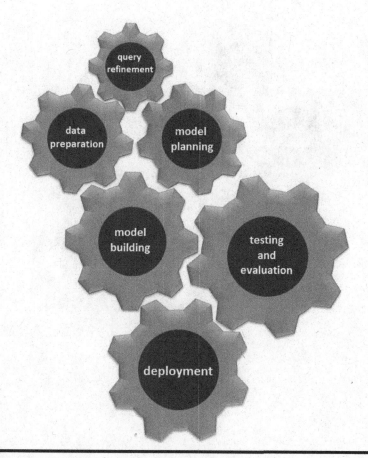

Figure 12.5 · **Analytics cycle.**

when a query is well defined; to build this needed experience, we propose some steps that can be considered for refining queries. One step is to eliminate ambiguous or uncertain terms. In question-answering systems such as IBM Watson (Lally et al., 2012), questions are analyzed, and their focus is identified. The focus characterizes the object of the answer such as questions starting with *who* have a person as focus and questions starting with *when* have a date as focus. Referring to Table 12.1, questions starting with *how much* have amounts as focus. See the motivating question in the fifth row in Table 12.1. That question starts with *do we*, but it is actually asking about trends of demographics in association with time periods. Other questions such as those in the sixth to eighth rows imply the need of a plan. When we propose a query refinement step, we suggest that these questions are stated in ways that make the focus clear. The other components that need to be clearly inferred are the technical type of analytics, the purpose of the data, and the products required to answer the questions.

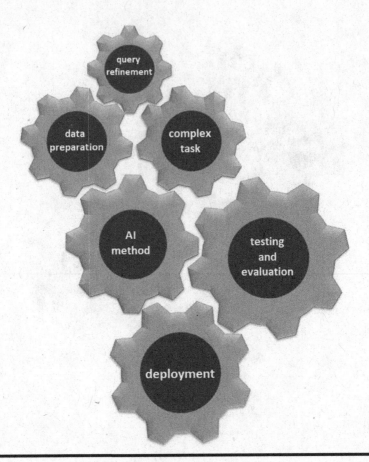

Figure 12.6 AI-aware analytics cycle.

Complex Task. This step is crucial for successfully using AI methods. From the motivating question, the data, the technical type, and products, and a clear complex task, must be identified. Figure 12.7 shows a hierarchy of analysis and synthesis tasks as they are usually discussed in AI. Note, however, that these tasks and their descriptions within this section are limited to structured data. Later on, we discuss unstructured data that relies on textual analytics.

The main categorization of complex tasks groups them as analysis or synthesis tasks. The general idea of analysis tasks is that they analyze an input to produce a result. Analysis types could be further categorized as classification and regression. Classification tasks examine the input to determine the class to which the input belongs. For example, the input is an image and the classification result is that the input is an image of a cat. The clue to recognize a classification task is that the classes are given in the input. This means that the input given includes the result, also called the label. For this reason, this classification task will be later implemented as supervised learning, i.e., because it includes the label.

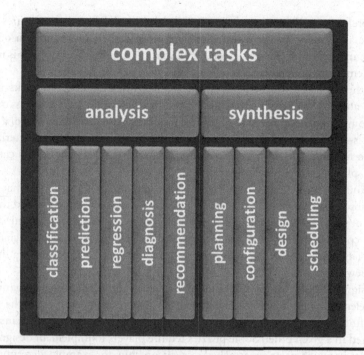

Figure 12.7 Taxonomy of complex tasks.

Regression differs from classification in that it seeks to identify trends or commonalities to project the same trend into the future. Regression can produce numbers as predictions, whereas classification indicates the class to which the input belongs. This does not mean that a prediction task can only be executed via regression. Prediction may be done via classification. For example, a prediction of revenue may result from the classification of inputs into an economic trend or activity level. In this example, the prediction is not a number, but a trend or activity level that can be later converted into a number.

Diagnosis is a type of classification task. The classes in diagnosis are diagnostics. Diagnosis can be contextualized in various domains such as medical diagnosis or troubleshooting, which is the name used for mechanical or computing contexts. The notion of troubleshooting is to eliminate sources of trouble. In essence, troubleshooting is the classification of these sources of trouble.

Recommendation is the task that produces results in recommender systems. The idea is that from a base of items, such as products, services, individuals, or organizations, are recommended to a user. The user produces the input to the recommender that may include two categories of information, namely, user particular characteristics and item particular characteristics. Information about characteristics of the user are used to create a user profile or personalization. Information about the items to be recommended are usually features of these items that are called preferences. Recommendation is an analysis task because the features of the item are analyzed with the features of the user and their preferences in order to identify an item to be recommended. The input of recommender systems is usually users, items, and preferences.

Synthesis tasks create structures. They differ from classification tasks in that they do not stop at analyzing the input to produce an output such as a class or diagnosis from a predefined list or to produce a number that reflects the reuse of a trend. Synthesis tasks create structures that have complexity and can be characterized by multiple features. We describe three complex tasks that fall under this category, namely, plan, design, and configuration.

The output produced by planning is a plan, and a plan is a structure that aggregates subplans or tasks, or subtasks. The plan and its tasks are represented through a series of variables that are assigned in different states. Plans start at an initial state and are completed when they reach the goal state. Each task of a plan is characterized by having the ability to change the values of the variables and moving the plan into a new state.

Design is a task that combines input elements into a structure or organization where elements may have functions or goals that need to be met so the design successfully meets its goal or goals. The design may require the elements to be organized in a given order. Some puzzles require players to implement design tasks. The order in which parts are attached to a silicon chip, for example, determines the success of the final structure.

Scheduling refers to defining the sequence of a set of steps. A popular application is in a manufacturing assembly line where parts need to undergo processes in different machines. The decision of an optimal sequence for each part that minimizes the idle time of those machines while maximizing the parts being manufactured describes the complexity of scheduling. Scheduling is also a task executed in organizations where employees need to cover uninterrupted shifts. Nurses in hospitals and crews in transportation services such as trains (Martins et al., 2003) have to schedule who works when. This is in essence the same task as scheduling exams or classes in schools and universities (Lim et al., 2000).

Configuration creates an organization of elements with a given set of goals. Examples of this task are the configuration of computing equipment, bicycles (Richer and Weber, 2014), cars, planes, cameras, and so on. Any product that can be customized is virtually configurable. The configuration is to match a user's needs.

AI Method. Different AI methods execute different complex tasks. This selection requires comprehension of AI methods that are beyond the scope of this chapter. This overview aims to prepare the reader to research AI methods in AI books. The books referenced in this section are further reading in these AI methods.

The data-oriented methods execute classification (Aggarwal, 2015) and prediction tasks. These are methods studied under machine learning and include neural networks (Bishop, 1995), where a decision whether to use deep networks (Goodfellow et al., 2016) or not depends on the amount of data available. A not-exhaustive list that includes the most popular methods includes decision trees, support vector machines, random forest, case-based reasoning (Richter and Weber, 2013), and naive Bayes (Russell and Norvig, 2014). Note that these methods are known to execute supervised learning, which means that the input data used includes information of the class to which each instance belongs. Classification can also be performed with rule-based reasoning, but this is not a data-oriented method, which means it is not amenable for large data sets and is not considered within machine learning.

When data is not labeled with a class, then the learning is called unsupervised. The most typical method is known as clustering (Aggarwal and Reddy, 2014). There are various types of clustering algorithms to choose from and selecting one will depend on specific characteristics of the problem. One of these characteristics is whether the number of classes is known or can be guessed and tested. Note that when clustering is used, the complex task may not be classification, but a step toward it. The actual tasks are called clustering or categorization, which means to identify categories.

Various AI methods execute the planning task (Ghallab et al., 2004; LaValle, 2006; Richter and Weber, 2013; Russell and Norvig, 2014). Some of the methods that execute planning are informed search algorithms such as A* and Dijkstra, and methods such as rule-based reasoning, case-based reasoning, and hierarchical task networks. Informed and uninformed search algorithms are also used for design, scheduling, and configuration tasks, as well as rule-based reasoning, case-based reasoning, and constraint satisfaction.

Recommendation can be executed with multiple methods. There are five major types of recommender systems, of which content-based and collaborative filtering are the most popular. There are also utility-based, knowledge-based, and demographic recommender systems. Content-based methods are typically implemented with case-based reasoning (Richter and Weber, 2013). Collaborative filtering recommenders are implemented with matrix factorization, which may use neural networks (Koren and Volinsky, 2009).

This step of the analytics cycle does not really end with the selection of the AI method. Once the method is selected, it becomes clear as to how the data are to be processed. Each of these methods require very different data preparation and processing. We recommend further reading for those methods.

12.5 Applications in Scholarly Data

Scholarly data refers to the set of published articles from conferences and journals where new knowledge is published in all fields of science, engineering, humanities, and arts. These publications are typically peer reviewed and are substantiated by theory or empirical studies through methodologies adopted in each field of study. This is the product of researchers whose job is to advance knowledge for the progress of our society. Scholarly data is a universe that retains the highest quality content learned by humans; a universe of knowledge that unfortunately requires tremendous effort to access.

What distinguishes scholarly data from all that we have discussed so far in this chapter is that scholarly publications are written in natural language, which is a data form referred to as unstructured data (see Richter and Weber, 2013, chapter 17). Analytics processes applied on unstructured data receive a different technical type: textual analytics.

This chapter illustrates how to implement the proposed AI-informed analytics cycle to answer a question with textual analytics. We start by posing a challenging question and then describing how to execute the first steps, *query refinement*, *complex task*, and *AI method*. For selecting a challenging question, we consider what we could do if we had perfect access to all the scholarly universe of knowledge. We propose to ask, based on scholarly knowledge, *what are the new jobs that will be most frequently offered within ten years or so?* The main steps are summarized in Table 12.2.

12.5.1 Query Refinement

We start by looking for ambiguity and uncertainty in the question, and then we analyze its focus, analytics technical types, and products. The adjective *new* is rather vague. Keeping this in the question forces us to define what *new* encompasses. The rule-of-thumb here is to determine the implications of removing the uncertain term. By keeping the adjective *new*, the question becomes about jobs that will exist and that did not exist before. By removing the adjective *new*, the question

Table 12.2 Query Refinement in Textual Analytics

Steps	*Contents*
Question Editing	What are the new jobs that will be most frequently offered within ten years or so?
	What are the jobs that will be most frequently offered within ten years or so?
	What are the jobs that will be most frequently offered within five to ten years?
Focus	Job fields
Technical type	Predictive analytics
Products	What are the advances in all fields in the last five to ten years? What are the topics contextualizing the advances in all fields in the last five to ten years? What are the most frequent topics contextualizing the advances in the last five to ten years?

is simply about jobs that will be sought in the future, regardless of whether they existed before or not. Of course, one alternative would be to conduct analytics for both, but for simplicity, let us remove the uncertain word.

The second uncertain expression is *ten years or so*. Based on comprehension of the data, which is one of the requirements for analytics, we use the assumption that advances reported in scholarly publications are about five to ten years ahead of their effective use in society as a job skill. Consequently, this information finds the match between the data and the question, which is that at the core of what we need to determine is in the advances discussed in scholarly data. We propose therefore to replace the expression *ten years or so* with *five to ten years*.

Considering that there are no uncertain expressions remaining in the question, we move to its focus. When asking for jobs, what level of specificity are we looking for? Is the question asking for job titles or industries that will be offering them? Again, we rely on comprehension of the data and consider that although scientific advances can give us details on what the processes would entail in different jobs, they do not tell us job titles. Consequently, we can affirm the focus to be about fields or areas of study, and not information specific to the detailed processes entailed in the advances. In fact, in order to make any use of the answer, it would not be beneficial to get a detailed list of job descriptions, but areas of study or topics that advances may have in common.

The question we pose requires predictive analytics, as it is a prediction task. In order to answer it, we need to consider which products we need for this prediction. The relationship between jobs and advances suggests that we need a descriptive analytics report with the advances in all fields in the last five to ten years. Note that the products require analytics of other technical types. We are interested in the topics contextualizing those advances, so we can determine which advances share the areas and will ultimately become the most frequently offered. Therefore, the other product needed is a report of the topics contextualizing those advances. Then, we will need to find common topics across various advances so we can identify the most frequent fields. The idea is to find common trends of topics across different fields that would suggest a direction or trend. It would be our assumption based on the comprehension of scholarly data that the most frequent jobs in the next five to ten years will be related to the most frequent topics contextualizing the advances in the last five to ten years.

12.5.2 Complex Task and AI Method

Although the main task seems to be predictive analytics, the analyst has to recognize that when data is unstructured, there is another large body of AI tasks and methods that require examination. When the data is textual, the methods required are from natural language understanding (NLU). In NLU, the complex tasks and methods are different from those described for an AI-informed analytics process when the data is structured. They are different because the real complex task is understanding, which follows a very different structure. In NLU, the primary concern is to learn a language model. The language model is what guides the decisions on how to execute multiple tasks such as search, or comparisons between words, segments, or documents. This chapter is limited in scope and does not cover textual methods, which would require another entire chapter. We briefly mention some of these methods in this illustration for the reader to appreciate the extent as well as the limitations of AI methods at the time this chapter was published.

We discuss the tasks following the sequence of questions. The first is, "What are the advances in all fields in the last five to ten years?" This question still needs to be further broken down to the question, "What are the advances described in this article?" With the answer from each published article, then the advances from the last five to ten years can be collected, and then their topics can be identified, followed by the advances that share topics. Unfortunately, this reaches a limit to NLU. Very recently, Achakulvisut et al. (2019) reported on an extractor that demonstrates this is not a task that methods from NLU are ready to perform.

Notwithstanding, we will continue our analysis as if this first step were feasible. Assuming we had a report with all the advances from all publications in the last five to ten years, this report would be a corpus of sentences, where each article's contribution would be likely reported in a set of sentences. To examine the feasibility of this task, we start from the estimate that all scholarly peer-reviewed journals publish a total of 2.5 million articles a year (Ware and Mabe, 2015). We estimate that each description of an article's core advance, commonly referred to as the article's contribution, could, on average, be described with a number of words similar to that of an abstract, which ranges from 15 to 400 words. This way we can consider an average of 300 words for each contribution for five years of 2.5 million articles per year, which amounts to 3 billion words. Fortunately, this volume is similar to the volume of words used to learn a language model in BERT (2018). BERT is the first of a class of algorithms that can learn contextual word representations in a language model. Note that there are other algorithms that learn contextual representations (e.g., Yang et al., 2019). In fact, progress in NLU comes quickly, making it difficult to keep up with this field.

In summary, if it were possible to effectively extract the advances described in scholarly publications, then we would be able to categorize their topics and find out what the most frequently offered jobs would be in ten years or so. In fact, had we overcome this impediment, the industry today would not have unfilled positions for data scientists.

12.6 Concluding Remarks

This chapter presents the role of AI in analytics and suggests applications in scholarly data. The chapter aims to emphasize the role of AI methods which are so far unexplored in analytics. With this purpose, it proposes an AI-informed analytics cycle. The analytics cycles provided in this chapter are depicted with gear cycle diagrams because the authors would like to emphasize the fact that changes in any of the steps are likely to impact all other steps. In practice, it means that any change in direction will require practitioners to revisit questions, purposes, and products.

Analytics is currently being practiced using AI methods from the second wave of AI, namely, machine learning methods. These methods are recommended to deal with large and complex data sets and are required to learn knowledge from data. There are, however, more methods in AI to be used in the creation and automation of the intermediary products required in analytics, such as those to create plans, budgets, and simulate potential results of different business strategies to improve decision-making. Harnessing AI methods beyond machine learning is likely to improve the potential of analytics.

This chapter presents the application of analytics in scholarly data, which is unstructured data. However, the descriptions of AI methods and complex tasks are focused on structured data. The combination of contents should provide a good overview of AI-informed analytics, but readers are encouraged to expand their knowledge with the various sources referenced herein.

References

Achakulvisut, T., C. Bhagavatula, D. Acuna and K. Kording. 2019. Claim extraction in biomedical publications using deep discourse model and transfer learning. *arXiv preprint*. https://arxiv.org/abs/1907.00962.

Aggarwal, C. C. Ed. 2015. *Data classification: algorithms and applications*. Boca Raton: CRC Press.

Aggarwal, C. C. and C. K. Reddy. 2014. *Data clustering: algorithms and application*. Boca Raton: CRC Press.

Alavi, M. and D. E. Leidner. 2001. Knowledge management and knowledge management systems: Conceptual foundations and research issues. *MIS Quarterly* 25(1):107–136.

Allen, J. 1995. *Natural language understanding*. New York: Pearson.

Bishop, C. M. 1995. *Neural networks for pattern recognition*. New York: Oxford University Press.

DARPA. 2019. Defense advanced research projects agency. AI Next Campaign. https://www.darpa.mil/work-with-us/ai-next-campaign (accessed: February 18, 2019).

Delen, D. 2018. Data analytics process: An application case on predicting student attrition. In *Analytics and knowledge management*, ed. S. Hawamdeh and H. C. Chang, pp. 31–65. Boca Raton: CRC Press.

Devlin, J., M-W. Chang, K. Lee and K. Toutanova. 2018. Bert: Pre-training of deep bidirectional transformers for language understanding. *arXiv preprint*. https://arxiv.org/abs/1810.04805.

Edwards, J. S. and E. Rodriguez. 2018. Knowledge management for action-oriented analytics. In *Analytics and knowledge management*, ed. S. Hawamdeh and H. C. Chang, pp. 1–30. Boca Raton: CRC Press.

EMC Education Services. 2015. *Data science & big data analytics: discovering, analyzing, visualizing, and presenting data*. Indianapolis: John Wiley & Sons.

Fayyad, U., G. Piatetsky-Shapiro and P. Smyth. 1996. From data mining to knowledge discovery in databases. *AI Magazine* 17(3):37–54.

Galloway, S. 2017. *The four: the hidden DNA of Amazon, Apple, Facebook and Google.* New York: Portfolio/Penguin.

Ghallab, M., D. Nau and P. Traverso. 2004. *Automated planning: theory and practice.* New York: Elsevier.

Goodfellow, I., Y. Bengio and A. Courville. 2016. *Deep learning.* Cambridge: MIT press.

Holmen, M. 2018. Blockchain and scholarly publishing could be best friends. *Information Services & Use* 38(3):1–10.

Huber, G. P. 1980. *Managerial decision making.* Glenview: Scott Foresman & Co.

Koren, Y., R. Bell and C. Volinsky. 2009. Matrix factorization techniques for recommender systems. *Computer* 8:30–37.

Lally, A., J. M. Prager, M. C. McCord, B. K. Boguraev, S. Patwardhan, J. Fan, P. Fodor and J. Chu-Carroll. 2012. Question analysis: How Watson reads a clue. *IBM Journal of Research and Development* 56(3.4):1–14.

LaValle, S. M. 2006. *Planning algorithms.* Cambridge: Cambridge University Press.

Lim, A., A. J. Chin, H. W. Kit and O. W. Chong. 2000. A campus-wide university examination timetabling application. In *AAAI/IAAI*, ed. R. Engelmore and H. Hirsh, pp. 1020–1015. Menlo Park: AAAI.

Liu, B. 2015. *Sentiment analysis: mining opinions, sentiments, and emotions.* Cambridge: Cambridge University Press.

Martins, J. P., E. M. Morgado and R. Haugen. 2003. TPO: A system for scheduling and managing train crew in Norway. In *IAAI*, ed. J. Riedl and R. Hill, pp. 25–34. Menlo Park: AAAI.

Moor, J. 2006. The Dartmouth College artificial intelligence conference: The next fifty years. *AI Magazine* 27(4): 87–91.

Pearlson, K. E., C. S. Saunders and D. F. Galletta. 2019. *Managing and using information systems: A strategic approach.* Hoboken: John Wiley & Sons.

Richter, M. M. and R. O. Weber. 2013. *Case-based reasoning: a textbook.* Berlin: Springer-Verlag.

Russell, S. J. and P. Norvig. 2014. *Artificial intelligence: a modern approach.* Upper Saddle River: Prentice Hall.

Robinson, A., J., Levis, and G. Bennet. 2010. INFORMS news: INFORMS to officially join analytics movement. *OR/MS Today* 37(5).

Simon, H. A. 1957. *Models of man; social and rational.* Hoboken: John Wiley & Sons.

Statista. 2019. Hours of video uploaded to YouTube every minute as of May 2019. https://www.statista.com/statistics/259477/hours-of-video-uploaded-to-youtube-every-minute/ (accessed: August 16, 2019).

Ware, M. and M. Mabe. 2015. The STM report: An overview of scientific and scholarly journal publishing. University of Nebraska – Lincoln. Technical Report. https://digitalcommons.unl.edu/cgi/viewcontent.cgi?article=1008&context=scholcom (accessed March 16, 2018).

Weber, R. O. 2018. Objectivistic knowledge artifacts. *Data Technologies and Applications* 52(1):105–129.

Yang, Z., Z. Dai, Y. Yang, J. Carbonell, R. Salakhutdinov and Q. V. Le. 2019. XLNet: Generalized autoregressive pretraining for language understanding. *arXiv preprint.* https://arxiv.org/abs/1906.08237.

Index

ABB, 194
ABB Ability™ Marine Pilot Vision, 203
ABB Ability platform, 194, 195
ABB Marine solutions, 205
ABB Smartsensor, 199, 202
ABB takeoff program, Industry 4.0
   background, 194, 195
   IIoT and digital solutions, value framework,
      194, 196, 197
   intelligent industry takeoff, 194, 196,
      198–201
Absolute trust, 49
Abstraction, 37
Academic dental clinic, missed appointments
   electronic dental records (EDRs), 152–154
   impact
      children and adolescents, 156
      dental prosthetic placement, 156
      diagnosis and treatment procedures, 156
      didactic and clinical training, 155
      increased treatment duration, 156
      orthodontic treatments, 156
      patient communication, 155
      productivity and revenue loss, 155, 157
      scheduling appointments, 155
   patient responses, fear and pain
      dental anxiety, 157–158
      dental avoidance, 158–159
   potential data sources
      clinical notes, 161
      dental anxiety assessments, 160
      staff and patient reporting, 161–162
ACE, see Automatic content extraction ontology
Action, data transformation, 40
Advanced AI-based solutions, 120
Agency, 36
AGI, see Artificial general intelligence
AI, see Artificial intelligence

AIDP, see Artificial Intelligence
      Development Plan
AI-informed analytics cycle,
      reinforcing concept
   analytics
      classification, 218–219
      complexity level of, 219–222
      cycle, 222–224
      query refinement, 224–225
      strategic planning, 219
   decision-making, 212–216
   scholarly data (see Scholarly data)
   three waves, 216–218
AI/ML systems
   ethics, 60–61
   performance measure, 56–58
ALC, see Analytics life cycle
Alexa, 125
AlexNet, 72
AlphaGo, 4, 84, 85
AlphaZero, 85
ALVINN system, 83
American Medical Association (AMA), 174
Amazon Alexa, 66, 71
Analytics cycle, 222–224
Analytics life cycle (ALC), xiii, xiv
ANN, see Artificial neural network
Apple's Siri, 71, 125
ArcFace, 74
ARIMA models, 89
Artificial general intelligence (AGI), 44
Artificial intelligence (AI), 21, 23–24,
      26, 29, 32, 41–42, 168; see also
      individual entries
   advanced analytics toward machine
      learning, 122–124
   artificial general intelligence (AGI), 44
   connectionism, 16

vs. data analytics
  AI-aware culture development, 62
  AI/ML performance measure, 56–58
  cybersecurity, 55–56
  data input to AI systems, 58–59
  data transparency, decision-making
    process, 61–62
  defining objectives, 59–60
  ethics, 60–61
  momentous night in Cold War, 54–55
deep neural networks, 16
definition, 216
descriptive *vs.* predictive *vs.* prescriptive,
  121–122
Dessa, 78
first wave
  categories, 217
  industries application, 216–217
  knowledge-based methods, 217
  machine learning methods, 217
history, 3–4
intelligent systems framework, 13–15
limitations, 44–45
machine learning, 42–43
narrow intelligence, 44
powered analytics, 22, 27
  combination of, 24–27
  data age, 23
  data analytics, 23–24
  examples, 27
  way forward, 28–29
race, 100
reasoning, 15–16
second wave
  data-oriented methods, 217, 218
  data science programs, 218
  data volume, 217
  machine learning methods, 217, 218
  problem, 218
super artificial intelligence, 44
systems, data input to, 58–59
technical vectors, 15
third wave, 218
Artificial Intelligence Development Plan
  (AIDP), 102–105
Artificial neural network (ANN), 8, 22, 66, 70,
  89, 169
Artomatix, 81
Aspect-level SA, 126
Atari 2600 games, 84, 85–86
Attention module, 68
Audio generation, 78–79

Augmented analytics, 28
Autoencoder, 69, 90
Automated insight-generation, 27
Automatic content extraction (ACE)
  ontology, 127
Automatic game playing, 83–85
Automatons, 5
Autonomous driving, 82–83
Autonomous ships, 203–204
  digitalization journey toward, 206
  steps, 205
Autonomous underwater vehicles (AUVs), 75
Autonomy, 4–5, 16–17
Auto suggest, 27
AUVs, *see* Autonomous underwater vehicles

Balanced scorecard (BSC), 134, 137
Benjamin, 77
BERT, 68, 71
Big Data, 3, 6
  and artificial intelligence, 120–121
  unstructured data
    challenge of, 119–120
    use cases of, 118–119
Black box algorithm, 48
Black Swans, 134, 136
Bordering, 49
Bounded rationality, 36
BRETT, 85
BrightLocal, 118
BSC, *see* Balanced scorecard
Budget allocation (Chicago data), 145, 147
Business ethics, 37
Business intelligence, 223

Cause and effect, 123
Cause-effect modified BSC, 141
Center for Strategic and International Studies
  (CSIS), 62
Chatbots, customer service, 128–129
Children's Fear Survey Schedule-Dental
  Subscale (CFSS-DS), 160
Chinese AI policy and global leadership
  A(Eye), 109–110
  Chinese characteristics, AI with, 103–104
  national security in, 104–106
  overview of, 100–101
  security/protection, 106–109
Chinese financial system, 102
Chinese innovation policy, 101
Clarifai, 75
Classical machine learning, 168

Cleaning, xi
Clinical notes, 161
Clustering, 38, 229
CNNs, *see* Convolutional neural networks
Cochleagram, 79
Cognitive bias, 46
Cognitive neuroimaging
   affordability and ability, 170
   brain images, 172
   brain structures and functions, 172
   brain visualization, 170
   definition, 170
   functional near-infrared spectroscopy
      (fNIRS), 171–172, 174–176
   machine learning (*see* Machine learning)
   methods, 170
   "Mosso method," 170
Common distance measures, 10
Complex decision environments, 38
Computing, 6
Content generation
   audio generation, 78–79
   image and video generation, 79–81
   text generation, 76–78
Continuous control, 137
Conversational speech recognition (CSR), 72
Convolutional neural networks (CNNs), 67, 68,
      71–73, 79, 169, 178
Corah's Dental Anxiety Scale, 160
Corpus-based methods, 126
Creativity, 15
Credit risk, 136
Credit scores, 23
Cross-Industry Standard Process for Data
      Mining (CRISP-DM), 224
CSIS, *see* Center for Strategic and
      International Studies
CSR, *see* Conversational speech recognition
Customer review analytics, 118
Customer service requests, 144
Cybersecurity, 55–56

DARPA, 15
Data age, 23
Data analytics, 23–24; *see also individual entries*
   advanced analytics toward machine
      learning, 122–124
   descriptive *vs.* predictive *vs.* prescriptive,
      121–122
Data availability, 6
Data-driven decision-making, 39–40
Data ethics, 37

Data lake, xi
Data quality, 138
Data readiness levels, 13
Data science
   analytics, 12–13
   applications, 11
   data engineering, 11
   data readiness, levels of, 12
   history, 2–3
   maturity model, 11, 12
Data science artificial intelligence (DSAI),
      xii, xv
Data science life cycle (DSLC), ix–xii
Data wrangling, xi
Decision environment, 38
Decision-making, 32, 33, 81–82
   automatic game playing, 83–85
   autonomous driving, 82–83
   choice step, 212
   contextual elements, 213
   conundrum, 33
   data, 214
   design step, 212
   energy consumption, 86–87
   gear cycle view, 213
   implementation and monitoring, 212
   information, 215
   intelligence step, 212
   intuition and reasoning in, 35
   knowledge, 215
   online advertising, 87–88
   problem-solving, 215–216
   process, 34
   robotics, 85–86
   semantic network, 212
   styles, 34–35
Decision types, 34–35
Deep autoregressive models, 69
DeepBach, 79
Deep belief networks, 90
DeepFace system, 73
Deepfake, 79, 80
Deepfake detection challenge (DFDC), 80
Deep generative models, 69
Deep learning, xi, xii, 7, 8, 124, 178
   artificial neural network (ANN), 169
   based NER models, 127
   computed tomography (CT), 169
   convolutional neural networks (CNNs), 169
   deep neural networks (DNNs), 169
   definition, 169
   fully convolutional network (FCN), 169

magnetic resonance imaging (MRI), 169
positron emission tomographic (PET)
            patterns, 169
Deep learning, in industry
    architectures, 67–68
    content generation
        audio generation, 78–79
        image and video generation, 79–81
        text generation, 76–78
    decision-making, 81–82
        automatic game playing, 83–85
        autonomous driving, 82–83
        energy consumption, 86–87
        online advertising, 87–88
        robotics, 85–86
    deep generative models, 69
    deep reinforcement learning, 69–70
    forecasting
        financial data, 90–91
        physical signals, 88–90
    overview of, 66–67
    recognition, 70–71
        in audio, 72
        in text, 71
        in video and image, 72–76
DeepMind Atari game, 84
Deep neural networks (DNNs), 7–9, 16, 72, 87,
        124, 169
Deep Q-networks (DQNs), 83–85
Deep reinforcement learning (DRL), 11, 69–70,
        81–83, 86
DeepStereo, 81
Deep Tesla, 83
Deep text models, 71
DeepTraffic, 84
Dental anxiety
    assessments, 160
    odontophobia, 157
    procedure type, 158
    treatment modalities, 158
    women *vs.* men, 158
Dental avoidance
    barriers, 158
    conservative dental restoration
            techniques, 159
    pain, 158
    poor treatment outcome, 159
    treatment fear, 159
Depot of Charts and Instruments, 2
Descriptive analytics, 12, 23, 152, 153, 219
Deterministic environments, 38
DFDC, *see* Deepfake detection challenge

Diagnostic analytics, 23, 152, 153
Dictionary-based methods, 126
Diffusion tensor imaging (DTI), 169
Digital powertrain, 202–203
Digital transformation, 184–186
    ABB Smartsensor, 199, 202
    ABB takeoff program, Industry 4.0
        background, 194, 195
        IIoT and digital solutions, value
            framework, 194, 196, 197
        intelligent industry takeoff, 194, 196,
            198–201
    autonomous ships, 203–204
    digitalization and AI, challenges of, 187, 188
    digital powertrain, 202–203
    future recommendations, 205–207
    integrated model, 191, 193–194
    objectives, 186–187
    people, competency, and capability
            development, critical roles, 207
    research approach, 186–187
    theoretical framework
        framework competency, capability, and
            organizational development, 190
        knowledge management and learning
            agility, data collection, 187, 189
        knowledge processes in
            organizations, 189
        transient advantages, 190–192
Digital transformation (DX) initiatives,
        22, 28, 29
Disengage, 191
DNNs, *see* Deep neural networks
Document-level SA, 126
DQNs, *see* Deep Q-networks
DRL, *see* Deep reinforcement learning
DSAI, *see* Data science artificial intelligence
DSLC, *see* Data science life cycle
DTI, *see* Diffusion tensor imaging
DX, *see* Digital transformation initiatives

Echo state network (ESN), 88
EHRs, *see* Electronic health records
Electronic dental records (EDRs)
    BigMouth Dental Data Repository, 155
    clinical decision support systems, 152
    data errors, 154
    data quality, 154
    dental schools, 152, 154, 155
    diagnostic and predictive analytics, 154
    electronic health records (EHRs), 152
    healthcare data, 154

private dental practitioners, 153
Electronic health records (EHRs), 152–154, 161
Empathy, 37
Energy consumption, 86–87
Ensemble methods, supervised machine learning, 8
EDRs, *see* Electronic dental records
ESN, *see* Echo state network
Ethics, 37
Evaluation, 40
Event extraction, 128
Examination of various cycles (EMC), 224
Exploitation, 191

Facebook, 74
FaceNet, 73
FakeNewsAI, 71
Financial data, forecasting, 89–91
Financial risks, 136
FNIRS, *see* Functional near-infrared spectroscopy
Forecasting
    financial data, 90–91
    physical signals, 88–90
Fuller analysis, 142
Fully convolutional network (FCN), 169
Functional near-infrared spectroscopy (fNIRS)
    applications field, 171
    changing optical properties of functioning tissues, 172
    gaming and brain activation
        addiction, 174, 175
        decision-making process, 175
        Huynh-Feldt test, 176
        Iowa gambling task (IGT) test, 175, 176
        neuropsychiatric and psychological disorders, 174
        oxyhemoglobin (HbO), 175
        prefrontal cortex, 175, 176
    neurovascular coupling, 171–172
    traumatic brain injuries (TBI), 173–174

Generative adversary networks (GAN), 69, 75, 79, 81
GeoVisual search, wastewater treatment plants, 75
Google, 87
Google Assistant, 66, 71, 125
Google Data Centers, 86
Google DeepMind, 78, 83
Google's PageRank algorithm, 45
Google's Street View project, 81
Graphics processing units (GPUs), 29

Hadoop, 6
Human and machine intelligence matching, 45
    human singularity, 45–46
    implicit bias, 46–47
    managerial responsibility, 47–48
    semantic drift, 48–49
Human computer interaction (HCI), 178
Human intelligence, 36, 37, 41
    analytical method, 38–39
    characteristic of humanity, 36–37
    "data-driven" decision-making, 39–40
    vs. machine intelligence, 41
Human singularity, 45–46
Huynh-Feldt test, 176

IBM, 124, 125
IDC, *see* International Data Corporation
IE, *see* Information extraction
ILSVRC, *see* ImageNet Large Scale Visual Recognition Challenge
Image and video captioning techniques, 76
Image and video generation, 79–81
Image classification, 72–74
ImageNet, 4, 13, 68, 72, 73
ImageNet Large Scale Visual Recognition Challenge (ILSVRC), 72, 74
Image super-resolution (ISR), 80
Implicit bias, 46–47
Information extraction (IE), 119, 127–128
Innovation, 15
Intelligent search, 26
Intelligent systems framework, 14
International Data Corporation (IDC), 21, 23, 28, 118
International Standards Organization (ISO/IEC JTC 1 Information Technology, 2015), 135
Internet of Things (IoT), 24
    competencies and capabilities needed in delivery of, 201
    customer value hierarchy, 196, 197
    framework, 200
Inter-organizational level learning process, 193
Intra-personal intelligence, 37
IoT, *see* Internet of Things
ISR, *see* Image super-resolution

KDD, *see* Knowledge discovery from databases
Key performance indicators (KPIs), 135–138, 141
    according to BSC perspectives, 139–140
    creating, based on open data, 141–142

financial resources management
perspective, 145–146
internal process perspective, 145–146
stakeholder perspective, 142–145
trained public servant perspective,
146–147
Key risk indicators (KRIs), 135, 138, 141
according to BSC perspectives, 139–140
creating, based on open data, 141–142
financial resources management
perspective, 145–146
internal process perspective, 145–146
stakeholder perspective, 142–145
trained public servant perspective,
146–147
K-means and k-nearest neighbors (KNN), 123
Knowledge
codification process, 189
decision-making, 215
generation, 189
representation and reasoning, 14
scanning/mapping, 189
transfer process, 189
Knowledge discovery from databases (KDD),
223, 224
KPIs, *see* Key performance indicators
KRIs, *see* Key risk indicators

Labeled Faces in the Wild (LFW), 73
Launch Phase, 191
LEGO blocks, 85
Lemmatization, 130
LFW, *see* Labeled Faces in the Wild
Linear bidding strategy (LIN), 88
Linguistically meaningful units (LMU), 129
Linguistic intelligence, 37
LMU, *see* Linguistically meaningful units
Long short term memory (LSTM) networks,
67–68, 71, 77, 79, 178
Lowercasing, 129
LSTM, *see* Long short term memory networks

MACE, *see* Mixture of actor-critic experts
Machine learning (ML), 6–7, 17, 25,
41–43, 120
approaches, 122–124
brain images, 172
challenges, 173
definition, 168
neuroimaging
deep learning, 177
learning algorithms, 177
pain measurements, 177
reinforcement learning, 10–11
resting-state signals, brain, 173
supervised learning, 7–9
SVM and kernel mapping, 173
unsupervised learning, 10
McKinsey Global Institute, 137
Made in China 2025, 102, 109
Magnetic resonance imaging (MRI), 169
Management AI (MAI), xiv, xv
Managerial decision-making, 32–33
bounded rationality, 36
conundrum, 33
decision-making, 33
decision types, 34–35
intuition and reasoning, 35
process, 34
styles, 34–35
Managerial responsibility, 47–48
Man Group, 91
Manual construction, 126
MarioNETte, 79
Medicine and healthcare analytics
descriptive analytics, 152, 153
diagnostic analytics, 152, 153
predictive analytics, 152, 153
Mental workload (MWL), 178
Mixture of actor-critic experts (MACE), 86
ML, *see* Machine learning
Modified Dental Anxiety Scale, 160
Monte Carlo tree, 84
Mosso method, 170

Named entity recognition (NER), 127, 129
Narrow intelligence, 44
Natural language generation (NLG), 128
Natural language processing (NLP), 22, 121,
124, 161
data analytics, 130–131
applications, 128–129
information extraction, 127–128
overview of, 124–125
sentiment analysis (SA), 125–126
text enrichment techniques, 130
text preprocessing, 129–130
NER, *see* Named entity recognition
Nervana, 90
Neural art, 81, 82
Neural machine translation (NMT), 77
Neural network, 8, 9
and deep learning, 123–124
NeuralTalk2, 77

NeuralTalk model, 76
Neural tensor network (NTN), 90
Neuroscience, 173
NLG, *see* Natural language generation
NLP, *see* Natural language processing
NMT, *see* Neural machine translation
Normalization, 129–130
NTN, *see* Neural tensor network
Numerai, 91
Nutch, 6
Nvidia's DAVE-2 system, 83

Odontophobia, 157
Online advertising, 87–88
The Open Racing Car Simulator (TORCS), 83
Operational decisions, 35
Organizational level learning process, 193

Parameter sharing, 67
Part-of-speech (POS) tagging, 130
Pattern recognition, 14
Perception, 39
Personalized e-commerce, 119
Physical signals, forecasting, 88–90
POS, *see* Part-of-speech tagging
Positron emission tomographic (PET)
        patterns, 169
Post-control, 137
Power usage effectiveness (PUE), 87
Pre-control, 136
Prediction, 39
Predictive analytics, 12, 23, 152, 153, 219
Prejudicial bias, 46
Prescriptive analytics, 13, 23, 219
Process to design an AI system, 138
PUE, *see* Power usage effectiveness

Q-learning algorithm, 70
Q-Table, 70
Quality, 119
    of data, 136
Quants, x

Ramp-up, 191
Ramp-up of digital services
    phased and customer focused, 198
    scaled and agile model for, 199
Random forest methods, 174
Rational decision-making, 50
RCNN, *see* Region convolutional
            neural network
RealTalk, 78

Real-time bidding (RTB) model, 87, 88
Recognition, 70–71
    in audio, 72
    in text, 71
    in video and image, 72–76
Reconfiguration, 191, 192
Recurrent higher-order neural network
        (RHONN) model, 89
Recurrent neural network modules (RNN),
        67–68, 71, 79, 81
Recurrent neural networks, 128, 178
Referred trust, 49
Region convolutional neural network
        (RCNN), 76
Regression, 38, 122, 123
Reinforcement learning (RL), 10–11, 69, 70,
        83, 123
Relation extraction, 127–128
Reputation management, 118–119
Residual architecture, 68
RHONN, *see* Recurrent higher-order neural
        network model
RL, *see* Reinforcement learning
RNN, *see* Recurrent neural network modules
Roadmap, 5
Robotics, 85–86
RTB, *see* Real-time bidding model

SA, *see* Sentiment analysis
Sample bias, 46
Scaled and agile model (SAFe), 196, 199
Scholarly data
    AI method, 231–232
    complex task, 231–232
    description, 229
    publications, 229, 230
    query refinement
        adjective *new*, 230
        descriptive analytics, 231
        predictive analytics, 231
        ten years or so, 231
Scientist of the Seas, 2
S-curve, digital technologies, 185
Security analysis, 3
Self-evaluation, 14–15
Self-guided learning, 14–15
Semantic drift, 48–49
SenseTime, 109
Sentence-level SA, 126
Sentient Technologies, 91
Sentiment analysis (SA), 125–126
Sentiment lexicon, 126

Show and Tell model, 76
Simon's decision-making model, 34
Simple decision environments, 38
Simple neuron model, 9
Situational trust, 49
Skype translator, 78
Smart cities development
    AI and strategic risk connection, 137
    concepts and definitions, 134–137
    key performance indicators (KPIs),
        135–138, 141
        according to BSC perspectives, 139–140
        creating, based on open data, 141–147
    key risk indicators (KRIs), 135, 138, 141
        according to BSC perspectives, 139–140
        creating, based on open data, 141–147
    methodology and approach, 137–141
    overview of, 134
SmartCitiesWorld/Phillips Lighting survey, 135
Smart data discovery, 26–27
Social credit score, 110
Social Credit System, 110, 111
Solar irradiance, 88
Space race, 100
Speech synthesis, 78
Speech-to-speech (STS) translation, 78
Spell correction, 130
SphereFace, 74
Spiritual intelligence, 37
SRGAN, 80
Stacked denoising autoencoders, 89
Statistical machine translation (SMT)
        approaches, 77
Stemming, 130
Stochastic environments, 38
Stopword removal, 129
Strategic decisions, 34
Strategic risks, 135, 137
Stroop task experiment, 178
Super artificial intelligence, 44
Supervised learning, 43, 122–123
Supervised machine learning, 7–9
Support vector machine (SVM), 178
    Parkinson's disease, 169

supervised-based algorithms, 168
Symbolic reasoning, 4
Syntactic parsing, 130
SyntaxNet, 130

Tactical decisions, 34–35
TBI, *see* Traumatic brain injuries
TensorFlight, 74
Terrapattern, 74
Tesla Autopilot system, 82
Text
    enrichment techniques, NLP, 130
    generation, 76–78
    preprocessing, NLP, 129–130
    summarization, 128
Text-to-speech (TTS) techniques, 78
Tokenization, 129
Tractable, 73
Traffic management/accidents, 142
Training data set, 122
Transfer learning, 44
Transformational leadership, 193
Translatotron, 78
Traumatic brain injuries (TBI), 174–175
Tree key factors, 145
Trogdor, 57, 58
Turing test, 41

Uncanny valley, 54
United States, 111, 112
Unstructured data
    challenge of, 119–120
    use cases of, 118–119
Unsupervised learning, 10, 43, 123

Variational autoencoder (VAE), 69
Vocal source separation, 72
Volume, 120

Watson, 125
WaveNet model, 78
Wild, Wild East, 112
Wind speed estimation, 89
World Trade Organization (WTO), 107

Printed in the United States
by Baker & Taylor Publisher Services